TRACY A.
North
and Lear... An expert
on working memory and education, she developed the internationally
recognized *Alloway Working Memory Assessment*. She blogs for
Psychology Today.

ROSS ALLOWAY, PH.D, CEO of Memosyne, Ltd, brings working memory
training to educators and parents. Ross developed *Jungle Memory*, used
by thousands of students in more than twenty countries.

Tracy and Ross edited an academic book on this topic (*Working
Memory*, Psychology Press), and their research has been featured on
the BBC, ABC News, The Huffington Post, Salon, the *Washington Post*
and *Newsweek*.

For more information and to take part in a
working-memory experiment:

website: www.docsalloway.com
Twitter: @docsalloway

THE NEW IQ

Use Your Working Memory to Think
Stronger, Smarter, Faster

TRACY AND ROSS ALLOWAY

FOURTH ESTATE • *London*

Fourth Estate
An imprint of HarperCollins*Publishers*
77–85 Fulham Palace Road
Hammersmith
London W6 8JB

This Fourth Estate paperback edition published 2014

1

First published in Great Britain by Fourth Estate in 2013
First published in the United States as *The Working Memory Advantage*
by Simon & Schuster in 2013

A catalogue record for this book is available from the British Library

ISBN 978-0-00-755036-4

NOTE TO READERS:
Names and identifying details of some of the people portrayed
in this book have been changed, and some people portrayed are
composites or are created for illustrative purposes.

Set in Minion
Printed and bound in Great Britain by Clays Ltd, St Ives plc

MIX
Paper from
responsible sources
FSC
www.fsc.org   **FSC™ C007454**

FSC™ is a non-profit international organisation established to promote
the responsible management of the world's forests. Products carrying the
FSC label are independently certified to assure consumers that they come
from forests that are managed to meet the social, economic and
ecological needs of present and future generations,
and other controlled sources.

Find out more about HarperCollins and the environment at
www.harpercollins.co.uk/green

For our little heroes,
M. and M.

CONTENTS

Intelligence That Matters

Does IQ matter? Perhaps it may matter to your school; perhaps to an employer when hiring, but does it really matter to *you*? This number—somewhere between 85 to 115 for most of us—seems to have lost its significance. Of course, you may be pleased to find that your number is closer to 115, but if you found that it was closer to 85, would you be all that concerned? If you answered "no" or "probably not", you're not alone. In an age when nearly any factoid can be had at a few taps of the keyboard, IQ—a measure of intelligence synonymous with the accumulation of information readily available on Google—seems outdated and even quaint in the context of everyday life. Is a 115 going to make it easier for you to cook dinner, help the kids with their homework, and answer the phone at the same time? Does a 115 help you find happiness when things aren't going your way? Will a 115 help you manage stress or resist the chocolate éclair? Will it give you a compelling response to the surprise question in the interview? The answer is no. The world we live in, the world that matters to us, demands a new conception of intelligence.

This book is about an intelligence that helps you succeed in the small things that comprise the ebb and flow of your life—like adapting a PowerPoint presentation for a new client, negotiating a treaty between warring offspring, and juggling football practise with the new product deadline. This intelligence is also deeply implicated in those meaningful moments as well, like when you were tongue-tied upon meeting the love of your life, or when you controlled your panic and found your five-year-old in the toy section, or when you came to accept the loss of a job and took the first step toward a new career. This book is about intelligence that matters.

PART I

The New IQ and You

1

Welcome to the Working Memory Revolution

In December 2005, a broker on the Tokyo stock exchange sold 610,000 shares of a company called J-Com, for the low, low price of 1 yen, an amount less than a penny. The problem is that he meant to sell one single share for 610,000 yen. Epic oops. In 2001, a London dealer sold *300 million pounds sterling*' worth of shares when he intended to sell only *3 million pounds*. The trade sparked a panic in the market that caused 30 billion pounds to go up in smoke.

Brokers may process mountains of information when deciding what to sell and buy, but in the heat of the moment, all it takes is just one extra piece of information—the ring of a phone, the flash of a screen, the thrill of being responsible for such a large sum of money— and their focus is lost. No longer able to process all the information, they struggle to check orders carefully. Trading is a profession that places high demands on a foundational cognitive skill called *working memory*.

By *working memory advantage*, we mean that this skill gives you a leg up, a boost in life. As you will discover, working memory offers you an advantage in a huge range of activities: from the everyday, like giving an important presentation at work, to the extreme, like ripping down an eighty-foot wave. It helped our evolutionary ancestors to advance from just surviving to thriving. It enabled our technological trajectory: from a bone club used for bashing to an iPhone used for connecting. By ignoring, overloading, or undermining your working memory, you put yourself at a huge disadvantage. But by focusing on your working memory, taking it into account, and improving it, the sky's the limit. We wrote this book in order to give everyone an opportunity to take advantage of this life-changing skill.

In the past decade, research on working memory has exploded. It is fast emerging as one of the most widely researched cognitive functions of the twenty-first century, and we have been leading participants in much of this research. Tracy developed a groundbreaking and highly accurate standardized working memory test for use by educators and has dedicated much of her research career to investigating the role of working memory in education and learning difficulties. Ross has focused his attention on developing exercises to improve working memory, and as the CEO and founder of Memosyne, Ltd., he developed working-memory-training software called *Jungle Memory* that has been used by thousands of students. Together, they have examined the role of working memory in a variety of contexts, such as how it changes when you get older; how it is linked to happiness; how it relates to lying; how it is affected by activities like barefoot running; and how it is influenced by social media like Facebook.

What Is Working Memory?

Working memory is our ability to work with information. More precisely, working memory is the *conscious processing of information*. By *conscious,* we mean that the information is on your mind. You are giving attention to it, shining a mental spotlight on it, concentrating on it, or making decisions about it. You are also intentionally ignoring everything else. If you are thinking about a stock trade, for example, you are filtering out the ringing phones, the jabbering of your coworkers, and the excitement of placing a $1 million order. By *processing*, we mean that you are manipulating the information, working with it, making calculations with it, or reformulating it.

The classic example of a job that requires a strong working memory is that of an air traffic controller, whose job is to maintain the safe and orderly flow of air traffic. With hundreds of planes taking off and landing every hour, an air traffic controller must have the mental agility to process multiple variables, such as equipment, weather patterns, traffic volume, precise communication with pilots, and quick calculations. In times of emergency, they must be able to make split-second decisions while effectively moderating the stress of knowing that the lives of pilots and passengers are in their hands.

We see a strong working memory giving us an advantage at play in many aspects of everyday life too. It allows you to listen to your spouse while checking your smart phone and making pancakes for the kids. It lets you complete a complicated spreadsheet in spite of interruptions from your constantly ringing phone and the din of annoyingly loud coworkers. Working memory gives you the ability to remain focused on the conversation with your dinner date while ignoring the urge to check the hockey score on your mobile.

Working Memory in the Brain

For more than the past decade, scientists have been using advanced brain imaging to examine how working memory functions in the brain. Their results reveal that using working memory involves a number of areas in the brain. On the next page are some of the major players:

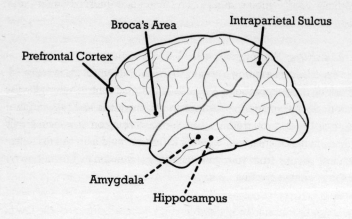

Major Players in Working Memory

Prefrontal cortex (PFC): The PFC is the home of working memory. Located in the front of the brain, the PFC coordinates with other areas of the brain through electrical signals and receives information from those regions so your working memory can make use of it. Brain-imaging scans show that when working memory is being used, the PFC glows while it fires thoughts to and works with information from the different brain regions. Working memory is the primary function of the PFC. Though the PFC is the area most often associated with working memory, it is important to note that scientists have also found activation in other areas of the brain, such as the parietal cortex and the anterior cingulate, when people perform a working memory task.

Hippocampus: The hippocampus is where the vast amount of knowledge you have acquired over your lifetime is housed for long-term storage. It is the location of long-term memory (LTM). Your working memory allows you to sift through all the information you have stored in your long-term memory, and pull out the bits most relevant to the task at hand. It gives you the ability to combine that stored knowledge with new information coming in, and to put new information into your long-term memory.

Amygdala: The amygdala is the brain's emotional center. When you are experiencing a strong emotion, like fear, your amygdala is activated. Working memory is also important to emotional control, managing the emotional information coming from the amygdala and preventing it from distracting you from the task you're working on. If someone yells "Fire!" in the cinema, your working memory would help you to control the fear coming from your amygdala so that you can exit in an orderly fashion without creating a panic.

Intraparietal sulcus: Located at the top back portion of the brain, the intraparietal sulcus is the brain's math center. When you need to perform calculations, such as in choosing the best mortgage loan or guesstimating how many more miles you can go on a quarter tank of gas, your working memory relies on it to get the answer. In fact, the intraparietal sulcus is so important to math skills that when researchers used mild electrical currents in order to take it offline, participants struggled to perform simple math tasks, like deciding whether 4 was bigger than 2.

Broca's area: Situated on the left side of the frontal lobes, Broca's area is involved in language comprehension and verbal fluency. Whenever you are writing or interacting with friends, family, colleagues, or a love interest, your working memory is processing information sent from this area. Whether you are a quick-witted verbal gymnast or you tend to stumble over your words depends in part on the strength of your working memory. We recently saw this play out at a wedding when the best man stood up to give the toast and then realized he had left his notes in the car. Instead of stumbling over a bunch of "ums" and "uhs," his working memory and Broca's area worked together to help him craft an eloquent, heartfelt toast on the spot.

What Working Memory Is Not

Whenever we give a presentation about working memory, someone in the audience raises his hand and asks, "Isn't that the same as short-term memory?" The answer is an unequivocal *no*. Short-term memory is the ability to remember information, such as someone's name at a party, this person's occupation, or the title of a recommended book, for a very short period. We usually don't keep this information in mind for long—a few seconds or so—and we would typically struggle to recall that person's name or the book title the following day. Working memory gives us the ability to *do something* with the information at hand rather than just remember it briefly.

Let's say you're at a business event and you meet Keith, a small-business consultant who mentions that anybody trying to start a business absolutely must read *The Essential Entrepreneur* by Smarticus McSmarty. You instantly recall that your friend Theresa is thinking about launching a new business venture, and you jot down the book's title so you can send her a text about it later. Your working memory is what helps you recall, from long-term memory, that Theresa wants to start a business and combine that with the new information that the book is great for entrepreneurs.

Working memory is also different from long-term memory. Long-term memory is the library of knowledge you have accumulated over the years—knowledge about countries, information about random news facts, memories about events from your school days, and even those annoying advertising jingles you heard on TV when you were a kid. Information may remain stored in your long-term memory for anywhere from a few days to many decades.

Working memory is what allows you to access that information and put it to good use. You can pull out information from your long-term memory, use that information in the moment, and then file it away again. Working memory is also the mechanism used to transfer new information into long-term memory, as when you are learning a new language.

Working Memory as a Conductor

You can think of working memory as your brain's Conductor. A conductor of music brings all the different instruments of an orchestra under control. Without the conductor, the result is a cacophony: the piccolo might tweet when the piano was supposed to play or the violins might be drowned out by a thundering percussion section. When the conductor walks out on the stage, chaos is brought to order.

In a similar way, your working memory gives you the advantage of control over the daily information onslaught: the emails, the ringing phones, the schedule that is constantly changing, the new math lesson that must be learned, your friend's disheartening Facebook update, the Twitter updates, the presentation that must be rapidly assembled for a potential client. In this ocean of information, where everything seems to be equally important, your working memory Conductor has two main functions:

1. It prioritizes and processes information, allowing you to ignore what is irrelevant and work with what is important.
2. It holds on to information so you can work with it.

Throughout this book, we occasionally refer to working memory as the *Conductor*, or the *working memory Conductor*, when discussing these functions.

For an illustration of how the working memory Conductor can give you an advantage at work, imagine for a moment that you are Mark, a middle manager in Microsoft's Tablet PC division, and the Tablet has been taking a beating from the iPad 700, which projects holograms. iPad 700 users love seeing their pictures and spreadsheets in three dimensions. You're called to a meeting where an inventor takes out a tablet called the FeelPad that can give holograms mass. FeelPad users can project images that can be touched and felt, not just seen. You are truly amazed. And because you are lower down the pecking order, you can just sit back and be enthralled because no one ever asks you a question at these meetings. Until today.

Bill Gates turns and looks directly at you. "Mark, will this give our tablet an edge?"

It is at this moment that you realize Gates mistakenly thinks you are the product manager. Your amygdala, the emotional heart of your brain, surges with terror. You can correct him, but then you know your career won't go anywhere. Or you can go with the flow and see where it leads. The Conductor takes over, and you decide to take a risk. Because you don't know much about the FeelPad's technology, you have to work with what you have just heard and cobble together an answer that combines the key features of the technology and how you think it will fit into the marketplace.

"Well," you say, "I think that the brand recognition of the iPad 700 is so formidable that it will mean considerable financial investment to make a dent in Apple's sales, but if the FeelPad can really make projections come to life, we may have a real iPad killer on our hands."

"Great," says Bill. "Apple wants to look at the technology too, and the inventor is giving us one day to make an offer. You have ten minutes to decide if we need to buy it."

Ten minutes? You go back to your cubicle to formulate a plan. That isn't enough time to come up with a detailed proposal, but it is enough time to assemble the most important technological information, market analyses, programming issues, and budget projections. Shutting out the ringing phone, the blinking email notice, and the low-level chatter, you modify a product launch plan with which you are already familiar and show that with the right software and viral marketing programs, the FeelPad can crush the iPad 700. Bill likes your plan so much that he makes you the project manager, and within a year, the FeelPad single-handedly turns around Microsoft's fortunes and you are promoted to vice president of new product development. Congratulations!

This remarkable change of fortune is a consequence of your Conductor working at optimum levels. It allowed you to pull out relevant information that you already knew, like product launch plans, and allowed you to synthesize it with the potential requirements of the new device. It also kept you on task and blocked distracting information, such as the ringing phone, the office chatter, and the surging fear that you may blow this opportunity. It allowed you to keep in mind the hardware, software, and finance data. It also allowed you to hold on to the information long enough to structure your plan.

What Working Memory Helps You Do in Your Daily Life

Working memory gives you the advantage of managing information in your day-to-day life from the time you're born until your golden years. Here is a quick preview of just a few of the many ways it helps you. We will explore many of these in much greater detail throughout the book.

Prioritize Information

A strong working memory helps you manage the stream of emails, texts, Facebook status updates, Tweets, and phone messages pouring into your life. Your Conductor allows you to process and prioritize all those data so you can quickly respond to the most important things first, make a mental note to deal with some things later, and efficiently shuffle the junk to the trash.

Focus on the Important Stuff

Life is filled with disruptions, and working memory helps us pay attention to what really matters. Torkel Klingberg of the Karolinska Institute in Sweden found that one of the important features of working memory is to selectively filter out distractions so we can focus on relevant information. For example, as we were putting the final touches on this book, we had a small electrical fire, our car died and had to be towed away, our refrigerator threw in the towel (resulting in mild food poisoning), and our babysitter had to take the entire week off due to a family emergency, leaving us with two rambunctious boys clamoring for our attention when we were supposed to be working. Working memory helped us deal with the emergencies, create a schedule to watch our sons, and then quickly shift our attention back to the book so we could finish and click the send button in time to meet our deadline.

Think Fast on Your Feet

You've got an interview for your dream sales job, and you are totally prepared for it—you've researched the firm, its clients, its competition, and its sales strategies. But the interviewer throws you for a loop with a wacky question out of the middle of nowhere: "You're meeting a client in an industrial estate with a gated parking lot. Where do you park?" "Huh?" You hesitate, then your working memory digs into your recent memory vault to recall that the interviewer had pointed to her car—backed into the parking space next to the exit gate—during your interview, and you quickly figure that where she parks is where she would want you to park, so you say, "I'd park right next to the exit." Ding, ding, ding! You get the job.

Take Smarter Risks

Your Conductor helps you zero in on the most essential information when weighing the pros and cons of any potentially risky venture and helps keep you from blindly going with the flow or following the crowd. For example, when that Facebook initial public offering you invested in takes an immediate nosedive, it's your working memory that helps you decide whether to dump your stock or hold on to it.

Learn More Easily in School

Kids use their Conductor every time they set foot in the classroom. It helps them to inhibit distracting information—like their classmates whispering near them—and to keep track of where they are in multistep tasks. It also allows them to access all the information they need, such as numbers or words, to complete an assignment. And, it lets them hold that information in mind and complete the tasks as quickly as possible.

Make Judgment Calls

Making quick decisions about your likes and dislikes, as well as how to act in certain situations, is a working-memory-intensive task. It may come as a surprise that even judging attractiveness relies heavily on working memory. When you spot someone across a bar, your working memory riffles through your hippocampus Rolodex for previous references of beautiful people. Then your working memory allows you to hold this information in mind while you compare the new person with the mental image and make a decision: Hot or not? The same process occurs as you decide whether you like a horror movie. Does the monster on screen measure up to the others stored in your hippocampus?

As far as actions go, your working memory is in control. If you get into a car accident and the other driver jumps out of his car and starts coming toward you in an aggressive manner, your working memory helps you quickly run through various scenarios to determine whether it's better for you to get out of the car or lock your door and call 911.

Adapt to New Situations

Have you ever wondered why some people who get laid off, divorced, or move across the country for a job transfer manage to land on their feet and thrive while others struggle to find their way? A strong working memory is the key to being able to switch gears and reinvent your career, jump back into the dating pool after years of marriage, or create a new life in a new home. Why? Because the working memory Conductor allows you to shift smoothly from thought to thought, to look at the world in a different way, and to think about old information in novel ways.

Stay Motivated to Achieve Long-Term Goals

Let's say you're finishing up your secondary education, and you aspire to an Oxbridge college. You may have high marks, but you still have to perform in your A-levels. If you study diligently, you can get the grades you need and stand a good chance of gaining entry to an elite institution. Working memory helps you keep your goal in mind and gives you the motivation you need to put your nose to the grindstone even when your friends are heading out to a party and invite you to join them. Working memory helps you say no.

Stay Positive in the Midst of a Dire Situation

Your Conductor is wired to organize emotions into those that are relevant and those that are not. The Conductor interprets signals from the amygdala, the primitive emotional heart of the brain that generates feelings of fear and anxiety, and then modulates those emotions to help us concentrate on positive thoughts. Later, we'll show you how this played out when Mario Sepulveda, one of the thirty men rescued from a collapsed Chilean coal mine in 2010, used humor to keep the group from devolving into chaos. Even during the gloomiest days underground, Mario was able to stay upbeat by focusing on the future.

Follow Your Moral Compass

Working memory helps you do the right thing in business, in social interactions, and even in your romantic relationships. It can help you stay faithful while others stray. Research shows that a good working memory gives you romantic self-control. People with a robust working memory manage to keep their relationship goals in mind and act to protect their relationship when something threatens it—like when an attractive coworker comes on to you during a business trip. Conversely, people with poor working memory are more vulnerable to giving in if an opportunity to stray presents itself.

Be a Better Athlete

There are times when a powerful working memory can be your best teammate. Let's say you're a tennis player. When the tennis ball comes bouncing to your side of the net, what shot do you make? Forehand cross-court, backhand down the line, lob, drop shot? Working memory helps you sift through the options and choose the best one, all while keeping in mind your opponent's position on the court. The more quickly your working memory can process all this information, the more likely you are to execute the shot well.

The Most Important Learning Tool: The New IQ

Our society has relied on IQ as the go-to measure of intellectual capability for nearly a century. The common belief is that the higher your IQ, the better your advantage in whatever you do. But a high IQ doesn't necessarily mean you will get what you want in life. On the other hand, how do some people with below-average IQ scores rise to the top to become business bigwigs, bestselling authors, or innovative inventors? What if we told you that IQ isn't the best measure of intelligence or the best predictor of lifetime success, especially not in the twenty-first century?

The modern IQ test has its roots in the early twentieth century. In 1917, as World War I raged on, the U.S. Army enlisted Richard Yerkes, the distinguished president of the American Psychological Association, to create a test to measure the intelligence of nearly 3 million army recruits. The army wanted to determine which men should be officers and which should be relegated to the lower ranks. Yerkes designed a test that measured the recruits' knowledge of facts and vocabulary, also known as crystallized knowledge.

But during wartime when nothing goes according to plan and you have to adapt to enemy tactics or lose, knowing concrete facts—say, that Rutherford B. Hayes was elected president in 1876 or that

Bismarck is the capital of North Dakota—isn't really helpful. Many of the men tagged for high-ranking positions failed miserably, while some men who languished in the lower ranks proved to have excellent military minds. The army quickly realized that Yerkes's test was identifying the wrong men for the job and abandoned it after six months. But the rest of society has continued to measure intelligence based on the amount of crystallized knowledge you have, and the modern IQ test doesn't look all that different from Yerkes's test. That's a big problem.

Thanks to Google and similar search engines, the world has undergone profound transformation in how we seek out, weed out, and absorb information. We live in the Google age. In cognitive terms, Google is great. It has considerably reduced the amount of intellectual resources that we previously had to dedicate to rooting out facts before we could do something with them. Because of Google, we no longer need to rely so much on crystallized knowledge—the memorization of facts, dates, or names—associated with IQ and the traditional concept of intelligence. With nothing more than a few clicks, we can pull up just about any information we need. But the key to intelligence today is being able to put those facts together, prioritize the information, and do something constructive with it. And there is one skill that gives you the advantage of managing all this information: working memory. *IQ is what you know. Working memory is what you can do with what you know.*

In one of her earliest research projects, Tracy compared students' grades with their IQ and working memory scores. She found that working memory could predict what grade they would get with far greater accuracy than IQ. In fact, if Tracy knew a child's working memory, she could determine his or her grades with 95 percent accuracy. In chapter 5 we will go into much greater detail about this study and other research showing that working memory gives you more of an advantage in the classroom than IQ. Here are just a few of the many fascinating and sometimes surprising findings we will explore in that chapter:

- A good working memory is the best advantage in school and is causally related to grades.
- Kids with good IQ scores don't necessarily have a good working memory.
- An average or even a high IQ doesn't necessarily give the student the tools for success in the classroom and beyond.
- IQ is linked to how rich or poor you are, but working memory isn't, which makes it a great equalizer.

The research on working memory also shows that the strength of a person's working memory influences far more than grades. An abundance of new evidence, which we present in this book, shows that the strength of your working memory plays a pivotal role in how successful you will be in many areas of your life, including whether you'll have the fortitude to work toward your long-term goals, whether you view the glass as half-full or half-empty, and even whether you'll be able to lay off the junk food when dieting.

How Working Memory Is Undermined

Unfortunately, many things in our fast-paced 24/7 society are working against us to weaken our working memory. And when working memory isn't operating at full speed, it puts us at a big disadvantage.

Information Overload

If your working memory isn't up to snuff, you could drown in the overwhelming flood of data. Todd learned about the impact of information overload the hard way. As a serial entrepreneur, the thirty-five-year-old father of three was no stranger to the frenetic pace of a Silicon Valley high-tech start-up company. He spent every day sitting in front of four computer screens that beeped and pinged and flashed email alerts, instant messages, websites, and Twitter feeds. His clients constantly called his home office, his kids demanded attention, and he was insepa-rable from his iPhone as he toggled between his home and office life. For more than a year, Todd had been looking for a buyer for his com-pany. But when a large company based on the East Coast emailed Todd saying that they were interested in acquiring his firm, the email got lost in the chaos of his life and he didn't discover it in his email inbox for over a week. If he hadn't finally stumbled across it when scanning back through his correspondence one evening at home, he might have lost what turned into a $2-million-dollar sale.

The Lure of Instant Gratification

In our *I want it now* society, we want immediate satisfaction. Our quest for the fleeting thrill we get from an impulsive purchase or from eating an entire bag of chips when we're on a diet, relegates working memory to the sidelines of the decision-making process. This is why we so often opt for smaller, more immediate rewards rather than waiting for bigger and better things, like a fat bank account, or a slim waistline.

Time Constraints

Being squeezed for time burdens working memory and makes you more likely to give in to impulse—whether you're confronted with a limited-time-offer purchase, for example, or trying to select the correct answers while taking a timed test, or even when faced with an ultimatum from a significant other to get engaged now or break up. In chapter 2, we look at how this plays out on eBay, where the ticking clock can overwhelm your working memory, making it more likely you will give into impulse and pay more than you should.

Stress

When the pressure is on, it can overload your working memory and sab-otage your performance at work, at school, or even on the pitch. Think of the angst that every team feels in a penalty shoot-out against Germany. Their reputation for flawless penalties transforms some of the world's best players into tripping toddlers. Stuart Pearce, Chris Waddle, Gareth Southgate—all these England players stepped up to take penalties in shoot-outs against Germany—and stress caused them to miss. Goodbye, glory.

Retirement

Sorry to burst your bubble, but if you've been dreaming about the day you can say good-bye to the 9-to-5 grind and hello to retirement, we have to inform you that retirement makes you dumb. Retirement marks not just a reduction of work, but also a reduction in thinking and, consequently, a reduction in your working memory strength.

Pain

If you've ever slammed your hand in the car door or spilled boiling water on your lap, you know that it's tough to think clearly when you're in pain. Scientists have discovered that pain, including chronic aches like a sore back or knee, may disrupt working memory.

Romance

What does romance have to do with working memory? In a 2012 study, Jeffrey Cooper and colleagues at Trinity College Dublin discovered that the PFC plays a big role in the first flush of attraction. They scanned the brains of nineteen- to thirty-one-year-olds on the prowl and showed them photos of potential mates. Some photos caused a burst of activity in parts of their PFC. Participants then went to a speed-dating event, and the researchers discovered that the stronger the activation in the PFC, the more likely the participants were to pursue a second date. If you find your working memory working overtime when you first meet someone, there is a good chance that you'll take a chance and ask them out.

Some exciting new research by Johan Karremans at Rodboud University in the Netherlands offers insight into why men often become tongue-tied when meeting a woman whom they find attractive. He found that men's scores on a working memory test were lower after they'd had a brief conversation with a beautiful woman. And intriguingly, he did not find this "attraction effect" in women after they'd had a conversation with a handsome man. His interpretation of his results is that because traditional gender roles require men to take the initiative in engaging in conversation with a potential mate, their working memories are more taxed by the process.

Video Games, Smoking, and Overeating

Whatever your guilty pleasure may be, it can take your working memory offline. A healthy working memory inhibits self-destructive habits, but engaging too often in highly addictive behaviors causes changes in the brain. Basically certain brain regions gang up and recruit your working memory into fulfilling the addictive desire, rather than stopping it.

How Working Memory Can Be Improved

As little as five years ago, people thought that working memory was fixed—that you were stuck with what you were born with. But research is showing otherwise. Think of working memory as like a rubber band. Some rubber bands are big, and some are small, but they can all be stretched. In the same way, we're all born with a certain level of working memory. But regardless of our genetic predisposition for a strong or not-so-strong working memory, nearly every one of us can stretch it to get a bigger advantage in life.

The lessons we've learned from our work with students to train their working memory with the *Jungle Memory* software Ross developed have confirmed that significant improvements are possible. Take the case of a young girl named Jasmine. She was often told that she needed to "try harder," but despite doing her best, she couldn't keep up at school or follow her mom's instructions at home. After being diagnosed with a working memory deficit, Jasmine used the *Jungle Memory* program for eight weeks and saw dramatic results. She improved her working memory by over 800 percent (an amazing result!) and started winning achievement awards at school.

Tracy has also seen significant improvements in clinical trials when she tested the working memory of students with reading and math difficulties. After they had trained regularly for eight weeks with *Jungle Memory*, they showed fantastic improvements in working memory; even more exciting was that their grades also improved—generally a whole grade point, such as from a C to B or a B to an A. Another study showed that they maintained all of these improvements eight months later.

Throughout this book, we introduce you to a host of simple working-memory-training exercises, so that you can get started on getting your working memory in shape as you read. And at the end of the book, we provide a quick hits training manual that you can use on the go to help keep your working memory sharp.

In the chapters that follow, we first draw on more than a decade of research and practical experience to explore why working memory is so vital in our lives and the role it plays in our general work aptitude and in our general life happiness, as well as in learning, overcoming addiction, and achieving in sports. In part II, we show you how working memory changes during our lives from childhood to old age and introduce encouraging evidence about how we can keep our working memory in good shape during later life. We also present specific tools for strengthening working memory—from the most effective brain training programs, to the best foods to eat (some of them may surprise you), to small but crucial tweaks in your daily habits that can make a big difference for your working memory. The chapters in part III imagine a future in which the world is designed to give our working memory the best advantage and look at groundbreaking research on how it gave our ancestors an evolutionary advantage.

Test Your Working Memory

To help you get a basic understanding of the strength of your working memory, here are two quick tests. For a more detailed measure of your working memory power, take the full online test at http://testwm.com.

Test 1

Below is a list of three-letter words. Don't look at it! Ask a friend to quiz you using the list of words. In level 1 of this test, your friend is going to read aloud two words, like *cat* and *bat*. You have to try to remember the two words, reverse them, and repeat them backward. *Tab. Tac.* In level 2, you have to do the same with three words. In level 3, it's four words. Most people are able to do level 1, but you need a strong working memory to complete levels 2 and 3 correctly.

Net
Top
Pig
Dab
Level 3

Tip
Car
Bun
Level 2

Lid
Dog
Level 1

Test 1. List of Words

Test 2

Level 1

1. Look at the pyramid below. Remember the triangle where the letter appears.

2. Now look at this picture. Does it start with the same letter as the letter in the triangle?

3. Here is another pyramid. Remember the triangle where the letter appears.

4. Now look at this picture. Does it start with the same letter as the letter in the triangle?

5. Now draw arrows to the triangles where the letters appeared, in the correct order.

Level 2

Follow the same directions as in Level 1.

1. Remember the triangle where the letter appears.

2. Does the picture start with the same letter as the letter in the triangle?

3. Remember the triangle where the letter appears.

4. Does the picture start with the same letter as the letter in the triangle?

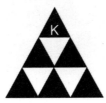

5. Remember the triangle where the letter appears.

6. Does the picture start with the same letter as the letter in the triangle?

7. Now draw arrows to the triangles where the letters appeared, in the correct order.

Level 3

Follow the same directions as in Level 1.

1. Remember the triangle where the letter appears.

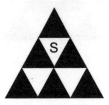

2. Does the picture start with the same letter as the letter in the triangle?

3. Remember the triangle where the letter appears.

4. Does the picture start with the same letter as the letter in the triangle?

5. Remember the triangle where the letter appears.

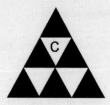

6. Does the picture start with the same letter as the letter in the triangle?

7. Remember the triangle where the letter appears.

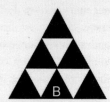

8. Does the picture start with the same letter as the letter in the triangle?

9. Now draw arrows to the triangles where the letters appeared, in the correct order.

Scoring

The number of letters you can remember in the correct order gives you an indication of the strength of your working memory. If you are like most adults, you were probably able to complete levels 1 and 2 of this test correctly. Data from thousands of people confirm that the average five-year-old can remember and process two things. Most adults are able to remember four or five items in the correct order.

If you didn't fare so well on these tests, don't get frustrated. You can always make an improvement. If you aced these assessments, don't get too smug. You need to continually challenge your working memory to keep it in tiptop shape. Doing brain training exercises, such as the ones in this book, can help optimize your working memory.

2

Why Working Memory
Is Crucial to Success

WE HAVE SPENT a lot of time studying what happens when our working memory Conductor fails to keep control—from kids struggling to keep up in the classroom to bad habits such as gambling and overeating and failing to meet deadlines at work. An overtaxed working memory may even be behind your feeling like a grump all the time, or an inability to control your wandering eye even though you've found "the one." At the heart of why working memory is so important in endeavors from work to school, to sports, to dieting is a core set of skills that a strong working memory enables us to exercise. To dig deeper into how working memory operates and how it enhances our lives, in this chapter we focus on this essential skill set, starting with perhaps the most distinctive feature of human life: our will—that is, the ability to choose for ourselves, to act, to carry out plans, to take responsibility for what we do.

Working Memory and Will

Your will affords you the wherewithal to go after the things you want in life: choosing a university, selecting a subject, chasing after a romantic partner, and vigorously pursuing a career. Why is working memory central to our ability to exercise will? Because exercising will requires evaluating, planning, and executing plans; keeping long-term goals in mind; controlling impulses; and overcoming obstacles—all of which rely on working memory skills.

We had an intense experience of the relationship between the working memory and will when we taught in El Salvador, a country known for danger. During our time there, grocery stores had guards armed with shotguns positioned by the milk and an area for you to check your guns and coats before you shopped. We quickly learned to deal with everyone in an exceedingly polite manner.

On our very last day in the country, we were driving on a well-traveled road when a car swerved and cut us off. Ross, who was driving, saw that one of many men in the car had a shotgun. He zipped his lips. Because of her line of sight, Tracy, in the passenger seat, didn't see the gun, and the red mist descended, and she used unmistakable, universal sign language to express her dissatisfaction. Fortunately, the men didn't notice the gesture or didn't care, and we continued on our way unharmed.

The way our two minds reacted so differently to the same incident is a prime example of how the will works. Joaquin Fuster, a professor of psychiatry and biobehavioral sciences at UCLA, once described the process by saying that the will must take into account a barrage of three kinds of information:

- *Internal information*—hormonal levels, mood, emotions, information from organs
- *External information*—the constant stream of information transmitted by the senses
- *System of Principles*—information—language, memory, values, culture, civics, and laws we are bound to

Our working memory Conductor takes all this information in, categorizes it, decides a course of action, and executes that plan. So let's see how Fuster's model may have played out in our driving mishap.

After slamming on the brakes to avoid the accident, Ross's Conductor rapidly processed the three kinds of information:

- *Internal information*: His amygdala was pretty pissed off and sent that information to his working memory.

- *External information:* Before he could hurl an insult, his working memory also brought to bear the sight of the gun and the number of men in the car.

- *System of principles information*: Cultural awareness that an expletive may provoke violence (as well as the painful awareness that he would be showing up to a gunfight with halting Spanish as a weapon).

His working memory weighed all this information, decided that there was no advantage to responding, and, in an expression of will, took the action of zipping his lip.

Now let's look at what happened in Tracy's mind. Her Conductor was also busy handling information:

- *Internal information*: Like Ross's, Tracy's amygdala fired off a message of anger to her PFC.

- *External Information*: Crucially, she didn't have the same external information—she saw only the car cut us off. Unlike Ross, she did not see the gun nor did she count the number of men in the car.

- *System of principles information*: Including an unmerited confidence in Ross's limited bilingualism to deal with any consequences. Also, the ethical sense that we had been wronged and deserved justice.

After weighing all this information in a matter of nanoseconds, her will elected to unleash a dramatic reply demonstrating her anger.

The exercise of will is not just a matter of being deliberative. It's more complicated than that and involves a complex juggling act of assessing information, modulating emotions, and thinking strategically. It's your

Conductor that helps you sift through all the data to come up with a plan, and in some instances, the best course of action may be a more aggressive go-for-it approach.

Let's say you have come up with what you think is a promotion-worthy idea for a new marketing campaign, and you excitedly share it with your immediate supervisor, Kathy. The next day, you overhear Kathy telling the marketing director about your idea and taking credit for it. Do you say nothing or stand up for yourself? Keeping the peace ensures that you won't irritate your supervisor, but it also means that you will probably be stuck in a cubicle for the foreseeable future. Telling the marketing director that it's your idea may upset Kathy but it could be your ticket to a big office and a major payday. You decide it's worth it, and it's your working memory that allows you to think strategically to come up with a clever way to let the boss know it was your idea without making Kathy look bad.

Delay of Gratification

Those who are able to delay gratification have a great advantage in life. By going for the fast buck, the easy way out, we lose the rewards that come with practiced patience, and as we will see in this section, it is our working memory that helps us achieve long-term goals. As anyone who has worked hard to move up the career ladder knows, it's the things you don't do as much as the things you do that make it possible to ascend the ranks. It is the times you don't go to happy hour with your friends so you can take night classes to advance in your career, don't plop down in front of the TV on Sunday for a football marathon when you need to prep for Monday's meeting, and don't call in sick for a "mental health day" just because you had a little too much fun over the weekend. The ability to set aside current pleasure for a greater reward is critical for success. But human nature has long been known to undermine this ability. Behavioral economist and psychologist George Ainsle is famous for his theoretical work on decision making and impulse control. In 1975, Ainsle drew together research demonstrating how people are much more inclined to pursue immediate rewards that are lesser rather than wait for a bigger reward later on. In one study, when participants were offered the choice of an immediate reward of $11 or a delayed reward of $85, they tended to take the smaller amount.

We now know that working memory plays a major role in this process, thanks to John Hinson and researchers from Washington State University. They found that when working memory is removed from the decision-making process, the average person opts for a smaller, immediate reward rather than waiting for an even better outcome. Hinson overloaded his participants' working memory with a large amount of information. Then when given a choice between accepting a small reward of between $100 and $900 immediately or waiting for a larger reward of up to $2,000, their working memory was unable to calculate which reward would be better in the long run. As a result, they followed their impulse and grabbed the smaller, immediate reward.

This study was echoed in research conducted by Bennedetto De Martino from University College London. He wanted to look at what was happening in the brain when people used their will to hold out for a larger reward. De Martino gave people a series of risk scenarios, but this time he scanned their brains using functional magnetic resonance imaging (fMRI). De Martino found that when people opted for the smaller but certain reward, they didn't really mull over the decision. Their emotional center, the amygdala lit up, and they made the easy, if unconsidered, choice. But when people controlled their impulse and chose the larger and uncertain reward, their prefrontal cortex, which houses their working memory, lit up.

Some people had a more automatic and stronger emotional response to these decisions: their amygdala showed greater activation. You may think that such people are more likely to always opt for the immediate choice, but when de Martino ran the numbers, he saw that the strength of their emotions didn't determine how likely they were to choose the immediate reward. In fact, it was how hard their working memory was working that influenced their choice. If their PFC showed less activation, they followed their impulses. But the greater the activation, the more likely they were to make the better choice.

Our Conductor's ability to delay gratification is also backed up by a decades-long series of studies from psychologist Walter Mischel, starting with his famous marshmallow test in 1968 and continuing with his most recent findings published in 2011. In the 1960s in his lab at Stanford University, Mischel offered more than six hundred children between the ages of four and six a marshmallow. Then he told them that he was going to leave the room, and if they could wait until he returned, they would get a second marshmallow. If they could not wait, they could ring a little bell that he left on the table, and he would return and let them eat the one marshmallow. Some of the children immediately popped the marshmallow into their mouths while others resisted temptation and held out for the greater reward of two marshmallows.

Although Mischel and his colleagues didn't call the marshmallow test a working memory task, we now know that it had many of the same features of a working memory task, such as keeping a goal or greater reward in mind, ignoring a distraction, planning, and executing strategies to divert attention. Based on what we now know about working memory, we understand that a child can manage only a limited amount of information, and they can easily be overwhelmed by a very tempting option, such as a single delicious, pillowy marshmallow sitting in front of them.

In order to overcome the urge to reach out and gobble up the marshmallow, they had to use their working memory Conductor to shift their gaze or, at the very least, their attention to something else. The kids used a variety of techniques to distract themselves from the fluffy treat: hiding under the table, covering their eyes with their hands, turning their chair the opposite way, or singing a song.

Mischel has tracked these children over the years, investigating whether their ability to delay gratification gave them an advantage in life. For example, in a 1990 follow-up study, Mischel compared the children's SAT scores with how they performed in the initial experiment and found that the longer a child had been able to wait for that second marshmallow, the higher his or her SAT score was.

In a paper published in 2011, Mischel and his colleagues retested the group. Now that they were in their forties, would they still be defined by how they performed as children? They selected the adults who as children were high delayers—they were able to resist the temptation to eat the marshmallow for longer— and those who gave in pretty quickly. In one testing session, they showed both a series of faces with different expressions—happy, fearful, or neutral—and asked them to press the space bar on the computer every time they saw a happy face but ignore the fearful or neutral faces. The groups performed similarly. In another testing session, the participants now had to press the space bar every time they saw a fearful expression and not when they saw a smiling face. It is a natural human impulse to respond to a smiling face, so this would require suppressing that natural inclination. Those who as children were low delayers, also had trouble not responding to the happy faces as adults; while those who had been high delayers as children, were able to control their impulses.

The next step was to find out what was happening in the brain, so they put the adults in a brain scanner while they were doing the same face task. When the high delayers had to resist the temptation to press the space bar in response to a happy face, the PFC was activated. But the low delayers were not using this area of the brain as much as the high delayers were. Instead, they were recruiting an area of the brain called the striatum, associated with automatized and unconsidered reactions.

Although Mischel didn't give specific details on the career successes of the participants, anecdotally it seems to be the case that the high delayers turned out to be more professionally accomplished. Carolyn, one of the high delayers, earned a Ph.D. at Princeton and is now a college psychology professor. Craig, a low delayer, moved to Los Angeles and has spent his career as a jack-of-all-trades. He is still looking for the solid ground on which to build his career. As Craig remarks, "Sure, I wish I had been a more patient person. Looking back, there are definitely moments when it would have helped me make better career choices and stuff."

We saw just how badly this lure of instant gratification can derail us in life with the recent financial crisis. The housing market lured home buyers into making unwise purchases in part by offering a highly appealing deal in the short term. Buyers' working memories were short-circuited, and they purchased increasingly expensive houses without considering how they were going to afford the payments or what they would do if the houses decreased in value. They went for the quick-and-easy profit.

The oversubscribed credit market, which contributed to the crash, was similarly designed to provide consumers with instant gratification. Want that new car but don't have the cash? Don't worry: go ahead and buy it at full price and make monthly payments for the next sixty months. Must have that Louis Vuitton bag but don't have £4,000 in your pocket? No problem; just charge it to the credit card with 18 percent annual interest rate. Need that HDTV *now* so you can watch the big game today? What's a 10 percent monthly charge added to the cost?

Salesmen put us at a disadvantage when they interfere with working memory, and we often walk away with impulsive purchases like the 4x4 Range Rover that we all know will never see an unpaved track. Have you ever paid more than you should have on eBay? We certainly have, and the reason is that online bidding overloads working memory. Let's say you're bidding on a home entertainment system that you could buy new at your local Argos for about £500. You find a used one online for a £49 minimum bid. *Fantastic deal*, you think. So you place your bid.

Each time the price changes, your Conductor has to work with the new numbers to determine if it's still a fantastic deal or, when you factor in shipping costs and the fact that there is no warranty, if it costs more than it is worth. At the same time, you have to use your Conductor to suppress the excitement coming from the amygdala, your brain's emotional center that is egging you on to *win*! Finally, as the clock counts down, your working memory has less and less time to process all the changing variables. The result is that you end up paying £300 for a possibly damaged entertainment system with no warranty.

Car dealers use the same tactic. They put you into a pressure cooker situation with a changing set of numbers to calculate, play on your emotions—*"If I speak to my boss, do I have your word that you are going to do a deal with me?"*—and give you a limited-time offer. Then you end up driving away from the dealer behind the wheel of a new car wondering why you paid more than you wanted to for a car that isn't even the color you wanted.

Psychologist Itiel Dror conducted an experiment that shows just how limited-time offers make us take greater risks than we normally would. In his trial, people were asked to play a simplified version of blackjack, in which players were dealt cards one at a time. Cards were worth whatever the number of the card was (a 7 of hearts was worth 7 points), and the numbers were added up with each new card. The goal was to avoid going over 21 points in total. The closer you get to 21, there's a much greater risk that you will go over with the next card, so after players get what they consider to be enough points, they usually hold, or stop taking cards. Participants were asked to play the game twice.

In the first round, they were allowed to take their time when making a decision to take another card or to hold. In the second round, they were given no time for reflection and had to make automatic decisions. Dror found that when they were forced to make a quick decision, they made bad choices. So if they had accumulated a large number of points, say 18, they were more likely to take another card even though it was highly likely they would go over 21. If they had no time pressure, they were far more conservative when they reached a higher number.

The irony in this allure of immediate satisfaction is that psychologists have found that the amount of pleasure you derive from that impulsive purchase dissipates considerably with the pain of making the payments. In order to achieve that fleeting feeling of excitement again, you need to plunk down your credit card for another new bag or gizmo. Eventually you may be perpetually chasing the thrill of the new purchase while placing yourself deeper and deeper in debt. If people really thought through a purchasing strategy of "owe more, enjoy it less," they would be far less likely to buy anything on credit ever again.

The ability to delay gratification and practice strategic allocation of our attention is vital in many areas of life. When you have a big test or a big project due the next day, your working memory keeps that squarely in mind so you can say no to the kegger at the fraternity or the happy hour get-together with coworkers. Your working memory keeps you from gobbling up the cheesy lasagna on your fiancé's dinner plate when you are trying to get into beach body shape for your island honeymoon that's three weeks away. The good news, again, is that you aren't stuck with the working memory you have now: you can strengthen it to shore up your ability to delay gratification and get the bigger rewards in life that you really want.

Focus and Multitasking

The ability to focus is another advantage that working memory gives us. Focus is crucial to learning and makes a big difference in our performance in school and beyond. In order to focus, your Conductor has to keep the goal in mind while making sure no other distracting thoughts overwhelm you. This is, of course, increasingly challenging in the world of nonstop email, Twitter feeds, and multiple windows open on our computers.

The fact that the strength of one's working memory makes a great deal of difference in this skill was demonstrated powerfully in a study that Michael Kane and colleagues at the University of North Carolina conducted in 2007, which measured the impact of working memory on people's ability to stay on task in the midst of demanding activities. They gave working memory tests to more than one hundred young adults and asked them to keep a week-long record detailing how often they experienced distracting thoughts or mind wandering. They found that the people with low working memory scores were often distracted, especially as the tasks got harder. In contrast, those with high working memory scores maintained their attention better.

Distraction isn't the only impediment to focus. We are all increasingly expected to multitask, and studies have shown that this demand to multitask taxes working memory and easily overwhelms it.

Let's take a look at what multitasking might look like in the brain. Imagine that it is seven o'clock on a Wednesday night, and you are helping your daughter, Gemma, with her long-division homework. The last time you did long division was twenty-five years ago, so it's not an easy chore, and you are firing signals between your intraparietal sulcus and PFC to stay on top of things.

All of a sudden, you hear your phone make the email "ding!" and you break your attention from long division. You have a big deal in your sights at work, and they need your help. You've got to respond with some critical information ASAP. You set aside the long division, and fire off a quick response. Now, back to the long division.

Psychologists call this skill *task switching*, and it is closely connected to your working memory abilities, as a colleague at the University of Geneva, Pierre Barrouillet, discovered in 2008. Barrouillet wanted to find out how switching from one task to another affects working memory. He gave the participants number tasks on a computer screen. Numbers were colored red and blue according to the task the person had to do. In the red task, participants had to decide whether numbers were larger or smaller than five. In the blue task, participants had to judge whether numbers were odd or even. The participants were given a chance to try it out and become used to the rules of both tasks.

Barrouillet could now test whether switching between the red task and the blue task would jeopardize performance. When the participants had to do only the red task, they were fine. But when they had to quickly switch between the red and blue tasks, their working memory was overwhelmed. It took them much longer to complete it, and they also made more errors.

One of the hardest realities of life these days is that there are certain times when you simply can't shift your attention from one task fully to the other but must do both at once. For example, you may find yourself having to answer an email from work while sitting in a meeting with your child's teacher, or take a call from school while navigating the highway on-ramp on your way to work. Can working memory allow us to do both, and will we be able to perform both tasks just as well as if we were focusing our attention on only one task? It depends.

In 2010, Jason Watson and David Strayer at the University of Utah tested the ability of two hundred people to handle a multitude of tasks. The participants had to drive in a simulator while using a hands-free phone. To make the task even more challenging, they had to listen to an audio of a series of words interspersed with math problems. This was a working memory task that required considerable mental agility: they had to use their working memory to retrieve mathematical information from their long-term library to solve a problem. At the same time, they had to keep track of a string of words in the correct order. On top of all this, they had to negotiate traffic in the simulator.

Out of the two hundred adults, the majority of them did worse in the driving simulator when they had to use their working memory at the same time. They took longer to brake than they should, and they tailgated a pace car. If you ever had to think through a work problem while driving or even decode your Aunt Mabel's cryptic and hastily scribbled directions in the days before GPS, you know your driving can suffer. The results of this experiment were clear: people perform worse when they have to do more than one task at the same time. Watson and Strayer also found that while most people are at least able to keep two possible tasks in their mind, when that number grows and they are forced to handle more than two tasks, their working memory Conductor drops the baton.

Scientists have known since the 1980s that performing two tasks at the same time undermines performance in both. But one additional discovery Watson and Strayer made was quite surprising: the rule that performing two tasks at once undermines our ability to do each well doesn't apply to all of us. Participants who had top working memory scores were able to do both the driving and the working memory task at the same time without any decline in the performance of either. For these "Super Taskers," as Watson and Strayer call them, their working memory was so good that it took everything in stride. If we improve our working memory, we can become more like the supertaskers.

Managing Information

Another major stress on our working memory is information overload: too much information can overwhelm our working memory.

One interesting study that shows this effect was conducted by researchers at Washington State University, who wanted to look at how

information overload can affect financial decisions. They gave participants a gambling task. They were presented with four decks of cards;
some cards won them money, and some lost them money. Remembering
what they'd won and comparing it with the cards they had turned over,
the best players were able to determine quickly which decks were able to
win them the most money and which decks were to be avoided because
of losing cards. But when players were also given random sequences of
numbers to remember, it took them longer to distinguish between the
winning and losing decks, and they ended up losing more money. This
shows that too much information can make you a bad investor.

This is all the more true on Wall Street. If you've ever seen the bank
of flashing screens at a broker's desk, you have a sense of the information overload they are up against. When deciding whether to invest in
a company, for example, they may take into account the people at the
helm; the current and potential size of its market; net profits; and its
past, present, and future stock value, among other pieces of information. Weighing all of these factors can take up so much of your working
memory that it becomes overwhelmed. Think of having piles and piles
of papers, sticky notes, and spreadsheets strewn about your desk, and
you get a picture of what's going on inside the brain. When information
overloads working memory this way, it can make brokers—and the rest
of us—scrap all the strategizing and analyses and go for emotional, or
gut, decisions.

This same breakdown in our analysis and decision making can happen to any of us when we're overwhelmed by a tsunami of information
at work. It can lead us to make emotional decisions at times when strategic thinking matters most, such as when choosing a new vendor. For
example, if you interview all twenty-three candidates who expressed
interest in the project rather than narrowing down the candidate pool
to five or fewer, your Conductor may lose track of all the data about
their past work experience and qualifications so you end up tossing all
that valuable information out the window and going with your gut. You
choose the guy who's an Arsenal fan because you're a huge Arsenal fan
too. That's not the smartest move.

Children are just as likely to suffer this same type of working memory overload when they are overwhelmed with information at school. When teachers introduce too much material at once, the Conductor loses control. This can cause even the brightest students to stop reasoning and start guessing on tests.

Too much information can even lead to what we call *catastrophic loss* of working memory. Our friend Sam was recently made redundant from his job because his company downsized. He had a six-month parachute to regroup and seek out new opportunities, but every time he sat down in front of his computer, he got distracted and overwhelmed. He would read emails from friends suggesting that he use his parachute to go travel in South America for three months. Other friends called recommending jobs, and the websites he surfed showed hundreds of possible career opportunities and directions he could take. He became paralyzed by the choices. In terms of working memory, too many choices equals too much information. Entertaining the myriad possibilities—traveling, becoming a firefighter, going back to school, writing the Great American Novel—caused Sam's working memory to crash, much like a computer does when too many programs are running at the same time. He became so frustrated that he gave up his search and started watching endless reruns of *CSI*. He suffered a bout of depression, related to his working memory overload. We explore the important link between working memory and mood disorders and general life happiness more in the next chapter.

It's important to know that being faced with seemingly limitless choices, or simply too much information, doesn't mean your working memory Conductor is doomed to fail. It's the way you deal with the steady stream of choices and data that determines whether you'll be inundated, like Sam, or able to quickly zero in on the best options and most important information for you. People who escape the crushing weight of too many choices don't allow themselves to entertain every single possibility or attend to every bit of information. They winnow down the options and sources to a more manageable number. We offer some tips about the best methods for doing this in our training manual at the end of the book.

Time Management

Another skill crucial for productivity is time management. These days we all have to learn the art of doing more in less time. But the problem, as we all know, is that even as new technologies help us to work faster—responding to email, reviewing important sales data or new documents, all before we walk through our office door in the morning—they don't always help us work smarter.

One downside of the new technologies is that they have given us many new ways to spend our time; we linger online, checking multiple news sources, travel deals, or sale items on our favorite websites. Instead of being productive, we end up wasting more time. Working memory plays a vital role in helping us keep on top of the time we're spending and complete the tasks at hand.

Cognitive time management is a term Katya Rubia and Anna Smith at King's College London used to describe how well we can estimate the amount of time we spend on a task, as well as manage the time we allocate to an activity. Their review of brain-imaging studies on cognitive time management revealed that the PFC is highly activated during tasks that involve timing. The theory is that working memory keeps track of passing time and modulates decisions about when to take action.

Managing Stress

One of the pervasive characteristics of life these days is stress, and unfortunately stress considerably undermines our working memory, as Mauricio Delgado of Rutgers University found. To test this in a study, Delgado created stress by submerging participants' hands in a bath of cold water. Though this may seem a procedure unlikely related to stress, it is a psychologically recognized method for inducing stress without harming participants. Delgado found that the stress undermined the participants' working memory to such a degree that when they were asked to determine the outcome of a series of financial investments, they tended to just give up thinking things through and use their emotions to give an answer.

The negative effect that stress has on working memory was also shown revealed in a study conducted by Amy Arnsten and colleagues at Yale University. They worked with rats to simulate stress by increasing their levels of protein kinase C (PKC). High levels of PKC are connected to increased stress: the more PKC there is in its system, the more stressed the rat. When the researchers raised the levels of PKC in the rats, their working memory literally shut down. As a result, they had impaired judgment, high levels of distraction, and displayed impulsive behavior. High levels of stress definitely have a negative impact on working memory.

But what's really interesting is that having a stronger working memory can also help inoculate you against stress. In 2006, Rachel Yehuda of Mount Sinai School of Medicine and her colleagues at Yale Medical School examined working-memory-type skills in a wide range of traumatic and stressful situations. They looked at combat veterans who had experienced posttraumatic stress disorder, those facing the loss of a family member, women in early stages of breast cancer, and those who had just survived a natural disaster. They found that skills associated with working memory played a big role in helping them to cope.

Calculating Risks

One final basic skill that contributes significantly to success in life and in which your working memory Conductor is integral is assessing risks and rewards in a variety of situations. Do you quit your dead-end corporate job to take a position with a start-up company that could either put you on the career fast track or leave you jobless if the business fails? Do you follow the family tradition and go to your parents' local alma mater, or do you enroll at a small liberal arts college thousands of miles from home? Do you accept the first job offer you get out of college or wait to see if something better comes up?

Risk assessment is also fundamental to the more menial aspects of our daily lives. Things as ordinary as driving regularly require a great deal of risk calculation. Should you speed up to make it through a yellow stoplight or slam on the brakes? Deciding requires your working memory to quickly assess the oncoming situation, the presence of any pedestrians in the crosswalk, and the possibility that a police officer might be lurking ahead. It's our working memory that allows us to juggle all this information in a split second. Think of all the daily tasks you do that require a similar assessment of risks, and you will realize how important working memory is.

So we've seen how important working memory is to the core life skills that allow us to achieve success, whether in school or work. In the next chapter, we introduce a fascinating set of findings that revealed that working memory is crucial to success in another fundamental aspect of our lives: our general happiness.

3

The Joker in the Mines

How Working Memory Makes Us Happier

MARIO SEPULVEDA, one of the thirty men rescued from a collapsed Chilean coal mine in September 2010, became famous for making jokes. During the sixty-nine days he and his coworkers were trapped in oppressive heat and total darkness deep in the heart of a dangerous mine, the forty-year-old's infectious sense of humor helped to keep the group from devolving into chaos. Even on the gloomiest days before the miners heard the sounds of drilling and a showering of rocks signaling that a rescue effort had begun, Mario found happiness by focusing on what he would do when he got out. He tried hard not to let the dusty air get him down and didn't complain about sleeping on damp cardboard with no sense of whether it was day or night.

Instead, he led efforts to find potential escape routes, made jokes to maintain his sanity and hold up group morale, and supported the younger miners who were often scared and hysterical. Whenever Mario got depressed, he kept his tears private so that the group would not lose their faith. After the tense rescue effort came to an end and the miners were lifted to safety, Mario gave the rescue workers rocks wrapped in tin foil as a gag gift for their hard work.

"We knew that if society broke down we would all be doomed," he told a reporter for the *Daily Mail*. "It was important to keep clean, to keep busy, to keep believing we would be rescued."

The international headlines dubbed him "Super Mario" because he was the one who kept the group from falling apart. They celebrated Mario's natural charisma, leadership, and positive outlook. But we have a slightly different take on the matter: we expect that Mario mobilized a healthy working memory to stay focused on the positive.

Although the understanding of the relationship between working memory and happiness is still developing, a growing body of evidence shows that working memory is involved in our ability to keep a positive outlook, even in stressful, threatening situations like the one Mario and his fellow coal miners faced.

The Science of Happiness

"Happiness depends on ourselves." This insightful gem, attributed to the ancient Greek philosopher Aristotle, elegantly summarizes what philosophers have long known: happiness is the consequence of decisions that we make in our lives. We can choose to be happy even in the most desperate circumstances. When Viktor Frankl, a key figure in existential therapy, was imprisoned in a concentration camp during World War II, he found meaning and a reason to live by focusing on his love for his wife. Instead of dwelling on his imprisonment, he made a choice to be happy by focusing on future goals. In the past decade or so, psychologists and neurologists have been employing sophisticated experimental techniques in an effort to understand what philosophers have known for so long. Working memory is at the center of their investigations.

Sara Levens and Ian Gotlib from Stanford University are two of the psychologists examining the role that working memory plays in happiness. In a 2010 study, they recruited a group of adults with depression and another group of adults without any history of the mood disorder. Both groups had to perform a working memory task that required them to evaluate the emotional expressions—happy, sad, or neutral—of a series of faces viewed on a computer screen.

As each face appeared on the screen, the participants had to judge whether it had the same or a different emotional expression as a face they had seen previously. The groups performed this task twice. The first trial does not require working memory because the participants only had to determine if the facial expression matched the one they had seen immediately prior (1-back). In the 2-back task, which does engage working memory, they had to determine if the facial expression matched the one they had seen two faces earlier. Here are examples of these tasks:

1-Back Task*

Sad   Happy   Sad   **Sad**   Neutral

2-Back Task

Sad   Neutral   **Sad**   Happy   Neutral   **Happy**   Happy

The words that are repeated in the 1-back or 2-back task are in bold.

Levens and Gotlib measured the speed and accuracy of the responses. There was no significant difference between the depressed and nondepressed groups on the 1-back task. The difference emerged when it came to remembering the emotional expressions on the 2-back task, the task that engages working memory. The depressed individuals were faster in matching sad faces, while the non-depressed adults were quicker in matching happy faces. The psychologists suggest that the way we use working memory to process emotions played a role in this difference. They conclude that depressed individuals were more likely to keep sad emotions in their working memory, while the non-depressed people keep happy emotions in their working memory. This suggests

---

* We have called this the 1-Back Task for ease of explanation.

that your working memory Conductor can be a double-edged sword when it comes to happiness: you can use it to fixate on the bad, or the good. Paraphrasing Aristotle, it's your choice. But as we will see, those with a stronger working memory tend to choose happiness.

To take her research a step further, Levens teamed up with Elizabeth Phelps of New York University to investigate what happens in the brain when people use working memory to process emotional information. They asked participants to perform working memory tasks in which they had to recognize positive and negative emotions. Participants were first shown a string of negative emotional words—like *murder* and *terror*—on a computer screen. They were then shown a single word (known as the target word) and asked to determine whether it was in the list of negative words they had just seen. The experimenters did the same with positive words. These tasks required the participants to use working memory to keep in mind the lists and then compare the target word with the lists. At the same time, the scientists observed the brain activity of the participants using functional magnetic resonance imaging (fMRI) scans. The scans revealed that blood rushed to the PFC, and the researchers showed that working memory plays a role in judging positive and negative emotions. But distinguishing between positive and negative thoughts isn't the same as feeling a negative or positive emotion. So does having a strong working memory actually help make us feel happier?

Working Memory Fires Up the Feel-Good Brain Chemicals

The human brain is coursing with chemicals that create happy feelings. Two of these feel-good chemicals are the neurotransmitters dopamine and serotonin. Dopamine is a pleasure and motivation chemical that is released in the brain whenever you do something enjoyable. The quick hit of dopamine produces a short-term feeling of euphoria, which encourages you to repeat the behavior. Serotonin is known as the Zen neurotransmitter because it is associated with feelings of deep and subtle satisfaction and long-term happiness. Serotonin is so critical to happiness that the most commonly prescribed antidepressants work by increasing its level in the brain.

Exciting research is showing some surprising links between working memory and the production of both dopamine and serotonin. One study from researchers at the University of California, Berkeley, used positron emission tomography (PET) scans to investigate the relationship between working memory and dopamine. The first step in this trial was to test the participants' working memory to identify individuals with high and low working memory. Then both the strong and weak working memory groups underwent PET scans to measure dopamine production in their brains. The researchers found that the brains of participants with good working memory made more dopamine, while those with poor working memory made less.

In another study conducted at the Heinrich-Heine University in Germany by Ruediger Grandt and colleagues, PET scans were used to examine whether there is any link between working memory and serotonin. The study revealed that when participants performed a working memory task that involved remembering a sequence of faces, they experienced an increase of serotonin that participants completing a non–working memory task did not experience. What we find particularly exciting about this study is that it is the act of using working memory that was linked to the surge in serotonin. In other words, simply using your working memory may make you happier. If you are feeling grumpy, you may want to try to engage in activities that use your working memory, to see if that dopamine and serotonin boost can improve your mood.

Working Memory and the Glass Half Empty

At the other end of the spectrum, we wanted to investigate how working memory is related to unhappiness, in particular, depression and rumination. *Rumination* is the term psychologists use when people fixate on things, often negative. It is an unproductive style of thinking that is difficult to control or stop, and it tends to be linked with strong emotions like worry and fear. It is like your working memory Conductor is playing the same sad song over and over again.

Susan Nolen-Hoeksema, a psychologist at Yale University, has been investigating rumination for more than a decade, and her research indicates that people who ruminate are more likely to develop depression; moreover, they experience more severe symptoms of depression. We wondered what effect rumination might have on working memory and discovered that emerging evidence suggests a relationship. Robert Hester and Hugh Garavan of Dublin's Trinity College artificially increased rumination on negative thoughts by showing adults lists of words with negative connotations like *murder, anger,* and *fight.* They found that rumination not only made people more depressed but also impaired their working memory.

In a related 2008 study, psychologists Jutta Joorman and Ian Gotlib gave two groups of people a task that required them to update information continually in their working memory, as well as trying to inhibit words with negative connotations. One group of participants was suffering from depression and the other was not. They found that the depressed individuals had more difficulty in not mulling over negative words, which inhibited their working memory.

We wanted to investigate these links ourselves, so we spent three months researching a group of more than one hundred twenty-somethings. We chose people in their twenties because these are the years in which people tend to move out of their parents' home, make new friends, and explore new ideas, and though this transition into adulthood can be exciting, it can also be a stressful time and result in a sense of feeling overwhelmed and even depressed. Because this age group faces so many challenges to their happiness, they presented a good opportunity for us to explore how working memory helps us to manage our emotions and stay positive.

The twenty-somethings in our study performed several cognitive tasks. First, they completed a working memory task from Tracy's

Alloway Working Memory Assessment (AWMA). We asked them questions such as, "Oranges live in water. True or false?" and then asked them to repeat the last word of the statement. Questions like this engage working memory because the brain is forced to hold the sentence in mind and decide if it's a true statement while repeating the last word. We then divided the participants into those with strong and weak working memory.

We also asked these young adults to complete questionnaires often used in hospitals and clinics to provide an objective measure of depression. This required participants to rate statements depending on how strongly they felt each applied to them during the past week. Some statements expressed negative feelings such as, "I was bothered by things that don't usually bother me." Others expressed positive feelings such as, "I felt hopeful about the future." Based on their responses, we determined whether they were depressed. We also measured their tendency for rumination using a similar questionnaire.

We had hypothesized that ruminators and depressed participants would have relatively poor working memory and that ruminators would be depressed. But when we analyzed the working memory scores, depression status, and propensity for rumination among the young adults, we made some very surprising findings: not all of the ruminators had low working memory scores, and not all ruminators were depressed. The ruminators who had good working memory were less likely to suffer depression compared to the ruminators who had poor working memory. Our interpretation is that though their working memory Conductor plays the same song, it is also strong enough to inhibit the negative emotions associated with depression.

Working Memory and the Glass Half Full

The results of our study on working memory, rumination, and depression were an exciting start because they revealed that people do use working memory to manage emotions, resolve problems, and avoid slipping into depression. Encouraged by these findings, we looked at the opposite end of the happiness scale to determine if a strong working memory makes people more likely to choose optimism.

To explore this question, we joined forces with the British Science Festival, a hugely popular annual event celebrating science, engineering, and technology. With help in promoting our study and inviting festivalgoers to participate in it, we were able to conduct another large-scale study involving thousands of adults. The scale of the study helped us understand how working memory influences happiness and if a strong working memory will make you more likely to see the glass half full.

For this study, participants completed a working memory test and filled out the *Life Orientation Test*, a clinical questionnaire that gauges levels of optimism and pessimism. We also asked participants to answer yes or no to the following questions:

1. In uncertain times, I usually expect the best.
2. I'm always optimistic about my future.
3. If something can go wrong for me, it will. I rarely count on good things happening to me.

When we looked at their responses, we found a correlation between the strength of working memory and level of optimism. Those with stronger working memory were more likely to have a high level of optimism, while those with weaker working memory tended to be more pessimistic. These results suggest that people with high working memory tend to be more hopeful and confident about the future, while those with weak working memory tend to be more pessimistic.

The research we have examined so far in this chapter suggests that a good working memory is associated with happiness and optimism. It's not a direct causal relationship because happiness is complex, and many factors—both personal and cultural—play into personal happiness. So although a strong working memory can't guarantee optimism, it can set your feet more firmly on the path to fulfillment.

One of the huge benefits of optimism is a longer and more satisfying life. Becca Levy's research at the University of Yale's School of Public Health demonstrated that older adults who are optimistic about aging live an average of 7.5 years longer than their less optimistic counterparts. An optimistic outlook is also associated with a healthier life. For example, Hillary Tindale and colleagues at the University of Pittsburgh found that optimism reduces the risk of coronary heart disease, which can lead to death. In their study of almost one hundred thousand women aged fifty to seventy-nine, they compared the 25 percent most optimistic with the 25 percent most pessimistic and found that the optimistic women had less risk of cardiovascular problems, as well as reduced risk for diabetes and hypertension. A study with men followed over a ten-year period found similar results: those who were optimistic were less likely to develop coronary heart disease as they aged compared to those who were pessimistic.

Less Is More

At the end of this chapter, we share some simple exercises to help you strengthen your working memory, but in the meantime let's take a quick look at a few coping strategies to improve both working memory and happiness.

In chapter 2, we introduced you to our friend Sam who struggled to wade through all the possibilities after losing his job. Too many choices result in psychological stress and unhappiness. A 2010 study by Hazel Markus and Barry Schwartz published in the *Journal of American Consumer Research* backed this up, finding that although American culture venerates choice and freedom, people often become paralyzed by unlimited choice and are less happy with their decisions as a result.

As you saw in chapter 2, an excess of choice can overload your working memory and lead to lots of negative consequences, including an increase in stress and anxiety, an inability to make a decision, and even ruminating over whether you've made the right choice. So one way to improve your happiness is to minimize the number of choices you have to make. At the office, for example, you might want to dedicate specific chunks of time to specific tasks and open only one program on your computer screen rather than toggling between multiple windows and switching back and forth between options.

At home, many of us feel that rushing our children off to five activities a day will improve their lives and make them happier. The reality is that offering your children too many choices of extracurricular activities may overwhelm them and reduce how well they perform in the activities they do pursue. By choosing a few activities and focusing on some relaxing downtime in which the family reconnects, there will be less working memory overload, and everyone will feel less stressed and happier.

Limiting your consumer choices will help too. At the supermarket, interesting packaging or new products compete for our attention. Sometimes it's hard to decide which of the ten different brands of the same product to buy. In order to limit the number of choices and not get overwhelmed, make a list of exactly what you need before you go to the market, and stick to it.

Our friend Sam who fell into depression because he couldn't decide what next job to pursue, found that narrowing his choices helped immensely. After a few weeks of his malaise, Sam's wife encouraged him to seek the advice of a career coach, who helped him focus on one or two more immediate tasks and goals. His working memory was then able to better digest the information he had to consider, his stress lifted, and he became happier. He was able to make a list of potential jobs and started sending out his newly updated CV. Two weeks later, he landed an interview.

Confronting Fears and Challenges

One afternoon Ann, a corporate lawyer who had recently made partner, discovered a large bump in her lower back. She immediately started worrying that it was a cancerous tumor, but since she was so overwhelmed with her new job responsibilities, she avoided going to the doctor and tried to put the situation out of her mind. But the more she tried to suppress the thought, the more she kept going over catastrophic possibilities in her mind. Within a few weeks, she was very depressed. She had trouble focusing on work, got distracted in meetings, made faulty judgments on cases, and started to forget to return phone calls to her clients. In short, her working memory was impaired.

Some fascinating research suggests that failing to address our problems undermines our working memory. One such study conducted by scientists at Harvard, Cornell, and the University of Texas researched the fight-or-flight mechanism in mice and found that mice who ran away from a variety of challenging situations (such as interacting with bigger, more aggressive mice) suffered weight loss, lower sex drive, and insomnia, and they had a change in levels of a protein called brain-derived neurotrophic factor (BDNF). Previous research has shown that low levels of BDNF are associated with both a compromised working memory and depression, but the exact nature of this complex relationship has yet to be determined.

The mice who interacted with the larger mice had regular sleep, a healthy sex life, normal eating, and no change in their BDNF levels. The authors suggest that the discovery has an important implication: dealing with your problems enhances resiliency. They draw on Rachel Yehuda's research on working memory and stress, which we discussed in chapter 2, to highlight how resiliency is evident after exposure to stressful situations and resilient people show optimism in the face of adversity. So let's return for a moment to Ann, who was busy at work and put off dealing with her problem. As a result, her working memory—and her work—was adversely affected by the stress. When Ann's best friend pleaded with her to get over her fear of going to the doctor and get the bump checked out, she finally decided to listen to her. The doctor took a biopsy, and it turned out that the bump was not malignant. The bottom line is if you avoid dealing with your problems, it can diminish your working memory and make you more susceptible to depression. This can have a knock-on effect, because a poor working memory also undermines your ability to deal appropriately with the fallout that comes from avoiding problems in the first place. By dealing with your problems head on, you at least have the benefit of a fully functioning working memory so you can adapt to whatever comes your way.

Be Still and Be Happy

Meditation has long been linked to a sense of calm happiness. In a 2007 trial, Richard Davidson and colleagues at the University of Wisconsin-Madison used functional MRI brain imaging to see what changes in the brain occur during meditation. The team enlisted expert meditators, many of whom had over 37,000 hours of meditation experience, as well as a group of novice meditators. As the participants meditated in the brain scanner, they were barraged with distracting sounds, such as restaurant noise, a baby cooing, or a woman screaming. The researchers found that compared to the novices, those with the most meditation experience were better able to filter out the distractions. The brain scans also showed greater activation of the PFC—the home of working memory—in the most experienced group. The PFC was recruited because the brain scans were conducted during *concentration meditation*, a form of meditation that involves focusing attention on a small visual image or on the breath, a technique that requires working memory.

Amishi Jha and her colleagues at the University of Pennsylvania took this discovery a step further and found a more direct relationship among meditation, a strong working memory, and feelings of happiness. She looked at U.S. Marines who were feeling stressed before they were deployed for duty. One group meditated for thirty minutes every day for eight weeks and the other group for twenty minutes a week for eight weeks. After that period, the participants were asked to rate their positive and negative moods. The group that practiced for thirty minutes a day had higher working memory scores at the end of the eight weeks and reported more positive moods than the group that meditated less. We would speculate that the improvement in working memory enabled the Marines to more successfully filter out negative, stressful thoughts and instead focus on positive thoughts, thus improving their moods.

At the beginning of this chapter we met "Super Mario," a man whose positive outlook allowed him to triumph over incredible adversity, and asked whether a strong working memory might have contributed to his happiness. Having examined the evidence, we think the chances are good. A strong working memory Conductor would have helped Mario ignore negative emotions and focus on the positive, even though there was every reason to believe that the miners might not be rescued. Also, because he was keeping himself busy—telling jokes, planning his children's future, looking for escape routes, and helping devise innovative ways to accomplish everyday chores while underground—which engaged his working memory, rather than brooding on possible doomsday scenarios—his dopamine and serotonin levels likely remained relatively high, preserving a feeling of well-being.

If you are frustrated because your coworkers are bombarding you with emails and IM jokes, strengthening your working memory Conductor can help you eliminate these extraneous distractions and focus on getting your project in on time. If you're feeling down because your spouse is complaining that the kids are arguing, the house is messy, and friends are arriving for dinner in fifteen minutes, building your working memory can help you focus on the fun to be had at the dinner party once you get your house in order and put the kids to bed.

Working Memory Exercises

Your working memory Conductor helps you to control your emotions, which is a big step toward experiencing more happiness. The following exercises will set you on the path to strengthen your working memory and gain better control over your moods and outlook.

1. Learn How to Manage Positive and Negative Emotions

An important step to happiness is being able to identify what makes you happy and what makes you sad. We use our working memory to focus on familiar emotional information. This exercise will help train your working memory to evaluate emotional words, so that you can learn to focus the positive, rather than the negative.

1. Below is a list of words. **Don't look at it!**
2. Ask a friend to read the list of words aloud.
3. Listen for repeating words. When you hear a repeated word that was read out three words before, do this:

   a. Snap your fingers
   b. Tell your friend whether the word is emotionally positive, negative, or neutral.

The answers are in bold on the list.

Word List

- *leaf*
- *unfortunate*
- *ecstatic*
- *sunny*
- *syrup*
- ***ecstatic***
- *thankful*
- ***syrup***
- *plank*
- *downer*
- *afraid*
- *friendly*
- ***downer***
- *thankful*

2. Have a Few Cups

In 2012, Lars Kuchinke and colleagues from Ruhr University, Germany, discovered that drinking 200 mg of caffeine, or about two to three cups of coffee or four cups of tea, improves how fast and how accurately you can recognize positive words, but not neutral or negative ones. While this study didn't examine if coffee drinkers are less likely to be depressed, one can point out that if coffee makes it easier to recognize the positive, it's a good thing.

3. Filter Out the Negative

When we ruminate, we can focus on negative experiences and emotions. This exercise trains your working memory to filter out negative feelings and focus on the positive ones.

Level 1: Instructions

1. Draw a line to connect the positive words and ignore the other ones.
2. Turn the page over and on a separate sheet of paper list all the positive words you've just connected.

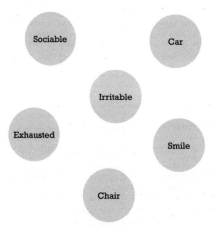

Level 2: Instructions

1. Draw a line to connect the positive words and ignore the other ones.
2. Turn the page over and on a separate sheet of paper list all the positive words you just connected.

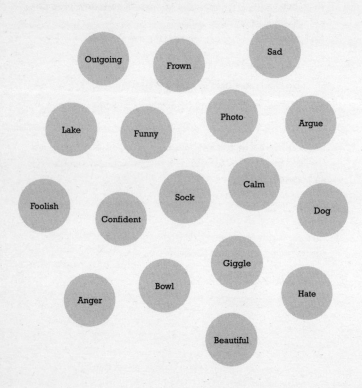

4. Prioritize Your Choices

This exercise helps you to relieve the stress you feel when you are overwhelmed with too many choices by helping you to prioritize what's most important.

1. Make a list of everything you do in an average day that places demands on your working memory—for example, checking Facebook, checking email on your phone, making breakfast. Your list may have thirty or more items on it.

2. Choose the tasks on the list that are the least important, and don't do them for a week. You might put your iPad in a closet, limit your time on the Web when you're working on your computer, or turn off your Twitter feed.

3. At the end of the week ask yourself the following questions:

    • Do I feel less stressed?

    • Do I feel more productive?

    • Was I able to focus more effectively on a task that I accomplished?

4. If you answered yes to all of these, seriously consider restricting the tasks in order to experience less stress. You may want to try and take out more tasks.

4

Failures, Bad Habits, and Missteps

WHEN YOU SEE wealthy athletes blow through millions of dollars and end up bankrupt, celebrities who seem to have it all throw everything away on a drug habit, or obese individuals continue to overeat in spite of having heart disease and diabetes, it's natural to wonder why they can't regulate their behavior. After years of research, we have found that out-of-control behavior is closely linked to working memory problems. In this chapter, we show you what happens when the working memory Conductor loses control.

When Good Fortune Goes Bad

In this down economy, who hasn't fantasized about winning the lottery? We certainly have. But should we beware of what we wish for? As you've probably heard, many people who win the lottery report later that they are no happier, and many ultimately find the large sums of money a burden rather than a blessing. This seems terribly ironic, but we think it may be related to interference with working memory and in a way that illuminates the role of working memory in impulsive behavior.

Take the case of Andrew Jackson "Jack" Whittaker whose $1 lottery ticket purchased at a gas station turned him into the biggest single U.S. lottery winner at the time: $314 million, which translated to a onetime payout of $113 million after taxes. If any lottery hopeful could handle a big win, you would think it would be Whittaker. He was already successful when he won. He had a net worth in the millions and was the president of a West Virginia–based contracting firm with more than one hundred employees.

In the flush of excitement, Whittaker pledged a portion of his winning to various organizations and set up a nonprofit organization to support low-income families. But it didn't take long before careful planning gave way to unbridled extravagance. The man who had made his millions with hard work and self-control was now thrust into a world in which he had so much money that he seems to have lost sight of its value and of his control in spending it.

In the first year, he had already spent $45 million. His personal plan of spending time with his wife of over forty years and adoring granddaughter never came to fruition. Instead, the *Washington Post* quoted him as saying, "If they want quality time with me, they have to get up earlier or go to bed a lot later." Between the trips to the racetrack and slot machines and buying property for development, it was no wonder he had less, not more, family time. And of course, Whittaker lived up to the stereotype of lottery winners by buying numerous cars and houses for himself, family members, and acquaintances. Five years after his win, he claimed that thieves had stolen a lot of money from him and that he was broke. He also had been charged with assault and drunk driving.

Although Whittaker's tale is not unique when it comes to big-ticket lottery winners, it is uncommon that such a tale begins with someone who was already wealthy. The reason this is relevant here is that Whittaker's case provokes the question: Why wasn't someone with experience in managing large amounts of money better prepared to manage his winnings better than most other winners? What turned him into such an impulsive spender?

Wilhelm Hofmann, from the University of Chicago Booth School of Business's Center for Decision Research, offers clues to the answer. He has spent several years researching decision making, impulsivity, and working memory. In a 2009 paper, he theorized a model of two significant influences in decision making—an impulsive system and a reflective system:

- *Impulsive system*: This system is automatic, unconsidered, and hedonistic, and it encourages us to do whatever feels good.

- *Reflective system*: This system is rational and involves strategic planning to achieve goals, deliberate judgment, and exercise of control. Hofmann directly links the strength of the reflective system with working memory.

Imagine that you're stranded alone on a life raft at sea, and you've rationed your supplies to give yourself the best chance of survival. Among other items, you've got a few chocolate bars, and you know that you should limit yourself to just one square a day. But there's a war going on inside your head. The impulsive system urges you to scarf down the whole chocolate bar—*C'mon, you're hungry. You need to eat the whole candy bar now.* The reflective system cautions you to stick to one square a day—*Don't give in to temptation. Make it last. It'll be better for you in the long run.*

Whether you gobble up the entire bar or ration it out depends on the strength of your working memory. According to Hofmann, the stronger your working memory is, the better your reflective system is at controlling your impulsive system.

Prior to the unexpected windfall, Whittaker had to exercise financial restraint to ensure that he didn't overspend. This required his Conductor to moderate spending by engaging the reflective system: *I really want that mansion, but I can't afford it.* But after his lottery win, he was in a financial position where any shiny thing that caught his eye—from diamonds to speedboats—could be had without reflection. Because moderation of his spending was no longer required, his Conductor basically retired from its job, and the impulsive system reigned unchecked. As Whittaker's self-control vanished, so did his lottery winnings. As one of Whittaker's friends aptly observed to *USA Today*, the win "overwhelmed him . . . the more you have, the more difficult it is to resist temptation."

Out of Control

Working memory plays a pivotal role in addiction, whether it's addiction to drugs, alcohol, cigarettes, overeating, shopping, gambling, pornography, or even video gaming. The stronger your Conductor, the easier it is to resist addictive behavior. The weaker your Conductor, the more likely you are to fall into the grips of addiction.

Have you ever wanted something so badly, been involved in something so deeply, or been fixated on something so intensely that nothing else seems to matter? Even if the object of your obsession is bad for your health, relationships, career, or finances? And even if it is ruining your life? You're certainly not alone. Just take a look at the numbers. More than 68 million Americans smoke. Nearly 30 million are affected by substance abuse, and another 22 million adults are addicted to Internet pornography. As many as 24 million are compulsive shoppers, and 6 to 8 million are problem gamblers. And don't forget the estimated 75 million adults and 12.5 million kids who are obese. Why do so many of us become enslaved to our bad habits and addictions?

The Addicted Brain

In 2011, the American Society of Addiction Medicine redefined addiction as "a chronic disease of brain reward, motivation, memory, and related circuitry." Nora Volkow, an eminent neuroscientist, psychiatrist, and director of the National Institute on Drug Abuse, is the leading researcher in the area of the addicted brain. The great-granddaughter of Leon Trotsky, Volkow is making her own mark on history with more than a decade of peer-reviewed research suggesting that addictive behaviors become compulsive because the brain's control mechanism is disrupted. Here is what is happening in the addicted brain.

Salience and Reward

Salience is the relative importance of an object or behavior, and *reward* is the pleasurable feelings we derive from that object or behavior. Salience and reward are closely linked in the addicted brain. Addictive substances and behaviors are extremely high in salience to addicts, which means they focus their attention on them. When addicted people engage in addictive behavior, the nucleus accumbens, located deep within the brain, releases a big hit of dopamine, the reward neurotransmitter. Eating a chocolate bar gives you a little squirt of dopamine; eating a hot fudge sundae with cookies 'n' cream ice cream, whipped cream, sprinkles, and nuts delivers a heftier dose of the neurotransmitter. And taking a drug like heroin causes a huge surge of dopamine. The reward that an addict gets from the dopamine gives that activity great salience, making it their singular focus.

Memory

People who have addictions remember the salience of the activity because the event is registered in both the amygdala and hippocampus. The brain's emotional center, the amygdala, registers the intense salience and reward and locks it into the memory bank, the hippocampus.

Drive

Drive is what motivates addicts to continue in their behavior. It pushes them to repeat the behavior again and again. Drive originates in the orbitofrontal cortex (OFC) and the anterior cingulate gyrus (ACG), brain regions often associated with working memory. Further research is necessary to determine the degree to which working memory is involved in drive. What happens when an addict craves a drug, is that their OFC and ACG become hyperactive and boost drive intensely. If working memory is involved in drive, it may be like a broken record, replaying the desire to procure the reward, over and over. Indeed, these regions of an addict's brain resemble those of people suffering from obsessive-compulsive disorders.

(Out of) Control

The control aspect in this process is located in the PFC, the home of working memory. For nonaddicts, the PFC helps them resist harmful behavior. For example, when you put your hand over the top of the wine glass rather than accepting another glass, your PFC has been activated to make that decision. But in the addict's brain, this behavior is reversed: when a person is engaged in the addictive behavior, the PFC is turned down to low. As you would expect, this diminished activity is associated with less self-monitoring and behavioral control. It's as if the Conductor has left the stage. The salience of how good the addictive substance or activity feels overrides the PFC's ability to rein in the behavior. When an addicted person craves something, as opposed to being engaged in the behavior or using the substance, the PFC increases in activation. While the person is craving, the PFC recruits working memory to bring up the past memories of the salience and reward, as well as to strategize how to satisfy the urge. In the addicted brain, the working memory Conductor, which should be *in* control, is *under* the control of the addiction.

The Addiction Process

In the addicted brain, working memory is recruited as a key component of the addictive process, helping to satisfy the addiction rather than inhibiting it. For illustrative purposes, this image shows the addictive process linearly, though the various stages may not always occur in this sequence.

We got a firsthand glimpse into obsessive behavior when Ross bought a really cool first-person video game about a week before Christmas in 2003. During the day, Ross was a mild-mannered academic, but at night he morphed into an ex–Navy SEAL working in the top-secret Third Echelon subbranch of the National Security Agency. Ross was entrusted with saving the United States from a breakout war with China. He used his stealth and considerable military acumen to stalk enemies and infiltrate their headquarters, even rescuing the United States from the detonation of a nuclear bomb.

You would think Tracy would have been proud of all his hard work and his determination to see the mission through. But in spite of the fact that Ross had single-handedly prevented World War III, she was concerned that he was spending too much time in this fantasy world. He did, after all, skip all of his favorite Christmas activities: going to the German Christmas market in Edinburgh with its steaming mugs of *glühwein*, hiking in the snow, making Christmas cookies and candy, and caroling on Christmas Eve. The video game had turned Ross into a veritable Christmas Grinch.

For Christmas Day, Tracy banned him from playing. And although Ross found himself moping about and fretting nonstop about what might happen if the game's shadowy criminal activated the nuclear device while he was celebrating the holiday, he realized that maybe Tracy was right: he had fallen into the grips of video game obsession. He snapped the disc in two and swore off video gaming for good, a pledge yet unbroken.

A lot of gamers are able to moderate the siren call of really awesome video games and do other things aside from assaulting the Sith Lord, winning the Grand Prix, or building a new civilization. But research shows that one in ten video gamers nationwide exhibit signs of addictive behavior. The web is full of stories from gamers who have become obsessed to the detriment of their work and relationships. Consider the following confession posted on a gaming website about addiction to a popular online game:

I had a wife, 3 houses, 3 cars, money in the bank. I stopped working. I went through a divorce. I had to sell a house. I had to sell a car. I have nothing in my bank account now, but good thing my game account is paid in full a year in advance. My credit is in ruins. I don't care.

Marriages are ruined, children neglected, and financial futures destroyed. The Chinese government's deep concern about the negative effect of Internet gaming addiction on many of its citizens may have been behind its ban of the popular online game *World of Warcraft* (*WoW*) in 2009.

That same year, a group of Taiwanese researchers led by Wei-Chen Lin undertook a groundbreaking study to discover what was happening in the brains of gaming addicts when anticipating a chance to play. They recruited ten heavy users of *WoW* who had made it to the top levels of the game by regularly playing over thirty hours a week. They also recruited ten nongamers who used the Internet less than two hours a day.

The researchers put them in an fMRI scanner and showed them a series of pictures, alternating between a neutral image and a *WoW* game image. It is important to note that they did not scan the participants while playing the game. They showed them pictures because they wanted to trigger a craving response in the brain.

As expected, the scans of the nongamer brains showed no difference between *WoW* images and the neutral images. When the *WoW* gamers saw the neutral images, their brains looked much like those of the nongamers. But when they saw the game images, the fMRI display screens lit up like a Christmas tree.

- The nucleus accumbens activated, anticipating the dopamine hit that came from playing the game—for example, when their character completed a quest, saved a friend, or slew a foe.

- The PFC powered up and put working memory to work to figure out how to get that dopamine hit by executing a plan to play the game.

The fact that this study looked at the brain activity when the participants were craving the addictive behavior as opposed to engaging in it explains why the PFC lit up. As we described earlier in the addicted brain model, craving changes the way the PFC and working memory function. The PFC and working memory, which moderate and control behavior in the nonaddicted brain, were in fact recruited in the craving process, enabling it, and finding a way to get that dopamine hit. When it comes to fulfilling a craving for an addictive substance or behavior, working memory becomes an enemy rather than a friend.

When Working Memory Failures Threaten Your Health

Is your working memory also working against you when you want to lose weight but can't seem to step away from the dessert tray? Do you just lack willpower? Or is something else preventing you from getting control over your eating? Consider Michael, a man from New York who weighed twelve hundred pounds. Partly encouraged by an obese mother, he liked to start the day with four bowls of cereal, toast, waffles, cake, and a quart of soda, and end it with a pizza. Michael tried diet after diet, but he was unable to control his urges.

New science suggests that some of us may in fact be addicted to fat. Considering that two-thirds of U.S. adults are overweight or obese, it is clear that a lot of us are eating more than our fair share of fatty foods, and it is having a devastating impact on our working memory. A 2007 study in the journal *Appetite* found that obese children perform worse on tests involving working memory compared to their non-obese peers. When you hit middle age, it doesn't get any better. In 2010, researchers from the University of Texas at Austin found that when obese individuals performed a working memory task, there was less activation in a brain area associated with working memory compared to normal-weight people or those who were just somewhat overweight.

In 2003, scientists at Boston University found that senior citizens who were obese and had hypertension had poorer working memory skills. Other research appearing in *Current Alzheimer's Research* in 2007 shows that being obese in midlife is linked to cognitive disease later in life. People who were obese in middle age were five times more likely to be diagnosed with vascular dementia and three times more likely to develop Alzheimer's. And don't think you're off the hook if you're just a little pudgy rather than outright obese. In this same study, people who were overweight were two times more likely to develop Alzheimer's or vascular dementia in their not-so-golden years. These studies with humans offer a useful first step in understanding the link between overeating and working memory. More recent research has benefited from using rats in order to more rigorously control experimental conditions—like altering brain cells or introducing electrical shocks—allowing scientists to learn how overeating can be addictive and ultimately impair working memory.

In 2010, neuroscientists Paul Johnson and Paul Kenny of the Scripps Research Institute in Florida set out to understand how fatty foods can act like a drug in the brain to send the reward system spiraling out of control. They took three groups of rats and fed them a variety of diets to see how fatty foods affected their brain and weight. Group 1—we'll call them the *smorgasbord* rats—enjoyed nearly unlimited access to high-fat foods, kind of like going to an all-you-can-eat buffet—including some human favorites like bacon, sausage, chocolate, and cheesecake. Group 2—we'll call them the *restrained* rats—had access to the same fatty foods but only for a short period once a day. Group 3, a control group—we'll call them the *healthy* rats—had access to only healthy rat food. Can you guess what happened? It's no big surprise that the smorgasbord rats ended up consuming twice as many calories as the healthy rats and quickly grew obese.

The researchers then conditioned the rats: every time a light went on, they would receive a mild electrical shock. The next time the groups went to feed, the researchers turned on the light and waited to see what would happen. The restrained rats and the healthy rats refused to eat when the light was switched on, but the smorgasbord rats went straight for their food. They had become so addicted to the fatty fare that the threat of a mild electrical shock couldn't deter them from scarfing down every bite.

Johnson and Kenny also wanted to explore more fully the role of dopamine in food addiction. As we've said, a person who becomes addicted to a substance tends to need more and more of it to get that same surge of dopamine. That's because an addicted brain has fewer dopamine receptors to receive the dopamine signals.

Johnson and Kenny wanted to find out what the smorgasbord rats would do if they had fewer dopamine receptors, so they inserted a virus in their brain to attack the receptors. The researchers expected that the rats would gradually adjust and eat less of the fatty food because it didn't provide the same dopamine high. Imagine their surprise when they found that the rats resorted to eating even more to try to achieve the same high.

So if you've ever wondered why it takes three candy bars to get the same satisfaction when it used to take only one, now you know that your brain might be compensating for the declining dopamine receptors. This also helps explain why some of us continue to gorge on fattening foods even though we hate the fact that we can barely zip up our pants, have type 2 diabetes, and are saddled with high blood pressure.

The research on diet and working memory also suggests that overindulgence in fatty foods directly assaults your working memory. Andrew Murray and colleagues at the University of Oxford took two groups of rats. Both were fed a healthy diet for up to two months and were given a working memory test for rats known as a radial maze task. This commonly used task for measuring working memory in rats uses an elevated platform with eight arms that extend from the maze in the center. The rats learn which of the arms have a food reward hidden out of sight at the end of the arm. A working memory error is counted when the rat goes to an arm with no food even though the animal looked there previously. This is considered a working memory task because the rat has to navigate the maze and at the same time hold in mind where it has already been. The researchers noted the scores of the groups.

After this test, they fed one group a high-fat diet for nine days and retested the two groups. The rats on the healthy diet blasted through the maze, and though they weren't perfect, they scored slightly higher than they did the first time. The rats on the high-fat diet took a lot longer to complete the maze than they did the first time and made more mistakes. The high-fat diet apparently diminished their working memory ability.

Other theories about specific foods that turn the brain reward system against us abound. In 2009, David Kessler suggested that it's foods that combine salt, sugar, and fat that do a number on the brain's reward system and lead to overconsumption and obesity. Sugar has also been implicated on its own, including high-fructose corn syrup, maltose, dextrose, and dozens of other sugar sources found in our food supply. As scientists attempt to pinpoint a single food, category of food, or combination of foods that trip up our reward system, it seems that it's when we overindulge in these foods that it becomes a problem. After all, it is important to remember that the human body needs fat for a healthy brain, needs glucose to think clearly, and needs salt. But when we overindulge, our working memory suffers.

When the Feel-Good Neurotransmitter Doesn't Feel Good

At the other end of the eating disorder spectrum are people with anorexia nervosa. Anna Patterson, a young woman who blogs about anorexia, was convinced that despite weighing eighty-nine pounds, she still needed to get rid of her "fat" stomach, and although she refused to eat, she couldn't stop fixating on food.

While it appears that people who eat too much do so at least in part because they've become addicted to the dopamine hit they get from an order of french fries or a piece of crispy bacon, new research has shown that people with anorexia don't respond the same way to dopamine. In 2012, Walter Kaye compared the brain activity of recovering anorexic women with a healthy group of women of the same age and used a PET scanner to determine the effect of dopamine in their brains. He gave both groups of women a single oral dose of the drug amphetamine, which resulted in a big dopamine release.

For most people, the dopamine hit equals pleasure, and as expected, the healthy women experienced feelings of pleasure and euphoria. When Kaye looked at the scans of the healthy women, he saw activation in an area containing the nucleus accumbens, which is filled with dopamine receptors.

Conversely, the brain scans of the recovering anorexics revealed activation in the dorsal caudate, a part of the brain that worries about consequences. In other words, for anorexic individuals, pleasure automatically brings feelings of guilt and worry. Sure enough, when the anorexic women were asked to complete a questionnaire on anxiety, they showed very high levels, lasting over three hours after having received the dopamine hit. For them, their out-of-control behavior was not about pursuing pleasure but rather a desire to avoid the feelings of guilt and anxiety that accompany the dopamine release that comes with eating.

Being "addicted to starvation," as biologist Valerie Campan calls it, or simply being hooked on self-control is also linked to working memory problems. It seems that too little pleasure can become just as addictive as too much, and working memory suffers in both extremes. In 2006, Australian psychologist Eva Kemps recruited a group of anorexic women and healthy women, and gave them a series of tests as well as a questionnaire about food. She found that the anorexic women reported having more intrusive thoughts about food, weight, and body shape. And while the anorexics and healthy women had similar IQ scores, she argued that the anorexics suffered from a diminished working memory.

In 2009, Arne Zastrow and colleagues at the University of Heidelberg took this further to look at brain scans of women with anorexia. They recruited a group of fifteen anorexic women and fifteen healthy women and asked them to perform a task that involved processing and monitoring information while they were in a brain scanner. The task was to keep a target shape in mind, like a circle or triangle, and press a button to identify this shape from other shapes. Another component of the task was that the target shape would change so the women had to mentally discard the previous shape and update their working memory with the new target. Clinicians commonly use this cognitive task to measure how quickly people can adapt when the rules of the game change.

As in the Kemp study, the anorexic women made more errors than their healthy counterparts, indicating cognitive inflexibility: they find it difficult to disengage from one idea and move to another, which may explain why they display rigidity in behavior. As you recall, a strong working memory helps you shift your focus, suggesting that working memory is impaired in people with anorexia. It is likely part of the reason that it is so hard for people with this disorder to shift from the notion that food is "bad" and to start thinking of it as something enjoyable that promotes good health.

The brain scans in Zastrow's study offered some insight into why this happens. The scans showed that a number of brain areas involved with motivation were underactive in the anorexic women. The healthy women also showed greater activation in their PFC, demonstrating that they were eliciting their working memory to solve the task. But the anorexic women did not show any activation in the PFC, suggesting that their working memory was on cruise control.

The disadvantages of a poor working memory are clear: when our Conductor falters we realize just how vital it is for our financial, psychological, and physical well-being. Having a poor working memory is linked to a greater risk for unhealthy habits and behaviors that can leave you bankrupt, addicted, obese, or all of these. And to exacerbate the problem, out-of-control behaviors may also drain your working memory or even recruit it to work against your best interests.

5

The Most Important
Learning Tool

Working Memory in School

IQ SCORES HAVE LONG been held as the benchmark for academic success. But in our own research, we found that relying on IQ to predict success is flawed.

When Tracy began investigating working memory, IQ, and academic achievement, she wanted to find out which cognitive skills were most important in predicting a child's success in school. For one of her first published studies, she recruited almost two hundred kindergartners and gave them a variety of tests, including working memory and IQ tests. When she compared their scores on these tests with their grades, she was taken aback by the results.

The students' IQ scores were surprisingly inaccurate in determining how well they would do in school, contrary to what you might think. According to her findings, students can have an average IQ score but perform poorly in school. For example, one of the kindergartners in this study, Andrew, had an average IQ score, but by the time he reached second grade, he was struggling to keep up with his classmates. If IQ was a good predictor of success, then Andrew shouldn't have had such a tough time in school. His IQ wasn't the reason he was doing poorly.

When Tracy looked at Andrew's working memory score, she noticed that it was low compared to his peers. In fact, if you stood him in a line of one hundred children of the same age, Andrew would be at the end of that line when it came to his working memory skills. Andrew's poor working memory score correlated to his poor performance in school.

The same held true for the other kindergartners. Tracy found that working memory could predict what grade students would get with far greater accuracy than IQ. In fact, if Tracy knew a child's working memory, she could determine his or her academic skills with 95 percent accuracy. When we looked at the youngsters' grades six years later, we found that working memory had such a powerful impact on learning that by knowing their working memory in kindergarten, we could also predict with 95 percent accuracy what their grades would be in the sixth grade.

In another study, Tracy wanted to identify the key cognitive skill required for success in learning the most basic school subjects: reading, comprehension, spelling, and math. She tracked nearly seventy students aged seven to eleven for two years. She tested their working memory and IQ and then compared those scores with their academic achievement in these four subjects. When she analyzed the data and compared working memory to IQ, she once again found that IQ contributed very little to achievement. On the other hand, working memory was the most important cognitive skill, and a strong working memory meant strong grades.

Other research groups have also reported this exciting finding of how working memory skills lay the foundation for school success. Linda Siegel, the Chair in Special Education at the University of British Columbia, Canada, has published several key pieces of research highlighting the importance of working memory in learning. In one study with seven- to thirteen-year-olds, she found that poor working memory can result in reading problems, as well as difficulty with arithmetic and computation.

British psychologist Rebecca Bull echoed this finding with British students and found that if students have poor working memory, they have lower mathematical ability because they are not able to process and work with all the necessary numerical information. Their poor working memory skills also mean that they find it difficult to integrate different mathematical concepts, something that is commonly required in solving word problems.

In the United States, psychologist David Geary at the University of Missouri–Columbia has spent nearly a decade investigating the importance of working memory in math skills. In one of his many studies, he followed children from kindergarten to fifth grade and found that those who struggled most in math had lower working memory scores compared to their schoolmates.

A wealth of research also points to working memory as the most important cognitive skill in language acquisition. Researchers from the University of California studied high school students over three years and identified working memory as the key skill that determined success in reading and comprehension. Adding to these findings are numerous studies from Susan Ellis Weismer and her colleagues at the University of Wisconsin–Madison. Weismer's work shows that working memory is critical for learning grammar as well as new vocabulary words. In her studies, the students typically have average IQ skills but poor working memory, so they offer an ideal opportunity to disentangle the contribution of working memory to learning from what IQ can offer.

Weismer has reported that even if students have average IQ skills, their poor working memory makes it hard to learn new words and remember the grammatical rules. In particular, she has found that people with average IQ but poor working memory have more difficulty learning if the information is presented quickly.

Tracy's contributions to the growing body of evidence on working memory and learning skills include another study in which she compared the IQ and working memory scores in six- to eleven-year-olds. In this study, she found a causal relationship between working memory and language (reading, writing, and comprehension) and math skills. The strength of the children's working memory determined how well they would do in these subjects.

With the evidence from Tracy and other researchers mounting, it has become crystal clear: if we want to know how well students will perform in the classroom, we need to look at their working memory.

These findings that a strong working memory is a big advantage in school, more than IQ, help to explain one of the mysteries of high IQ children, also known as gifted children.

Rethinking Giftedness

Jeff was one of those precocious children who was inquisitive about the world and seemed to know more than anyone else in his kindergarten class. Most people would probably assume that Jeff has a high IQ. And they would be right. A child needs to score at least 130 on an IQ test in order to be deemed gifted. When schools are identifying gifted children, they may take other factors into consideration, but many rely heavily on IQ scores.

You would probably also assume that Jeff grew up to be a successful professional—a top business executive, a lawyer, or a doctor. But that wasn't the case. He bounced from job to job for years before ending up being a handyman. What happened? If Jeff was one of the "gifted" students, shouldn't he also have been highly successful? You would think so, but we have found that the general concept of giftedness isn't quite that simple.

Giftedness is a notion that has intrigued psychologists for almost a century. Lewis Terman is one such psychologist who devoted much of his life's work to the study of this intriguing topic. In the early twentieth century, he developed one of the first tests to assess intelligence, the Stanford-Binet IQ test, and is credited with coining the term *gifted child*. In a long-term study, published as the *Genetic Studies of Genius*, Terman identified a select group of children who scored in the top 1 percent on IQ tests and tracked them throughout their lives. This seminal research left a legacy of furthering our understanding of giftedness, but it also raised a perplexing question that still lurks today.

When Terman's colleague, Melita Oden, compared the one hundred most successful of Terman's protégés with the one hundred least successful from the same group, she found a difference in their chosen professions. While the top one hundred included doctors, lawyers, and scientists, the bottom group included pool cleaners and carpenters. What was surprising was the fact that these two groups barely differed in their IQ scores.

So why did some gifted students excel while others didn't? Many people, including educators, assume that if gifted students aren't performing well in the classroom they simply aren't trying hard enough. But is this truly the case?

Tracy uncovered some evidence to explain the problem when she was offered the chance to work with the National Association of Gifted Children. She was thrilled because she knew this would be a great opportunity to explore why some gifted students are successful throughout their lives while others end up in menial jobs. Probing this mystery, she gave a group of gifted students both IQ and working memory tests. The results showed no clear link between IQ score and the strength of working memory. Although all of the kids had a high IQ, they didn't all score at the top of the scale in working memory. In fact, their working memory scores ran the gamut from low to high.

Tracy found that students with a high IQ but low working memory are more likely to be underachievers, and students with both a high IQ and a strong working memory are most likely to excel. To show how this relationship between working memory, IQ, and academic achievement might play out in the classroom, imagine two high school students, Madison and Emma. Both girls have a high IQ and are in the same English class for gifted students. Both possess all the right facts: the names of important authors and literary works, the spellings and definitions of words, and important dates in literary history. But the difference between the two girls shows up when they have to write an essay comparing and contrasting *Fahrenheit 451* and *Nineteen Eighty-Four*.

Madison, who has a low working memory, struggles to connect the relevant themes in a coherent and logical manner. Emma, who has a high working memory, deftly draws together all the information in a compelling way. Madison gets a C on her paper, while Emma earns an A. Which of these two students is going to be more successful in the long run? Emma. Which cognitive skill made the difference in Emma's success? Working memory.

Based on the growing body of evidence about working memory and achievement, we propose that it is time to rethink the notion of giftedness and how it is measured. Rather than defining giftedness as having a vast store of knowledge as is measured by IQ, our society and school systems should start recognizing giftedness as the ability to succeed in the classroom and beyond. And because working memory has emerged as the best predictor of academic achievement, we would argue that schools should use working memory tests to measure giftedness rather than relying so heavily on IQ.

What About Learning Styles?

A prevalent argument in the education research community is that learning styles hugely influence how well students will do in school. The learning styles theory argues that individuals learn best in different ways. A popular framework for learning styles is one that separates Verbalizers from Visualizers, and Wholistic thinkers from Analytical ones.

- *Verbalizers*: People who prefer language-based learning

- *Visualizers*: People who prefer learning with pictures and images

- *Analytical*: People who prefer to focus in on the details when learning

- *Wholistic*: People who prefer to look at the big picture when learning

To see how a student's preferred learning style affects them in the classroom, imagine that you are back in your high school science class—*okay, stop cringing!* The subject for today: glaciers and their formation. The teacher presents a slideshow of the various stages of glacier formation, using nothing but photos of Yosemite National Park. You get the basics of glacier formation immediately because you respond best to information that is presented with images. But your classmate Brandon would prefer to see slides containing text that explained the glacier formation process, so he has to work harder to understand the material. And another classmate, Ali, has trouble grasping the concept because the teacher focused solely on the nitty-gritty details about the various stages of glacier formation without offering any information about the big picture.

The theory of learning styles would argue that you would ace a quiz given after this lesson while Brandon and Ali wouldn't fare so well. A proponent of the learning styles framework would argue that depending on the type of learner that you are, you will excel in one subject but not necessarily in another. For example, Richard Riding at the University of Birmingham suggests that analytical thinkers tend to do better in school because their more detailed outlook allows them to come quickly to the heart of any problem. Verbalizers also do well because teaching is presented using written information rather than pictures so they can gain the most from it. But Riding's theory may be missing a crucial piece of the puzzle.

Tracy conducted a study with a group of British secondary school students to look at working memory, learning styles, and academic outcomes. In the United Kingdom (as in the United States), secondary school students take a standardized exam that assesses their knowledge in a range of subjects like English, maths, science, history, and geography. When Tracy gave the students a popular learning-styles questionnaire and then tested their working memory using her standardized test battery, the results were surprising: students with good working memory excelled at all subjects, regardless of their learning style preference. The visualizers did just as well as the verbalizers in all subjects, and wholistic thinkers scored just as highly as analytical ones.

While this may seem puzzling in the context of the learning style framework, it makes perfect sense to us. Students who have good working memory are able to adapt their learning style to different learning situations, regardless if information is presented with pictures, text, details, or the big picture. Although they may have a certain preference for acquiring knowledge, they won't be held back if information is not presented in their preferred learning style.

A More Level Playing Field

Because working memory is so important for success, your potential for achievement is not determined by the side of the tracks you were born on. Why? While IQ is closely related to how much money your parents make, and where you live, working memory abilities are evenly spread across society.

Meet two American eight-year-olds who seem to have nothing in common. Dominique lives in a ten-bedroom mansion and rides to school every day in a sleek Mercedes. After school, she is chauffeured to an equestrian training facility for horseback riding lessons or to her parents' country club for tennis lessons. Jorge is a first-generation American who lives in a one-bedroom apartment with his immigrant single-parent mom, his grandmother, and his two younger brothers. Every morning, Jorge walks over a mile to school, and when he finishes class, he heads straight home to babysit his two brothers and take care of his grandmother until his mom finishes work.

By now, you can probably guess that when these two youngsters took an IQ test, Dominique outscored Jorge. This isn't surprising to us. That's because IQ is closely linked to parental income: the more money the parents make, the higher their children's IQ is. It is also the same with a parent's education level: the more schooling a parent has achieved, the higher their child's IQ is, likely because educated parents are able to provide more opportunities and exposure to experiences that are captured by IQ tests.

But as Tracy discovered, this doesn't mean that Dominique will likely have a higher working memory score than Jorge. Tracy looked at kindergartners and compared their working memory scores with their parents' education level. A striking pattern in this group (and one that she has found in other studies) is that a child's working memory scores do not depend on parents' education level. It doesn't really matter if Mom and Dad have their GCSEs or a Ph.D.

We wanted to put these findings to the test so we looked at data on postal codes that Tracy had collected from children from different parts of the United Kingdom. Using a marketing database that divides neighborhoods based on their postal codes into different socioeconomic levels, we were able to identify students from low-income areas, as well as those from wealthy neighborhoods. We compared these children's scores in standardized tests of IQ as well as working memory. IQ tests typically measure what you know, like a verbal index of the knowledge that you have accumulated about the world. In contrast, working memory tests measure what you can do with what you know.

As you can imagine, the lower-income children, who may not have had the same opportunities as their peers, scored considerably lower on the IQ tests. However, when it came to the working memory tests, the two groups had very similar scores. In other words, both sets of children had the underlying skills necessary for success. This suggests that if children from lower-income backgrounds are afforded the same learning opportunities as higher-income children, they should be able to achieve academic success.

To see why the strength of working memory is such a deciding factor in learning ability, let's look at what learning in the classroom requires of a student, starting at the beginning.

One Small Step for Preschoolers, One Giant Leap for Working Memory

Entering kindergarten is a momentous event in a child's life. It signifies coming of age and a break with his or her previous existence. Gone are the days of one-on-one attention from parents or babysitters. Gone are the daily routines that cater to a child's individual needs, behaviors, personality, and learning style. For example:

- Johnny, who may be overly active and learns best when he is allowed to wiggle, jump around, and shout the answers, will need to learn to sit still.

- Mary, who understands information more quickly when it is presented with a picture, now has to copy words from the board or sentences without any images.

- Tim, who thrives when challenged with harder material, now has to wait for his peers to catch up with him.

With classroom sizes reaching thirty or more students, it would be extremely challenging for teachers to match lesson plans to the myriad behavioral styles in the room. In fact, it would be pandemonium: Johnny—and maybe a couple of others—would be hopping like kangaroos, Mary would be expecting the teacher to draw a picture of Jack and Jill fetching a bucket of water, and Tim would be rushing on to the next lesson before the others had absorbed the material. For most kids, going to school represents the first time in their lives that they are required to adjust their behavior to meet a set of expectations rather than having Mom and Dad make compromises to cater to them.

In cognitive terms, the move from the playroom to the classroom is the equivalent of Neil Armstrong stepping from the spacecraft to the moon, of learning to swim in a stormy ocean, of taking a walk through a pitch-black forest—a profoundly challenging and hitherto unknown world. It is as if a child's working memory Conductor, used to managing a few instruments, is abruptly thrust in front of a large orchestra. Children now have to copy information from the board, inhibit the desire to pet the cute class hamster, ignore the whispers and giggles all around them, follow complex spoken instructions from a stranger, resist the temptation to turn their worksheet into a paper airplane, and of course, learn how to read, write, and do arithmetic. Working memory makes it possible for them to cope with this brave, new world.

Children must constantly use their Conductor in the classroom.

- To inhibit distracting information, like their schoolmates whispering near them or the bright pink of the backpack in front of them. It also helps them to keep track of where they are in a multistep task.

- To work with the information—the numbers, letters, or words they need to think about to complete an assignment.

- To hold the information for a limited amount of time, as well as helping them complete the tasks as quickly as possible.

In terms of the types of information children must be able to process, working memory is vital to doing a good job with all of the main classroom tasks: reading, writing, and arithmetic. In each of these, working memory will be called on to process one or the other of two basic types of information, or both at once:

- Verbal information: things they can read and hear
- Visual information: images, numbers, maps, and patterns that they can "see" when they close their eyes

Reading

Reading is primarily a verbal activity involving the two language centers, Broca's area and Wernicke's area, which help us comprehend what we read and hear. These regions were discovered in the nineteenth century when neurologists Paul Broca and Carl Wernicke came across patients who had brain damage in those regions and struggled to speak. The role of working memory in understanding verbal information is just as critical because it helps children to keep their place while reading, as well as to remember what they have read in order to understand the context and fuller meaning.

Let's say that young Marion has to read the sentence, "The rowboat floated in the water alongside a playful dolphin." For an adult, this is very easy and automatic, but a child reads much more slowly. The Broca's and Wernicke's areas will sift through the sentence to find the meaning of each word and stop at any word she doesn't know, for example, *alongside*.

Marion's working memory Conductor helps her break up the compound word. She first works with *along*, which is shuttled to the Broca's and Wernicke's areas. Her working memory discovers that she knows the meaning of that word. Then it does the same with *side*. Next, the Conductor brings both of the definitions back together to get a good sense of the meaning of the word *alongside*. Finally it updates the sentence with the newly discovered meaning, and she understands that the dolphin is near the boat.

Writing

While we were writing this book, our older son woke up one morning around 6:00 a.m., before either of us were ready to get up. Ross poured him a bowl of cereal, sat him at the kitchen table, which was strewn with notes for the book, and went back to bed. When Ross woke up, imagine his surprise and gratification when our son proudly presented him with this handwritten text (the image on the left is the text our son was copying; the image on the right is his writing).

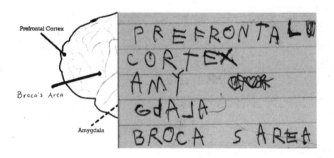

Son's writing

At the time, our son was learning to read and found it challenging to decipher words that are more than one syllable, so this was strictly a writing exercise for him. It required his working memory to manipulate both verbal and visual information. The verbal information is the letters, and the visual information is the order in which they appear. We have taught our son to read by sounding out the letters rather than memorizing words as sets of letters. Initially this method is slower going, but it will give him the tools to read any word he wants rather than being limited to what he memorized. He also tends to write in uppercase.

Let's look at the second letter he wrote. When he wrote the word *Prefrontal*, it was a complex verbal task. His Broca's and Wernicke's areas helped him to identify the letter r and speak it, and his working memory helped him hold it in mind. He then used his working memory to convert the lowercase r into an uppercase R, and hold it in mind as he wrote R on the paper.

Furthermore, his working memory had to process a large amount of visual information. The words *Prefrontal Cortex* were positioned at the top of the illustration and surrounded by white space, which made it relatively easy for him to keep his place when writing it. His Conductor had to hold on only to the preceding letter and the letter he was currently working with at any one time. So when he started to write *Prefrontal*, he had to work only with P (the letter he had already written) and R (the letter he was writing), R and E, E and F, and so on, until he had spelled the whole word.

But when he went to write the next word, he had to process two other pieces of information. Now he had to use his Conductor to hold the words he had already written (*Prefrontal Cortex*), as well as the next word in the list, and the letters that comprised it. As you can see in the figure, rather than following *Prefrontal Cortex* with *Broca's Area*, the information overload became too much, and he skipped down to *Amygdala*.

Based on the results of our study on working memory across the life span, the average child our son's age can hold only two pieces of information in mind, so we were proud parents to see that he was processing more than two pieces of information at the same time. And the fact that he persevered despite an overwhelmed Conductor is great to see. (Now if he would only eat his spinach.)

Arithmetic

$$12 + 9 = ?$$

This arithmetic problem may seem like a cinch to answer, but for a young school child, it may be daunting because it involves several steps that hinge on working memory. If you've ever had trouble adding a horizontal math problem, the breakdown below of the steps involved will show you why it's harder than it looks. Here's a step-by-step look at what's going on in your brain:

> Step 1: Take *2* and *9* and send them to the intraparietal sulcus (IPS) to perform the first part of the calculation.
> Step 2: Put this answer, 11, in your working memory.
> Step 3: Use your working memory to carry the 1 (from 11) and add to 1 (from 12).
> Step 4: Update your working memory with 2. Combine 2 with 1 (from 11) to get the answer: 21.

This math problem is especially tricky because it is presented horizontally rather than vertically. Frequent errors in this problem include children writing 121 because their working memory wasn't up to the task of keeping track of where they were in the problem.

In a study of more than 200 seven- and eight-year-olds, Tracy found that a youngster's working memory score was directly related to his or her ability to solve arithmetic problems. Working memory is a key player in keeping numerical knowledge in the correct order to solve the problem.

When Classroom Struggles Emerge Later in Life

Have you noticed that some children do fairly well in elementary school, but when they get to junior high, high school, or college, they start to struggle and fall behind? They aren't saddled with a learning disorder, like attention deficit hyperactivity disorder or dyslexia, but they just can't seem to keep up anymore. These students can baffle and frustrate teachers and parents alike, who can't quite put a finger on the reason why. The reason is often a poor working memory.

In a large-scale study involving more than three thousand children, Tracy and her research team wanted to find out why some children seem to develop learning problems as they get to higher grades. For this study, she examined data on younger (five- and six-year-old) and older (nine- and ten-year-old) children. She found that the gap between students with poor working memory and their peers gets wider as they get older. In the younger group, only a third of those with low working memory achieved very low scores in tests of language and math. However, when she looked at the older students with low working memory, the proportion with low test scores had nearly doubled.

There are a number of reasons that explain the increase in learning problems as children age. In lower grades, the teachers often repeat instructions and provide memory support to aid learning. As students get older, they are expected to be more independent in their learning, and students with poor working memory struggle as a result. In addition, class material becomes more complex, and a poor working memory can't handle the increased challenge.

The troubles become even more pronounced in higher education. When Tracy tested a group of nearly four hundred college students to find out what skills predicted good reading, spelling, and comprehension scores, she found that working memory played the important role. Certainly at university level, students are required to do complex analyses with the material they are given. Not only do they have to hold more new information in mind, but they are also expected to be creative in finding solutions to problems, coming up with compelling arguments in essays, and presenting innovative ideas that go beyond rehashing existing research to shed new light on a subject.

When it comes to learning, working memory continues to play an important role throughout the life span. That's what Lynn Hasher and Rose Zacks concluded from a review of the research on working memory and aging. They analyzed several studies on language skills and reading comprehension and concluded that poor working memory underlies problems in these areas. In particular, they highlighted one study in which older and younger people had to read some grammatically complex text, a task that places a heavy demand on working memory. The older adults who had poor working memory were more likely to have difficulty making sense of the text compared to the younger generation. Hasher and Zacks also discuss how some older adults are still able to perform very well, and we'll learn more in chapter 9 about working memory as we age.

Working Memory and Learning Disorders

Step inside any classroom and you will likely find at least a couple of students who have special needs or learning disorders, including attention deficit hyperactivity disorder (ADHD), dyslexia, and autism. There is a tendency to view these conditions as separate issues with specific differences, and although this is true on one level, they often share a common disadvantage: a poor working memory. The link between working memory and these learning disorders is complex, and researchers, including ourselves, are still in the process of discovering the exact nature of this relationship. Here is a glimpse at what has been discovered thus far.

ADHD

Nine-year-old Jason can be a disruptive force in the classroom. He incessantly kicks the desk in front of him—*bang! bang! bang!*—unexpectedly pops up out of his chair, and talks when it isn't his turn. He also has trouble completing his homework and is prone to daydreaming while the teacher is talking. Jason isn't trying to be a troublemaker. It's just that he is one of the 9 percent of British children who have ADHD. But does that mean that Jason isn't smart? And what exactly is preventing him and other kids with ADHD from reining in their behavior and staying focused on their lessons?

Students with ADHD often have an overactive motor cortex, which means that they are more likely to wiggle, jump, and shout—often at the most inappropriate times. If they do manage to be quiet, it is because their Conductor is working very hard to control their behavior. But because their Conductor is so busy reining in their actions, it isn't available to help them understand a new concept, copy from the board, or read. Their Conductor can't handle double duty: either learning has to give or the child's behavior does.

In 2005, Tracy had the opportunity to investigate the relationship between working memory and ADHD in schoolchildren when she led a United Kingdom government-funded project. After comparing the working memory scores of almost one hundred students with a clinical diagnosis of ADHD to those of their peers without the disorder, she found that the majority of the students with ADHD had very low working memory scores. This finding is supported by brain-imaging scans that have found that students with ADHD have a smaller PFC, possibly affecting their working memory.

There isn't enough evidence to date to definitively say that low working memory *causes* ADHD, but there appears to be a combined effect, with ADHD weakening working memory on the one hand, and low working memory exacerbating ADHD on the other hand. Here's an analogy that might clear up the relationship. Let's say your thumb hurts. It's sprained, and you have a big splinter in it. If you take out the splinter, it might lessen the pain, but you would still have the sprain. You have two different problems, but by improving one of them, you can probably use your thumb better. It's the same with working memory and ADHD. From what we currently understand, they are two separate issues, but if you strengthen one of them, the child's ability to learn may improve.

The link between poor working memory and ADHD is so strong, in fact, that working memory tests are often used as one of the diagnostic tools in identifying ADHD. Parents or educators who suspect that a child might have ADHD would be wise to assess the child's working memory to help determine if the learning disorder is indeed the problem.

Dyslexia

Fourteen-year-old Taylor has always had a tough time in school. She said she was "stupid" because reading was really difficult for her and she never did well on essay tests. It turned out that she had dyslexia, which is associated with confusing certain letters like B and D, misspelling words based on phonetics (like *frend* instead of *friend*), and transposing numbers (writing 14 instead of 41).

Some psychologists suggest that poor working memory is an underlying factor in dyslexia. We use working memory to keep language in mind, and the Conductor has to keep in mind the relevant speech sounds and concepts necessary for identifying words and understanding text. Because we also use working memory to keep information in the correct order, students, like Taylor, can often get confused because their Conductor loses track.

The connection between working memory and dyslexia can persist even to adulthood, as Tracy discovered in a recent study she conducted with college students. When she compared the working memory scores of the students with dyslexia to a typically developing group of students, she found that those with dyslexia had lower scores on the tests requiring them to process words and language. This confirmed that dyslexia is related to problems with working memory.

Autistic Spectrum Disorder

Martin, age ten, loves dinosaurs and can recite just about anything you might want to know about *T.rex*, stegosaurus, or triceratops. But ask him how he's feeling or tell him a joke, and you're likely to get nothing more than a blank stare from him. Martin has autism, which is linked to a number of issues, including problems with communication and social interaction, as well as a tendency to overfocus on a narrow range of interests.

What's causing these problems is a billion-dollar question. Decades of research on autism have yet to bring to light any concrete findings about causes. And although investigations into the association between working memory and autism have confirmed a link, they have not pinpointed working memory as a cause.

In Tracy's research with an autism charity, she found that children with autism find it hard to keep in mind all the necessary information for language processing. Because social interactions are inherently linguistic in nature, with communication between people relying heavily on verbal exchanges, children with autism can struggle to understand social situations.

In this same trial, Tracy saw evidence that students with autism spend too much time on the details and have difficulty seeing the bigger picture. For example, one student was given a working memory task where he had to answer true or false to a statement and then remember the last word in the sentence, such as, "Dogs can play guitars." The student spent a long time thinking about this and finally answered, "Well you can teach a dog!" His intense and extended scrutiny of this sentence meant he had forgotten what he had to do next in the task.

Brain-imaging studies on students with autism have found that they have a smaller corpus callosum, the thick band of nerve fibers that divides the brain into two hemispheres—right and left. The corpus callosum allows information to pass from one side to the other. As a result, students with autism can end up working with the equivalent of a single-lane street while their peers have the benefit of a four-lane highway to transmit information. This may mean that information takes too long to reach its destination. Combine that with the tendency to overfocus on thoughts, and you can see that there can be a veritable traffic jam in the brains of autistic children.

Does this mean that all children with autism have low working memory scores? No. Working memory skills can vary depending on where a school-age child is on the autism spectrum. For example, a high-functioning autistic student may display average working memory skills.

Can strengthening working memory help to unblock the traffic jam? Research on the potential benefit of working-memory training for individuals with autism is still in its infancy but showing promise. The

Center on Research on Individual Development and Adaptive Education of Children at Risk in Germany, where Tracy gave a presentation in 2012, is investigating forms of training that may have a positive effect on working memory in children with autism. We offer more detail about working memory training later in this chapter.

From the Research Lab to the Real World

As awareness increases about working memory and its importance for learning, there is a surge of interest in implementing working memory strategies in the classroom and at home. When Tracy began her research, she had to spend a lot of time reaching out to educators and parents. As her message about the importance of working memory caught on, they began to beat a path to her door. Now she fields inquiries on a daily basis from parents, teachers, special education teachers, school psychologists, administrators, school boards, and policymakers, all of whom are searching for practical ways to harness the power of working memory.

For parents of problem students, discovering how working memory influences learning can be a welcome relief. At the end of one of Tracy's presentations, a mom approached her with tears in her eyes. She said that her eleven-year-old daughter had been having lots of trouble in her schoolwork and that the teachers had basically written her off. After hearing about the role of working memory in learning, this woman said that she felt that there was some light at the end of the tunnel for her daughter and that she was so excited to learn that there were ways that she and her teachers could support her daughter.

Other parents have lamented to Tracy that school counselors told them that their children shouldn't even bother applying to college because they wouldn't be able to handle the higher-level demands. But when these same kids were given working memory support, they got into college, and some of them graduated with honors.

In some cases, teachers seek out Tracy's expertise looking for answers to help a single student, like thirteen-year-old Adam, who was breaking equipment in class. His teachers wondered if he had a problem with attention, if the class material was too complicated, or if he lacked the motor skills to control his movements. An assessment determined that Adam had ADHD and poor working memory, which made it hard for him to control his behavior and frustrated him. With this information, his teachers created an individualized plan for him, including shorter periods of time devoted to learning. For example, instead of having him do two math problems in a row, they would have him do one, take a break, then tackle the next one. The change allowed him to better control his behavior and improve academically.

Other schools are interested in implementing a system-wide approach that focuses on working memory. Such is the case with a school in England that is renowned for providing outstanding support to students with reading problems. Administrators there had heard about Tracy's research and invited her to give a presentation. Tracy outlined a number of simple changes teachers could make in their teaching methods, including some of those listed in the Working Memory Exercises and Strategies section at the end of this chapter. These strategies free up working memory so students are better able to focus on their reading.

In the United States, a growing number of schools are seeking Tracy's help to adopt a more working-memory-friendly approach to learning. In one school district in Kansas, students are being tested with the *Alloway Working Memory Assessment* (AWMA) and are using *Jungle Memory* for working memory training. The school is also implementing some teaching methods and classroom strategies that reduce the load on working memory.

In spite of the mounting evidence, not all teachers or administrators are aware that working memory can make a difference in learning. At one K–12 school where Tracy spoke, an art teacher told her before the presentation that she didn't think working memory would be relevant to her classes. But after listening to Tracy's presentation, this instructor approached her again and admitted, "I realize now that *everything* I say and do in class involves working memory. When I'm giving instructions or telling my class to use certain techniques, I'm making demands on their working memory. It makes a difference how many directions I give."

Some teachers don't think that focusing on working memory is necessary because they already have memory aids in the classroom. Memory aids, such as a number line or alphabet on the wall, are common in elementary schools. But students with poor working memory may not be able to use these memory aids effectively, or their Conductor can't manage using the memory aid *and* do an assignment at the same time. When teachers are aware of this and help these students use the memory aid, they can solve the problem.

These are only a few of the many ways that working memory is already making a difference for thousands of students in schools around the country and around the world.

Working Memory Training for Higher Achievement

Schools and parents who are eager to take advantage of working memory to increase academic achievement are increasingly turning to computer-based training programs. *Jungle Memory*, one such program, is specifically designed to target working memory skills critical for academic success. It also trains students to pay attention and process information and challenging concepts more quickly.

So far, our research has shown that *Jungle Memory* helps improve grades and working memory in average students, those with general learning difficulties, and those with learning disorders, such as dyslexia or autism. In one study, Tracy found that after eight weeks of *Jungle Memory* training, students with learning difficulties improved up to ten standard points in language and math. This is like improving from a C to a B or a B to an A. They also improved in working memory. For scientific validity, the results were compared with those of a control group that received extra tutoring but did not use *Jungle Memory*. The control group didn't show significant improvements in working memory or learning.

In clinical trials conducted in partnership with the organization Dyslexia Scotland, Tracy found that students showed significant improvements in standardized tests of working memory after training regularly with *Jungle Memory*. Their scores on standardized tests in language and math were also better after training. Tracy presented these findings at meetings of Dyslexia Scotland in 2010 and 2011.

We were also curious to know if working memory training could improve learning ability in children with autism, so we conducted a trial with high-functioning autistic students. Specifically we wanted to find out if using *Jungle Memory* could improve working memory and grades in autistic children. We split the participants into three groups: Group 1 used *Jungle Memory* four times a week for eight weeks, Group 2 used *Jungle Memory* once a week for eight weeks, and Group 3 did not use *Jungle Memory* during the eight-week period.

We gave all of the students standardized tests of IQ, working memory, and learning at the beginning of the trial and eight weeks later at the end. The findings showed that students with autism who used *Jungle Memory* four times a week showed significant improvements compared to the other two groups. Their working memory scores improved from low to average, and their grades increased by an average of 5 points, or the equivalent of going from a B- to a B+. To ascertain if the results were long-lasting, we retested each of the groups eight months later and found that the improvements remained in the group that trained four times per week.

As researchers, we spend a lot of time crunching numbers and analyzing data, and uncovering results such as these can be very exciting. But nothing is more rewarding than hearing firsthand from the parents of a child with a learning disorder just how much *Jungle Memory* training has helped that child. This is from the mother of nine-year-old Carson:

> Carson enjoyed *Jungle Memory* and made steady improvement as the weeks went by. He has been attempting to read more challenging books since the study and I feel that this was a good opportunity for Carson to feel positive about his ability. I have seen his teacher at school today, and she informed me that there had been

an improvement in Carson's word recognition and spelling and that he had a score of 7.5 compared to 0 last year.

Putting the Focus on Working Memory in School

The discovery that working memory is so vital to learning has huge implications for our schools and the way we educate our children, both at school and at home. Knowing a child's working memory can be a great advantage for teachers: a powerful tool we can use to transform their learning outcomes, which is why we should test the working memory of all children. By testing students' working memory, we can determine their strengths and weaknesses. With assessment results in hand, teachers can gain a better understanding of why some students aren't performing up to their abilities, which students need extra help in specific areas, and which students aren't being challenged enough. This information allows teachers to better allocate their time and efforts in the classroom and helps them figure out the best ways to work with each student to increase his or her academic achievement.

Knowing students' working memory scores can also create a powerful shift in thinking. For example, rather than assuming that an underachieving student is just being lazy, teachers and parents may realize that the student has a working memory problem and that a few adjustments can help that student be more successful. Similarly, educators and parents who previously thought that students with certain learning disabilities were incapable of improving their academic outcomes may come to understand that enhancing working memory or lightening the load on working memory may facilitate their child's learning. In the Working Memory Exercises and Strategies at the end of this chapter, we offer a number of simple techniques teachers can use to prevent working memory overload in the classroom.

Catching learning problems earlier in life can also contribute to alleviating the tremendous financial strain on cash-strapped education systems. Earlier in this chapter, we explained how poor working memory can lead to greater learning problems as a child progresses in school.

For example, if a seven-year-old child who has trouble with language skills doesn't get the help she needs, she may be struggling in every subject by the time she is twelve years old. Trying to deal with the problem at this late stage in her education requires a much greater investment in terms of time, effort, resources, and finances. Addressing learning problems early will help reduce overall costs.

Helping students overcome learning problems at an earlier age could also help reduce dropout rates and improve U.S. education rankings compared to other high-performing countries. In America, one student drops out every twenty-six seconds, and only 75.5 percent of students graduate from high school, according to America's Promise Alliance. On the international scene, the United States is lagging behind in education. Of thirty-four countries, it ranked fourteenth in reading, seventeenth in science, and twenty-fifth in math, according to the Programme for International Student Assessment. To fix these problems, especially when public schools are facing greater funding cuts, we need innovative solutions. The emerging body of research and real-world results point to working memory as an effective, affordable way for U.S. schools to improve learning outcomes.

Working Memory Exercises and Strategies

For Teachers

Test Working Memory

Tracy developed the *Alloway Working Memory Assessment* (AWMA), the highly accurate standardized working memory assessment, to empower schools and teachers with the knowledge they need to improve learning outcomes. The AWMA has been translated into almost twenty languages and has been used in thousands of schools around the world, but millions more schools could benefit from getting an accurate profile of their students' working memory.

Support Working Memory

Knowing a student's working memory is only the beginning. We have identified a number of strategies that support working memory to improve learning. The overall goal in supporting working memory is to reduce working memory demands that are unnecessary so students can use it on the things that matter.

—Routine, Routine, Routine—

Every time you introduce something new to the class, such as the concept of fractions or a new book to read, you are making a demand on students' working memory. In order to best learn the new concept or grasp the new reading material, students should be able to focus their working memory on the learning process. Unfortunately, that often isn't the case because many teachers unwittingly add working memory demands on their students.

Many teachers, for example, break routine by mixing up their lesson plans or doing things in a different order than they usually do, such as asking students to take out their rulers first when they usually take out their graph paper first. This creates an additional demand on working memory because the students now have to consciously do something differently than they have before. This should be avoided whenever possible. Once you have found a routine that works, stick with it. You want students to use their working memory for the fractions and the new book.

—Yellow Dots, Red Dots, Green Dots—

Everything in the classroom should have its proper place. Markers need to go with the markers, dictionaries need to go on the shelf, and construction paper needs to be in the proper drawer. Children who spend a lot of time searching for the pencils or water paints may forget why they needed them in the first place. This is particularly important for students from kindergarten to sixth grade, when children often move things and leave them strewn about. To help keep everything in its place, try a simple color coding strategy: use yellow dots on books, red dots on all writing or painting instruments, and green dots on all types of paper.

This way, students will have a visual cue to help them remember where to find things, which frees up working memory for learning tasks.

—Break It Down—

Understanding instructions is one of the most demanding tasks for a student's working memory. They have to keep the set of instructions in mind as well as execute each one in the proper sequence. Too many instructions can easily overwhelm a student or a whole class. The more instructions you add, the harder it becomes, and the more likely that a student will give up on an assignment. Solve this common problem by knowing what your class can handle.

Working Memory Skills by Age

Age	Number of Instructions According to Age
5–6	2 instructions
7–9	3 instructions
10–12	4 instructions
13–15	5 instructions
16 and over	6 instructions

—Go Back to the Basics—

Too often in a classroom, students have yet to master the fundamentals when they are asked to perform a complex task. A good example is reading comprehension. Let's say a student is asked to explain the meaning of the sentence: "She grabbed the corner of the box and picked it up." A student who doesn't yet know that *or* makes the sound *awr* will use up his or her working memory trying to figure out the word *corner* and will not be able to process what it means in the sentence. To fix this, drill the basics of sounds and letters so that they become automatic during reading. This means students will not have to actively work with these sounds and letters, freeing up their working memory to comprehend the sentence.

For Parents

Turn Off the Unlearning Tool

Just as classrooms support working memory by avoiding practices that undermine it, parents can do the same thing. One of the most important things you can do is to turn off the TV. Kids' brains are very plastic. As infants, toddlers, and schoolchildren, their neurons are laying down the links that will define who they are and how they react to things. If you want them to learn to laugh, laugh a lot. If you want them to have a good vocabulary, speak to them often. If you want them to enjoy the outdoors, let them play outside. If you want them to be passively entertained, have a short attention span, and struggle to think, plop them down in front of a device that encourages all these things—the TV.

Based on what we know from work by Dimitri Christakis, there is good reason to switch off the television. In 2004, he published a study that followed more than twelve hundred children for six years, testing them at ages one, three, and seven. What he found was astonishing: the more time children spent watching TV daily at ages one and three, the more likely they were to have attention problems at age seven.

If you want to encourage your child's working memory, limit TV, especially when they are very young. The American Academy of Pediatrics suggests that children under two years old avoid TV altogether. For those older, they suggest no more than one to two hours a day of educational, nonviolent programs. In place of all that TV time, encourage children to exercise their working memory by turning ordinary objects into something extraordinary: boxes become spaceships, spoons become swords, Mom's shoes become glass slippers, and Dad's shoes become a pair of rocket boots.

Read to Your Children or Have Them Read to You

Aside from the fact that kids love having their parents read to them, being able to understand a story that is read aloud requires them to use their working memory. At the end of the book, ask them questions about the story so that they can use their working memory to think critically about what they just heard. One caveat: don't give in when children ask to hear the same story over and over. As a tale becomes well-worn, it turns into a recitation of something they already hold in their long-term memory and no longer requires them to use their working memory. Challenge their working memory by frequently reading new stories.

As a parent, it's easy to become bored with children's stories and therefore spend less time reading. Ross grew to loathe a very engaging but eventually tiresome children's book that our older son loved. Ross decided that if our son wanted to be read to, he would have to listen to works that Ross enjoyed, such as John Milton's *Paradise Lost*, bits of Shakespeare, and histories like *King Harold's Saga*. Ross was happy to find that if our son didn't understand something, he would ask, and the two would have a discussion about the book. If you tire of children's stories, try reading from books that interest *you*: a biography of a U.S. president, a memoir of a business bigwig, or an adventure tale of survival in the wild. Your child may not understand everything, but they might surprise you. Encourage your child to read to you too. Depending on his or her age and ability, this may be a single word, a sentence, a page, a chapter, or more.

Make Simple Recipes

Making quick-and-easy recipes engages working memory. Give your child a recipe with just a few ingredients, like pancakes (flour, milk, eggs, sugar, butter) or fresh pasta (egg, flour, olive oil). Make sure you read the steps ahead of time rather than having him read from a recipe. This ensures that he will be using his working memory to hold the steps in mind at the same time he is working with the ingredients. Have all utensils and ingredients ready to go before you start.

Kids' Fresh Pasta Recipe

1 egg
1 cup flour
1 tablespoon olive oil

1. Pour flour in a mound on a cutting board, and make it into a volcano with a big hole in it.
2. Break the egg, and put it and the oil in the volcano. Carefully mix the egg, oil, and some flour from the sides without breaking the sides of the volcano.
3. Squish it using hands and fingers so that everything is mixed, and then shape it into a ball and sprinkle flour on top.
4. Flatten the ball into a sheet with a rolling pin, and sprinkle flour on top. Roll the pasta sheet into a tube shape.
5. Ask Mom or Dad to cut the tube with a knife perpendicular to the tube so that little spiral wheels are formed. Unroll the wheels into noodles.

Because each instruction combines more than one step, give your child the instructions one or two at a time depending on his or her age and working memory. For children up to age eight, try one step at a time. Children over age eight may be able to handle two steps at a time.

Draw from Memory

Use the following method for a fun way to engage your child's working memory:

1. Show her a picture (for example, a car, a beach, or a famous painting).
2. Take the picture away.
3. Ask her to draw or paint the picture from memory as much as she can.

Working memory is required in this activity because children have to hold the picture in mind at the same time they are drawing it. Make sure that it is a picture they haven't seen before. This will ensure that they are using their working memory to hold it in mind rather than their long-term memory.

6

The New Mind-Body Connection

Working Memory in Sports

HAVE YOU EVER wondered why some athletes choke under pressure while others seem to have ice running through their veins? Why some skiers willingly hurtle themselves down black runs at breakneck speeds while the rest of us mere mortals panic just thinking about it? Why your golf game got *worse* after those pricey lessons? Why some players appear to throw in the towel before a match has even begun? Why athletes have a reputation for being simple-minded? Or why you never seem to get any better at five-a-side even though you've been playing the sport since you were ten years old? These are the kinds of questions that have haunted elite athletes, coaches, fans, weekend warriors, and duffers alike for decades. The answers lie in working memory.

As recreational athletes and sports fans, we decided to explore the relationship between working memory and athletic achievement, and here we introduce the many findings that have been made. We also introduce how the physical activities you engage in might affect the power of your working memory.

A number of fascinating studies have been revealing the ways in which working memory is involved with athletic achievement, finding that it's important to call on working memory at some times and to circumvent it at others: it can be either an advantage or disadvantage, depending on the situation. This is a tricky balance, and being able to switch from engaging our working memory to bypassing it is one of the talents that can make a big difference in how well you play. During much of the time that we're playing a sport, it's best if we are "in the zone," so that our movements are immediate and largely subconscious, and this requires that our working memory be turned way down. But we must also be able to call on our working memory at any given moment in order to analyze a situation and come up with a strategy for our next move. Think of Serena and Venus Williams, who have to perform rapid calculations that help put them in the right place at the right time on the tennis court to execute a screaming down-the-line backhand winner. Or consider what American football quarterbacks like Tom Brady must do, reading the defense and drawing on their extensive experience and working memory in order to decide whether to pass, and to which player, or to hand the ball off to a running back instead.

The fact that working memory is called on a great deal while playing sports was backed up by a study done by Swedish researchers in 2012. The researchers compared professional soccer players with non-athletes on a range of cognitive tests, including working-memory-type tasks. Both male and female soccer players from the European higher and lower divisions scored higher than the non-athletes. But the most interesting finding was that the players in the higher divisions scored the highest of all in these tests. The authors suggest that good players develop their working memory as a result of their constant training. In the time pressure of a game situation, the players have to learn to use their working memory to assess the situation, compare it to past experiences, come up with creative alternatives, and make a quick decision. So the next time you see some brawny player, don't think of him as unintelligent.

The key to getting the right balance of working memory engagement (and not interfering with getting in the zone) is in achieving enough mastery of the basic moves of a sport so that we can execute them without having to think about it, which frees up our working memory to be on guard and to activate it when we need it.

To see how working memory can get in our way when playing a sport, think about a time you've tried to learn a new sport, or a difficult new technique, such as switching from a one-handed to a two-handed backhand in tennis, or going from skiing to snowboarding. Trying to learn how to execute all of the things an instructor tells you to do can be totally overwhelming. Tracy experienced this when she accompanied Ross, an avid skier, on a trip to the Swiss Alps. She had never skied before and signed up for a lesson. Her instructor spoke perfect English and was a stickler for detail. Before she could move down the slopes, she was given a mental checklist. Hips had to be at a precise angle relative to the back. Arms had to be in an exact position, knees had to be bent to a specified degree, and skis had to be properly edged.

The instructor had told her to remember all of these instructions and say them to herself as she took her first run down the bunny slope. *Hips? Check. Arms? Check. Knees? Check. Skis . . . Plop!* Down she fell after about fifteen seconds. All of the instructions kicked her working memory into high gear, and when this happened, the areas of her brain that coordinate movement and balance froze. To see why this is true, take a look at what we call the working memory motor learning circuit, which is what is engaged when we are being taught a sport. It involves three steps.

Working Memory Motor Learning Circuit

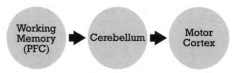

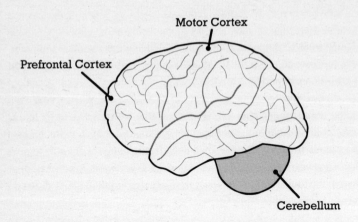

1. You hear a set of instructions that your working memory processes using your brain's cognitive hub, the prefrontal cortex (PFC).
2. Your PFC shuttles those instructions to the cerebellum, the brain's coordination center, to mentally rehearse the movements.
3. Finally, your cerebellum passes the instructions on to the region of the brain responsible for voluntary movement, the motor cortex, which commands your muscles to move in accordance with the instructions.

Think of these three steps like a "bump-set-spike" sequence in volleyball. Each player has to get to the ball and execute his or her role in the sequence quickly so the teammates can subsequently make their play. If any one of the players makes an error, the whole sequence falls apart, and you lose the point. Or, depending on your sport, you fall on your butt in the snow, strike out, or hook the golf ball into the sand trap. The more information you're trying to pay attention to, the more likely it is that one of the players is going to slip up.

Being in the Zone

To see what accounts for the difference when we are in the zone, seeming to make all the right moves without even thinking about it, compare Tracy's experience learning to ski with the way Ross, already a good skier, learned how to "carve" on that same ski trip. Carving is an advanced turning technique in which a skier leans dramatically to one side while shifting onto the edges of the skis, and it makes you feel as if you are turning on rails. Ross had been trying to figure out how to do it for a few years without any luck. So while Tracy was taking a beginner lesson, he took a carving lesson. His instructor, unlike Tracy's, didn't do much talking, which turned out to be a plus.

Rather than verbalizing detailed instructions, the instructor simply took out a rope and had Ross hold on to one end while she held on to the other. Then she motioned for Ross to lean as far over as he could so the sides of his knees were about an inch from the slope and his skis shifted to their edges. Voilà! Without a single verbal instruction, Ross understood exactly what it felt like to carve simply by leaning his body that far over. All he had to do was replicate that feeling.

On his next run, he was carving. After years of trying to think his way into a carving turn, he was finally actually doing it. Without a mental checklist to be keeping track of, his working memory wasn't engaged in the motor skills of the activity—rather, it was freed up to help him navigate the tricky terrain.

Ross's instructor had bypassed the working memory motor learning circuit and allowed Ross to tap directly into the cerebellum–motor cortex (C-MC) loop to get a feel for carving rather than a cognitive understanding of it. When this loop is activated, the cerebellum and motor cortex effectively turn working memory into a benchwarmer and work as a finely tuned duo, and there's no conscious thinking involved. You just perform, seemingly effortlessly. This is being "in the zone."

Cerebellum–Motor Cortex Loop

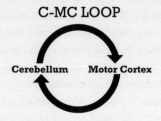

Choking When the Pressure's On

Have you ever found yourself with the ball in an intense soccer game and flubbed the shot on goal? Or wanted to make a great golf shot to impress the group you're playing with and then hit the ball right into the trees? You aren't alone. Even professional athletes who earn millions can choke under pressure. Who can forget England goalkeeper Robert Green's agonizing (and failed) attempt to grasp the ball after fumbling a routine save in the 2010 World Cup? Or Rory McIlroy, one of golf's emerging superstars, wasting a seemingly untouchable four-shot lead going into the final round at the 2011 U.S. Masters in Augusta, only to wind up ten strokes behind the eventual winner? Anyone who's played a sport knows about choking, but what you may not know is that working memory has a great deal to do with it.

Scientists who study sports and working memory have found that you are more likely to succumb to the pressure of competition if you learn a sport or a new skill by using the working memory motor learning circuit. That's what Richard Masters, chairman of the Institute of Human Performance at the University of Hong Kong, discovered when he carried out a series of experiments examining the role of working memory in sports performance.

In one study, he assigned participants to two groups to learn how to putt in golf. He gave one group very detailed instructions on how to putt, based on leading coaching techniques. This group had to use the working memory motor learning circuit in order to remember the instructions and match them up to what they needed to do physically.

Masters didn't give any putting instructions to the second group while they practiced their stroke. Instead, the group had to randomly generate letters every time they heard a tone from a metronome. In doing so, Masters was "distracting" their working memory so that they could not use it as part of learning how to putt.

Both groups had to complete one hundred putts per session over five consecutive days. On the final day, the pressure was on: Masters told the participants that they could receive more money if they performed well and that an expert golfer who had played at the British Open would closely evaluate their performance. In order to verify that these "incentives" were stressful, Masters monitored their heart rate, gave them an anxiety questionnaire, and recorded how much longer it took them to complete their putts. As he expected, the incentives had the desired effect, and the participants showed considerable performance anxiety on the final day of putting. Although both groups experienced performance anxiety, only the group that had learned the set of instructions using the working memory motor learning circuit showed a decline in their putting performance. Because they had been thinking when learning the movements, their Conductor wasn't free to manage their anxiety. In contrast, the group that didn't use their working memory to learn to putt didn't do any worse when under pressure, because their working memory was free to manage their stress.

If you tend to turn in a subpar performance when it really counts, go ahead and blame it on the working memory motor learning circuit.

Kicking Working Memory Off the Practice Squad

"Practice makes perfect" is one of the most common adages in sports. But it isn't 100 percent accurate. As we've shown, practicing while scrolling through a mental checklist can be detrimental to performance. That's why we'd like to suggest changing this maxim to "practicing *without working memory* makes perfect." How do you do it? Here are two working memory–free practice techniques we refer to as: the fatigue and fundamentals (F&F) factor.

You might think that trying to learn a new sport while you're utterly exhausted would be counterproductive, that you'd be too tired to retain anything. Well, you'd be wrong. Acquiring new motor skills when you're completely spent is actually one of the best ways to lock those moves into your brain.

If you've ever participated in a competitive organized sport, you may have experienced what is commonly called Hell Week in America, when coaches and trainers attempt to push players beyond their physical capabilities and work them to utter exhaustion. In the world of American high school and college wrestling, every week is *Hell Week*. Although wrestling matches last no more than seven minutes, training sessions can last for hours and hours and include power lifting, explosive plyometrics, sweat-inducing sprints, and dynamic calisthenics. Why? It isn't just to torture the athletes. Coaches know when athletes are pouring with sweat and gasping for breath, they tend to learn new moves far better. Here's why it works:

When you are exhausted, your working memory is considerably diminished. That's what Terry McMorris and his colleagues at University College Chichester discovered when they tested the effects of fatigue on working memory in a group of athletes. In order to bring about fatigue, the athletes were subjected to high heat and humidity for two hours. Immediately after this, they had to perform a series of physical and cognitive tests. The researchers found when the athletes were fatigued, their working memory performance dropped.

What this means is that when you're dog-tired, you can tap directly into that C-MC loop. And that's a good thing if you're trying to learn a completely new motor skill, like how to inline skate, ride a horse, or dance the tango. It's also effective if you're simply adding a new move to activities you already engage in, like learning how to inline-skate backward when you already know how to skate going forward, how to jump fences when you already know how to ride a horse, or how to dance a hip-hop routine when you already know how to ballroom dance.

Now for the "fundamentals" part of the F&F factor. When you hear the word *fundamentals*, the first sport that comes to mind probably isn't skateboarding. After all, it's a free-wheeling sport that's associated with rebellious teens. But the art of skateboarding at a high level boils down to one thing: practicing the fundamentals. Just ask Rodney Mullen. Widely hailed as the most influential and significant skateboarder in the history of the sport, we were thrilled then Mullen agreed to speak to us about the importance of drilling the basics.

Mullen invented the most commonly performed tricks in skateboarding, including the flat-ground ollie, where skaters pop up into the air from a standstill or while moving. Though an ollie may look like a simple jump, it is surprisingly complex and can be broken down into a number of submovements: the crouch-down, popping the board up, jumping, sliding the front foot up to the nose the board, and lifting the rear foot while keeping contact with the board, Mullen explained to us. If he were approaching this trick for the first time, he wouldn't rapidly speak the steps to himself. At less than a second, the trick is just too fast for that. But he could practice each element separately and memorize how each one feels.

That's a practice technique Larry Vandervert has been studying. He has found that deliberate practice drills individual movements into the motor cortex. The cerebellum then learns these routines through repeated episodes, which leads to layers of learning. These layers are built over time and on top of each other. The result is an increase in automaticity and efficiency of the action, meaning you don't need to tap into your working memory to perform them.

In striking similarity to Vandervert, Mullen describes his practice process as blanketing, where each submovement is like a blanket that he layers on top of other blankets. Mullen spends hours and hours perfecting each blanket before folding them together—practicing hundreds of crouches before adding a pop-up, before adding a jump, and so on. Think about what would have happened if Mullen had tried to do an ollie before he'd mastered each of those moves separately. He probably wouldn't have gotten much air, if any.

That's the key for perfecting your own practice routine. We all have a tendency to want to rush past the fundamentals and go for the flash. But it's better to break down the movements of your sport and practice each of those submovements before linking them all together. Yes, it can be boring to practice catching a pass in basketball and not sinking the layup or tossing a tennis ball into the air and not whacking a big serve. But with those movements eventually locked into your brain, your working memory is free to calculate and execute the flashiest and most effective plays in the big-pressure moments when it counts.

Calling Working Memory off the Bench and into the Game

One of the biggest benefits of the C-MC loop is that once you've mastered the basic skills of your sport, working memory is freed up to help you innovate and respond to situations that you didn't expect. You can practice, practice, practice, but when you find yourself on the field, the course, the court, or the slope, you are going to face situations that you didn't expect, things that you couldn't practice for, things with which the C-MC loop is unfamiliar. That's when you need working memory to come in off the sidelines and rejoin the team.

If you've ever seen a televised round of golf in St. Andrews, Scotland, with the howling wind and the horizontal rain, you know that even the most seasoned players can be thrown off their game. Nevertheless, the unexpected can also bring out the best in players, and result in a thrilling round of golf. This is also the case for mere mortals.

Ross played basketball in high school. In one game, his coach told him to stay on the outside and take perimeter shots. But all of a sudden, Ross saw a slight opening between defenders on the key. To penetrate it would require a sequence of moves that he had never linked together before. Leading with a shoulder, he made a larger space between defenders, spun around under the basket, and sank a reverse lay-up.

At the time, he had no idea how in the world he pulled it off because he had never practiced it before. But now he knows that his working memory made it happen. He had drilled all of those individual moves separately, and his Conductor calculated the sequence and sent it to his cerebellum, which passed it to his motor cortex.

Ross was able to improvise his reverse lay-up because of what Larry Vandervert calls the *predictor model*. This model is based on research by Patricia Goldman-Rakic, an American neuroscientist, and Per Roland at the University in Denmark. According to the predictor model, when we are presented with the unexpected, which is a regular feature of playing a sport—whether that's another player having made a fake move or a ski slope becoming unexpectedly icy—working memory is used to strategize the best course of action and identify the movements required. The PFC, the home of working memory, then sends the message to the cerebellum and the motor cortex to execute the action based on the required force and duration of the movement, such as how hard you need to hit or how high you need to jump. In this way, according to the predictor model, your working memory can help you face the challenges of a fast-moving game of tennis or break through a tough basketball defense. In more extreme sporting challenges, it can also save your life.

Take the case of Alex Honnold, a world-record-holding solo free climber. Free soloing is rock climbing with consequences. You climb without ropes, clips, or any other aid to get to the top. When you're climbing well, it's just you and the rock, but if you make a mistake, it may be just you and the valley floor. Honnold is best known for climbing extremely challenging routes on sheer faces and is one of only a few who has free-soloed the granite face of Half Dome in Yosemite. Honnold is so good that most of the time the C-MC loop is uninterrupted when climbing these routes.

We interviewed Honnold to find out how and when he calls on his working memory during his climbs. As he described it to us, his brain is on cruise control most of the time. He has all the required movements drilled into his cerebellum and usually doesn't have to think while performing them. In particularly challenging sections, however, he has to enlist his working memory.

In rock climbing, there is something known as the *beta*. It is a proven sequence of moves determined to be the best way to climb through challenging sections. For Honnold, the problem with betas is that they are generally designed for people climbing with ropes, and because they have the security of being anchored to the wall, they are more willing to take risks. With no ropes tethering him to the rock, Honnold often has to disregard the beta and problem-solve on the spot. That's exactly what happened to him on a thousand-foot wall near Nevada. As Honnold explained it to us, he had been on autopilot for most of the climb, but there was a problem just as he was nearing the top.

"I got up high on the route near the top, and it was pretty obvious what I should do," Honnold told us. "I could see the chalk marks from previous climbers, and then I could see this huge hole that people had been jumping to. I needed to get to that hole, but since I was soloing, there was no way I would jump. That was out of the question." Honnold had to come up with an innovative solution to get to the hole without jumping. "I kept probing that corner thinking there must be some way other than jumping and found this little tiny hole and then after several attempts, I found a new sequence where I could sort my feet out differently and reach up to the hole." Honnold can thank his working memory for springing into action to help him blaze the new path to the top.

Flipping the Working Memory Switch On and Off in the Face of Fear

The key to top performance is being able to switch working memory on and off. And sometimes this may be a matter of life and death. When you're engaged in activities that involve a good deal of danger—say, whitewater rafting in Class 6 rapids, mountain biking down treacherously steep terrain, or riding a monster 80-foot wave—an active working memory can add to the danger or even be deadly. Why? For the same reason that the working memory motor learning circuit can trip us up. As big-wave surfer Laird Hamilton aptly puts it in his book *Force of Nature*, thinking "gets in the way of your body."

So it's a good thing that in the face of fear, our working memory is naturally turned down. Consider what happens in the brain when we are confronted by a danger. What we experience as fear is, in terms of brain chemistry, the amygdala recognizing a threat—say a fifteen-hundred-pound grizzly bear running toward you—and signaling the release of two action hormones, epinephrine (also known as adrenaline) and cortisol (the stress hormone). These two hormones act to make the body and brain ready for "fight or flight." Epinephrine gets your blood pumping, makes your airways bigger, and sends blood to the muscles, while cortisol increases the blood sugar in your body. Epinephrine makes your body stronger; cortisol gives it high-octane fuel.

When these hormones turn your body into Superman or Superwoman, they also turn down the dimmer switch on your working memory. Numerous studies have found that the more cortisol and epinephrine in your bloodstream, the smaller your working memory is. Scientists have subjected people to all sorts of stressful situations and have found that the more fearful you are, the less you think. And that's a good thing. With working memory turned down low, you access the C-MC loop, allowing your cerebellum to communicate directly with your motor cortex, telling it to jump, punch, duck, or run much more rapidly than if you had to think everything through.

But working memory is still absolutely critical in fear-filled sports. To see how, let's take a look at big-wave surfing, also referred to as "tow-in" surfing because surfers get towed into the waves by jet skis. A big-wave surfer like Laird Hamilton goes through three major stages to ride a monster wave: releasing the rope of the jet ski, dropping down the face of the wave, and turning at the bottom to exit the wave. Before he drops in, his working memory is likely fully functioning. In order to release the rope, Hamilton has to *decide* to let go. To do this, he has to calculate the precise moment to do so, and indeed determine if it is possible to drop in at all.

You might think, given the explanation about how fear turns the working memory down, that a surfer's working memory would be impaired in this situation. After all, who wouldn't feel anxiety, or outright terror, about the danger if he drops the rope at the wrong time? But a fascinating study has shown that the amygdala doesn't fire off the action hormones at this stage of anticipation. In a 2008 study, Sarita Robinson and colleagues at the University of Central Lancashire exposed ten men to a helicopter underwater evacuation training exercise, a highly stressful experience that simulates being upside down in a sinking helicopter and having to find a way to exit the craft and swim to the surface. In this experiment, the researchers found that the men's cortisol levels didn't increase significantly before the stressful event, only after the event. This indicates that working memory is still in full force while anticipating a dangerous experience.

Once Hamilton is on the wave, his amygdala likely goes into turbo drive, putting his working memory on standby so that the C-MC loop takes over to enable rapid and subconscious responses to the dynamic variables of the wave. When everything goes perfectly, Hamilton emerges safely out of the wave, and his working memory won't be required until he gets ready to drop in on the next wave. But when something unexpected happens, for example, when a wave is bigger than anticipated, Hamilton needs to call on his working memory to survive.

Applying what we know about working memory and sports, we have a unique take on one of Hamilton's most intense experiences to date, described in harrowing detail in Susan Casey's *The Wave*. On December 3, 2007, a break off Maui roared with walls of water reaching fifty to one hundred feet. As Hamilton dropped into one wave, he quickly realized that it was breaking too fast and was going to come crashing down on top of him. Hamilton had to snap out of the hormone high and reactivate his working memory to make a choice to abort halfway down the face.

But how to do so? He couldn't go back over the top of the wave because it was already closing perilously over his head. He made the decision to punch right through the wave so he would come out the back. The plan worked, but he then found himself directly in the path of another thundering eighty footer. His tow-in partner, Brett Lickle, grabbed him just in time and gunned the jet ski's engine. But they couldn't outrun the menacing wave, which slammed them under the water. Wave after wave thrashed the pair. In the tumult, a fin on Hamilton's board sheared the muscle on Lickle's leg to the bone, leaving him rapidly bleeding out in the sea. Lickle needed a tourniquet or he would die, but all the gear was in the jet ski, hundreds of yards away. Hamilton had to flip the switch once again to activate his working memory to solve the problem.

Hamilton's working memory likely managed at least five pieces of information: the ever-advancing waves, his own pain and exhaustion, his friend's distress, the need for a tourniquet, and how to make one when they had no materials at all. His working memory Conductor prioritized the information, quickly moving the last two items to the top of the list. Looking down, he realized that his stretchy wet suit would work as a tourniquet, and he pulled it off and tied it above Lickle's wound. He had bought some time, but now he had to get his friend out of the surf.

He realized that swimming all the way to shore was impossible in the conditions, so he set off for the jet ski. Once he made it, though, he realized that he didn't have the electrical lanyard required to start the engine. Lickle had lost it in the thrashing. Hamilton was going to have to tap into his working memory to work with what he had, but this one was going to be a stretch. Looking in the glove compartment, he found a set of iPod earphones that he was able to cannibalize and start the engine.

In this life-or-death situation, how was Hamilton able to flip the switch to reactivate his working memory? Why didn't he freeze in the face of fear like most of us would? There may be a clue in research from Mustafa al'Absi and colleagues at the University of Minnesota. For al'Absi's study, a group of healthy adults agreed to participate in a stressful situation—preparing and delivering a series of public speeches—specifically designed to raise their cortisol levels. While in that stressed-out state, they had to perform a working memory test.

When al'Absi's team took blood samples from the volunteers, they discovered that some of the participants didn't produce as much cortisol under stress as others. What we found most interesting about this study was that the people with lower cortisol levels performed better than their more stressed-out peers in the working memory test. This suggests that in fearful situations, people who produce less cortisol are better able to access their working memory for problem solving than people who pump out more of the stress hormone. Of course, we haven't analyzed Hamilton's blood, but we would venture to guess that he might be one of those individuals who produce less of the working-memory-dimming hormone.

So being as deft as Laird Hamilton at switching our working memory on and off may be somewhat a matter of our biology. But all of us can get better at sports if we practice in the ways that allow us to circumvent working memory in order to learn the moves so that we don't have to think about them. This will free up our working memory to be more alert and on the ready to help us navigate the tricky surprises we have to confront in any sport.

When Sports Do a Number on Working Memory

As scientists who have spent years developing training tools to enhance working memory, we are constantly seeking ways to pump up mental power. By contrast, we are also trying to identify the behaviors and activities that put working memory at risk. Unfortunately, some sports fall into this category; specifically, contact sports, including football, boxing, and rugby, can damage your working memory. Ironically, though these sports are often working memory–intensive, they can also damage your working memory.

Sure, we all love watching a hard tackle. However enjoyable the spectacle, evidence is mounting that it comes at a cost to many players, both young and old. The longer you play contact sports like rugby, boxing (think Muhammad Ali), even lacrosse, hockey, and football— yes, heading the ball counts as "contact"—the greater the likelihood is that you will experience a concussion. And concussions can have a huge impact on working memory, which in turn can lead to impulsive behavior, depression, and dementia. Even if you don't experience the effects immediately, you may find yourself with debilitating cognitive problems in the long term.

Immediate symptoms of a concussion include dizziness, confusion, disorientation, and headache. These symptoms are often the result of chemical damage. When the brain is working properly, it is a perfect chemical machine, but when you hit your head hard enough, the impact disrupts the delicate balance of neurotransmitters, potassium, calcium, and glucose.

A concussion is like putting your brain through a blender: everything gets mixed up. The neurotransmitters spill out from the brain cells, causing a huge release of potassium from the cells. Potassium has an electrical charge, and the excess that is now outside the cells causes a change in the polarity, affecting brain function. In attempting to restore the balance, the cells go into overdrive to vacuum the potassium back up with specially designed pumps, but this requires more energy, in the form of glucose, than the brain has readily available. As a result, the brain goes through a sugar crash. If a second concussion happens before the brain has recovered fully, the damage can be even greater, because the brain lacks the energy to restore the chemical balance.

You would think that it would be easy to know if your brain had just gone through the blender, but research shows that you may not even realize that your brain has been injured. And a doctor or a team physician might not know it either. A study from Thomas Talavage and colleagues at Purdue University concluded that a person may suffer a concussion but have absolutely none of the telltale signs—no headache, no dizziness, no disorientation.

For this study, Talavage and his team of researchers placed sensors on the helmets of American high school football players over the course of a season. They found that after players were hit with concussive force, many of them didn't experience any symptoms. Moreover, team physicians who examined them did not give a diagnosis of concussion. However, when the players were scanned using fMRI, evidence of trauma was clear.

Working memory suffered a lot of damage. The researchers tested the players' working memory before the season started and then again at its conclusion. They found that in all of the players, working memory was poorer and had to work harder to perform the same tasks that had been accomplished with less effort at the beginning of the season.

The consequences are not just short term. Repeated brain trauma can devastate an athlete's working memory over the long term. Research from Boston University Medical School shows that multiple concussions cause the buildup in the PFC of an abnormal form of a protein called Tau, which forms *neurofibrillary tangles*—collections of twisted fibers found inside nerve cells. If you've ever attempted to unravel a knotted ball of Christmas lights, you will have some idea of what Tau buildup looks like. A devastating disease called frontotemporal dementia is associated with the buildup and can cause a lack of judgment and inhibition, compulsive behavior, loss of appetite control, and the inability to form complete thoughts.

To keep your working memory in tiptop shape, skip the contact sports or wait until they have reduced the risk of concussion. But don't use that as an excuse to become a couch potato. A growing body of evidence shows that inactivity weakens the brain. Physical activity that doesn't involve getting punched in the face or knocked out can actually strengthen your working memory. In our own research, we have found one activity in particular that can pump up your brain power.

Run for Your (Working Memory) Life

When Bruce Springsteen sang, "Baby, we were born to run," he wasn't kidding. Christopher McDougall's *Born to Run* has popularized the idea that running, particularly endurance running, is what the human body has been adapted to do. And running over long distances is one thing we can do better than any other mammal on the planet. This particularly human expertise means that you have it within yourself to run down a deer (if you really wanted to).

You are a long-distance running machine: your gluteus maximus twists your hips, moving your legs; your feet act like springs taking the energy from each step and recycling it to the next; your torso counter rotates against your twisting hips; and your swinging arms act like mass dampers helping you to maintain stability. Perhaps most important, lacking any fur and having a large number of sweat glands, you are great at dumping heat when running. Quadrapeds like deer and antelope cool down by panting, but they can't pant and run at the same time, so if they run for too long, they become *hyperthermic*, or overheat.

According to Daniel Liberman at Harvard University, these physiological differences combined to allow our ancestors to run down prey over distance, causing the prey to overheat until they were easily dispatched. Liberman speculates that the ability to hunt meat in this manner was crucial to meet the calorie demands of our big brains: we ran, in part, to think. Though most of us no longer need to run for food, our brains improve with running. Research has shown that it makes us less likely to be depressed, generates new brain cells, releases a wonderful cocktail of endorphins, and helps us deal with stressful situations.

It also improves working memory, according to a study from the University of Illinois. Researchers there wanted to see if exercise increased working memory, and if so, which type of activity had the greatest effect. The team compared the effects of running versus weight lifting, and what they found could cause a lot of bodybuilders to rethink their workout. Lifting weights provided no measurable improvement in working memory, while running boosted mental performance. The biggest benefit seemed to come immediately after running, when working memory abilities spiked. But even a half-hour after running, working memory was still better than before exercise.

One of the reasons that running may be so good for working memory is that it activates the PFC. Japanese scientists, including Mitsui Suzuki at Nihon Fukushi University, used optical imaging, a technique to look at the effect of running on the PFC. He placed a cap with a series of laser diodes and light sensors on his participants. As the lasers shine, the sensors determine how the light is absorbed by the brain, which allows them to determine how much hemoglobin is in a particular area. The greater the concentration of hemoglobin, the greater the activation.

The study volunteers exercised on a treadmill at a slow walk (a little less than 2 mph), a fast walk (a little more than 3 mph), and a moderate run (about 5.5 mph—around an eleven-minute mile). Suzuki found that walking slowly or fast did not increase hemoglobin levels in the

PFC at all. Running, however, increased the amounts significantly. In other words, running gives your PFC a workout. Suzuki theorizes that this may be because running can be unpredictable and requires controlled attention to changes in gait and speed, a working memory skill that fires the PFC.

If the controlled attention required in running relies on working memory, does running with a higher degree of controlled attention lead to a better working memory? To find the answer, we started from the ground up and took off our shoes to test the effects of barefoot running. Harvard's Liberman has been at the forefront of research that has shown how going barefoot considerably improves running mechanics.

For nearly 2 million years before Nike appeared, the original and natural running shoe was the bare foot. The prominent heel pad on modern running shoes encourages your foot to strike the ground heel first, causing a jarring impact that travels through the joints of the leg. In contrast to shod runners, barefoot runners often land midfoot or forefoot and comparatively less jarringly, leading to less injury when it is done correctly.

Because most runners come to barefoot from wearing shoes, their form needs work. Feet land far off the center of mass, too hard, and hips don't twist as they should. To correct this requires an increased proprioception of a number of things at the same time. Are your feet landing beneath your hips? Are you running gently? Are your feet landing in a straight line or a zigzag?

When you have all of these down, exteroception comes into play. You have to pay attention to sight stimuli (things you can see) and, something else shod runners take for granted, touch stimuli (things your feet can feel). You have to look and feel where you are landing because if you don't, it hurts. Landing on glass, a sharp stone, or even a twig can be very painful for feet that are used to stomping about with shoes on. Barefoot runners tend to think of runs in terms of how they feel on their feet: rough, soft, smooth, slippery, cool, or warm.

We undertook a study to find out if the extra cognitive input from barefoot running translates into cognitive benefits, the first study of its kind. We asked a group of barefoot runners and shod runners to fill in an online questionnaire and take a series of working memory tests. The questionnaire included items such as what kind of terrain they ran on and what they wore on their feet, if anything.

When we looked at the data, we found a fascinating result. It turns out that what you have on your feet when you run is very important to your working memory. The barefoot runners had higher working memory than those who ran with shoes. This makes sense.

As a family, we loved spending many hours of our weekends running barefoot through thinly cut trails in the Pentlands, outside of Edinburgh, bouncing through moss, jumping over streams, gently dancing over sharp rocks, and avoiding the occasional pile of sheep-recycled grass. Though we had loads of fun, we quickly learned that if we didn't pay attention, we'd find ourselves tumbling down a hill or slipping and landing on our backsides.

While that's true whether you're running with shoes or without them, barefoot runners have the added stimuli of touch. One potential benefit of this extra sensation is a heightened awareness of the environment around them. We think this is because when you are running with shoes, you can select what you focus on, ignoring the pebbles and twisting roots. But barefoot runners are aware of nearly everything under their feet—there is little irrelevant information because they need to be aware of most of the ground in order to avoid a painful misstep. This processing of a larger volume of stimuli may account for the fact that barefoot runners have a higher working memory.

Seeing proof that running, and barefoot running in particular, pumps up working memory power is exciting because it suggests that it is possible to improve our mental abilities. When we work our body, we work our brain.

Working Memory Exercises

Strategies 1 to 6 are designed to help you learn a new skill or improve your moves by keeping working memory in the "off" mode so you can tap directly into the C-MC loop. We also offer a few tips for all you coaches, instructors, and parents so you can improve your teaching techniques and get the most out of your players.

1. Learn from the Best

Your cerebellum can be filled with all the right moves, or all the mediocre moves. Whatever moves you learn in the beginning are the ones that you will have in your arsenal when you are competing, so choose an instructor with a proven record of teaching perfect technique.

Quick tip for coaches: Choose the best copycats. If you are deciding who makes the cut, prioritize athletes who can pick up and mimic a skill quickly, not necessarily those with the most game experience.

2. Opt for One-on-One Lessons

If you are learning a sport for the first time, stay away from group lessons and spring for one-on-one private sessions. They may be more expensive at the outset but could end up costing you less—in terms of both money and frustration—in the long run. Private lessons ensure that you get the instructor's full attention, which will help you learn new skills faster and more correctly, so you may need fewer lessons overall.

Quick tip for coaches: If a player isn't performing on the field, it may be because he or she never learned the skills properly. Help the player out with a one-on-one session where you break down his or her performance and show this person how to execute movements correctly.

3. Zip the Lip and Focus On the Feel

When you are learning a new skill, seek out coaches who don't give a lot of instructions and aren't overly chatty. Too much talking means too much working memory, which gets in the way of the C-MC loop. The best coaches help you get the feel for the motion and know when to shut up. One of the best things you can do is to stop asking questions and just try to copy the form you are being taught. Questions mean working memory. Copying means feeling.

Quick tip for coaches: Learn to shut up. Imagine how you would teach a skill if you had tape over your mouth. Then give it a try.

4. Take Advantage of the Fatigue Factor

Fatigue is a great way to lock down working memory. Being too tired to think makes it much easier for your cerebellum to absorb the feeling of athletic movements. The next time you want to learn how to swing a golf club, don't head straight for the driving range. First, go for a run, do push-ups, or do jumping jacks until you feel fatigued.

Quick tip for coaches: If you are teaching a new skill, allocate more time to "warm up" that day than you usually do so you can pre-fatigue players.

5. Break It Down, Drill It, Then Put It Together

Every movement in sports—from an ollie in skateboarding to a forehand in tennis, a spike in volleyball, a jump, or a sprint—is made up of multiple submovements, and the whole movement can be ruined by getting just one of those parts wrong. Drill each submovement separately to lock it into the C-MC loop. Then when you link the moves together, it will flow more automatically without having to think about it.

Quick tip for coaches: Understand that drilling submovements can be very boring for the person who's learning. If you're working on sub-movements one day, be sure to add a little fun to your sessions in other ways.

6. Turn On Working Memory When You Need It

After the C-MC loop has established how to perform the movements correctly and automatically, it is time to reintroduce working memory into your activities. We recommend doing this in two stages. Be sure to master the stage 1 exercises before trying stage 2.

Stage 1: Do the following simple tasks, which require you to use working memory during your practice sessions. Then when it's time for the big match, your working memory will be free to strategize, counter your opponent's moves, or deal with high-pressure situations.

> • While practicing, count backward from 1,000 by threes: 1,000, 997, 994, 991 . . .
>
> • While practicing, say the alphabet backward: z, y, x . . .

Stage 2: Replay a movement or a series of moves in your head that are different from the movement or moves you are performing at the moment. For example, if you are playing basketball and doing a pick and roll, think about taking a fading jump shot. If you are playing golf, imagine the perfect drive as you are putting. This is tremendously demanding and is almost guaranteed to mess up your performance at first, so don't try it on game day. Save it for practice. Once you get the hang of it, you will be able to better use your working memory to think outside the box and be more creative.

Quick tip for coaches: Play the opposite game.

Stage One: Drill your players repeatedly in a particular movement, say jumping or sprinting. As they are doing the movement, shout out the name of the movement. For example, "Jump!" or "Sprint." This primes them to carry out the movement every time you shout its name.

Stage Two: Now ask them to do a different movement like a push-up when you shout "Jump." This will force them to use their working memory to inhibit a trained response and carry out the push-up.

Stage Three: Add more and more movements with contradictory instructions. "Jump" = push-up, "Push-up" = sprint, and so on. By using their working memory to carry out the action, they will be better prepared to use it during competition to come up with innovative solutions.

7. Lace Up Your Running Shoes (or Not) and Go for a Run

Going for a run is a great way to give your working memory a workout. If you'd like to get the benefit of the extra processing demands that come with adjusting to the terrain beneath your feet, consider going barefoot. With training, it is possible to run on almost any terrain—even snow and ice. Ross used to be able to run just a mile a week until he took his shoes off and *slowly* worked up to a thirty-three-mile barefoot run in the Pentlands. Ready to give it a try? The web is full of sites with great advice on barefoot running, but here are a few tips to help you get started:

- Start at home by walking around barefoot on your own floors.
- Walk outside on the sidewalk, grass, and pavement.

  When you get your confidence up, break into a jog for a hundred feet or so.

  Add just a little more distance every time you try it.

  Always know your own limits, and if in any doubt, stop.

- Whatever your goal, get there as gradually as you can. If you rush at all with barefoot running, you will get injured. If you take it slow, anything is possible.

8. How to Beat Germany (or Any Other Team) at Penalties

So many fans have been crushed by the abject failure of their national teams in penalty shout-outs against Germany. Use the science of working memory to change their anguish into triumph.

Kick not think: Thinking about how you will take the penalty when the moment arrives invites working memory into the CM-C loop and is guaranteed to trip you up. Exclude working memory by targeting a particular area of the goal in practise, until hitting that spot is like breathing. On match day, you will be able to hit your target without thinking.

Kick and think: Pressure is inevitable during a shoot-out. Prepare your working memory to manage it by undertaking activities like mental math, or reciting the alphabet backward during penalty practise. This way you will become used to hitting the target while your working memory is engaged.

Pressure familiarity: Now familiarize your working memory with managing the pressure. Dare teammates to speak the unspeakable things fans do when you make a mistake, to ding your shiny new Ferrari, or to tell you your team will be relegated if you miss. Get emotional (that's the point), but control the emotion with your working memory and hit your target.

PART II

Growing and Improving
Working Memory

7

Working Memory Across the Life Span

IN PRIOR CHAPTERS, we've seen the many ways in which working memory is vital to our success and happiness in life. Now it's time to explore how working memory evolves throughout our lives and how we can preserve it as we age. In this section, we examine a range of brain training exercises, such as Sudoku, to find out if there are any benefits for working memory. We also look at how eating the right foods and making habits of some simple daily practices can boost working memory.

How does working memory develop? When is it at its peak? How does it change as we age? We decided to try to answer these crucial questions by launching a large-scale study of how working memory ability develops and changes over the course of our lives. In this study, we tested the working memory of kids as young as five, teens, and adults up to eighty years old—from a range of demographic backgrounds—and our findings shattered many of the accepted notions about working memory. In this chapter, we share those findings as well as findings from a number of studies conducted by other researchers as we take you on a journey from working memory's progression from a spark inside the womb to its vibrant flame during adulthood and on to its dimming as we age. The good news is that although our working memory will almost certainly diminish somewhat as we enter the twilight of our lives, there are many things we can do to protect it and even limit the worst debilitations, such as dementia.

The Birth of Working Memory

The roots of working memory begin to form during a baby's gestation in the mother's uterus. As the body grows and develops, so too does the PFC. Early on, neurons lay the structural foundations for what will eventually become a complex and richly connected control center from which working memory will emerge. By the time a baby is born, his or her PFC has the largest number of neurons that it will ever have. Undergoing attrition, the neurons begin to die off, until around sixteen years of age, when numbers stabilize. Early on in life, too many neurons can be a disadvantage. For example, in 2011, Eric Courchesne and colleagues discovered that children with autism have an excess of neurons in the PFC, around 67 percent more. As the neurons of a healthy PFC are being pruned, those that remain are rapidly forming connections that will exponentially increase after birth.

Working memory seems to emerge from these connected neurons very quickly indeed. As parents, we noticed this ourselves when our younger son was a baby and was interested only in hearing new stories. He would throw down a familiar book. Psychologists have long observed that babies prefer new things to old ones. Give a baby a colorful toy key ring, and she'll gaze intently at it *until* you wave an orange fuzzy ball in front of her. Then she'll drop the key ring and focus in on the bright ball. Show her a black-and-white stuffed penguin, and the orange ball will be forgotten as she zooms in on the penguin. Psychologists call this behavior *novelty preference.*

Because infants haven't yet learned their numbers or letters, you have to get creative if you want to test their working memory. Lisa Oakes of the University of Iowa did just that when she tested working memory by capitalizing on babies' interest in new things. She showed babies two screens with one square on each screen: the square on one screen always remained the same color, while the square on the other screen changed colors. Because of their preference for novelty, four- to six-month-old babies consistently paid attention to the screen with the changing square. This means that they were able to use their working memory Conductor to hold the previous color of the changing square and recognize that the new color was different. But when Oakes added an extra square to each screen, the infants did not show a preference for either screen. Their Conductor was overloaded: they couldn't hold all the squares in mind.

What we find most interesting about Oakes's study is not just that very young babies show evidence of working memory, but that this skill rapidly increases over a short time period. While the working memory of four- to six-month-olds was overloaded with more than one changing square, ten- to thirteen-month-olds could remember and compare up to three different colors. Oakes speculates that the difference between the working memory abilities of the two groups is a direct consequence of the rapid development of the PFC during the period between six and ten months.

Just as we have seen in experiments involving adults throughout this book, we can see the front of babies' brains being activated during a working memory task. With adults, researchers usually use an fMRI machine or a PET scan to look at brain activation, but for obvious reasons it's inappropriate to subject babies to the strong magnetic fields of an fMRI machine or to inject them with the radioactive marker necessary for a PET scan.

Fortunately, Martha Bell from Virginia Polytechnic Institute came up with a non-invasive solution that allows us to understand what is happening inside a baby's brain. She decided to use electroencephalography (EEG), a test that measures electrical activity in the brain using sensors placed on the scalp. Using EEG, Bell gave babies a working memory task that involved locating a stuffed animal. When the babies were able to successfully locate the toy, they had a much stronger electrical signal in the frontal area of the brain than when they didn't find it.

This is yet another sign that working memory is developing at a rapid pace in infants. As parents, we have been watching with great interest as working memory evolves in our own children. For example, our younger son has absolutely loved ducks since he was about six months old. Whenever we said "quack, quack," he would light up with a big smile, and whenever we read a certain picture book to him, he would get very excited when we got to the page with pictures of ducks. But when he reached thirteen months of age, something changed. He took that book and immediately flipped ahead to the page with the ducks, showing us that his working memory had taken a major step forward in its ability to process multiple pieces of information. In this instance, his Conductor was processing his love of ducks, the fact that the book had pictures of ducks, and where those pictures were in the book. These types of scenarios often go unnoticed, but they represent significant leaps in the development of working memory.

I Think, Therefore I Am and You Are

One of the fascinating findings regarding the development of working memory is that it is necessary for what psychologists call theory of mind. *Theory of mind* refers to an awareness of self, an awareness that others may perceive the world differently from you, and an awareness that you may need to adapt aspects of yourself to fit in to your environment. Philip Zelazo of the University of Toronto argues that development of working memory is closely linked to the emergence of self-consciousness in children, and in a series of experiments, Stephanie Carlson shows that working memory is a crucial component of how children understand the motivations of others.

The working memory Conductor is critical for self-awareness because it allows us to give attention to the unity and ownership of ourselves. It helps us keep ourselves in mind, recognize we are not other people, and they are not us. According to the eminent neuroscientist Joaquin Fuster, working memory is the cognitive process most closely associated with self-awareness. *Self-awareness*, generally occurring around two years of age, is the first stage in a child's developing theory of mind. The next stage is *other-mindedness*, which is an awareness that others may perceive the world differently from him. Other-mindedness occurs around age four to five. Research suggests that the stronger a child's working memory is, the better he is able to understand that others have a mind of their own and may see things in another way.

Theory of mind can be traced back all the way to ancient and early modern philosophy. If you remember anything from your Philosophy 101 class, you probably remember two phrases: "Know thyself" and "Cogito ergo sum" (I think, therefore I am). Both Socrates (who often repeated the first statement) and Descartes (who is responsible for the second) argued that self-awareness was the starting point for knowledge. We can't know anything about others or about the world around us if we do not know ourselves. Psychologists agree that theory of mind follows the same progression: *First* we are aware of ourselves, and *then* we become aware of the perspectives of others outside ourselves. The working memory Conductor is so important to this progression because it allows us to keep our own perspective, as well as what we imagine the perspective of others to be, active in our minds.

We had a vivid experience of how a child's awareness of self and of others can interact. When our older son was five years old, he was in desperate need of a haircut. His brown bangs had been covering his eyes for weeks, but he adamantly refused to let us cut his hair. After much negotiation, we finally got him to agree to a minor bang trim. It fell to Ross to perform the delicate operation, and he took tiny snips— a little here, a little there—to ensure that any mistakes could be corrected. With each cut, he complained, "I don't need a haircut," "I don't like it," and finally he refused any further trims, covering his head with his hands. "What's wrong, buddy? The haircut makes you look handsome," Ross said in a desperate appeal to his vanity. Our son sharply replied, "I don't like your handsome. It makes me not look like me."

Thanks to a well-developed theory of mind, made possible by a Conductor that allowed him to give attention to elements of himself, our son was aware that his hair was one of those things that makes him who he is. Moreover, in criticizing Ross's view of handsomeness, he was consciously processing another's perception of him.

We first verified our son's developing self-awareness a few months before his second birthday, when we gave him what psychologists refer to as the rouge test. It is an exceedingly simple and elegant way to find out if a child is self-aware, and you can even try it on your own child. Just get some red lipstick (or any other color that contrasts with your child's skin) and put a mark of it on his nose without drawing attention to what you are doing. Then put a mirror in front of your child. If he touches his nose, as our son did, he recognizes that he is the person in the mirror. If he doesn't touch his nose, he doesn't recognize himself. In terms of working memory, touching his nose implies that he is able to combine two pieces of information: the image in the mirror with the image that he has of himself in his mind.

An easy way to test other-mindedness is the false belief task, which determines if a young child is able to understand that people can have a different set of beliefs from her, which will motivate her actions accordingly. It works like this: A young child is shown a packet of M&Ms and is asked to guess what is inside. She will usually answer, "M&Ms."

The experimenter then opens up the packet to reveal that a pencil is inside. Now the experimenter asks the child what her friend will guess is inside the packet if she is shown it. Most three-year-olds will say, "A pencil." However, by the time they reach five, they are able to understand the concept that other people are not aware that the experimenter has replaced the M&Ms with a pencil and so will guess, "M&Ms."

The role of working memory in facilitating the development of other-mindedness was verified by Mark Alcorn and his colleagues at the University of North Colorado. When they gave children between three and five years old the M&Ms task, they found that those with better working memory skills were more likely to realize that other children would guess M&Ms. They also found that working memory is necessary to inhibit the impulse to say "pencil" and also to keep in mind that the other person didn't have the same perspective they had. For a young child whose working memory skills are not yet fully developed, this false belief task is very difficult.

As your child's working memory matures and his sense of other-mindedness develops, he comes to the next milestone in theory of mind: an ability to tell sophisticated lies. A 2009 review of almost twenty brain-imaging studies on deception in adults found that the most extensive area of activation was found in the PFC, the area associated with working memory. The study looked at both simplistic denials and sophisticated deceptions. Simple denials are just saying "no" or "yes." Sophisticated lies are the ones that take into account a complex set of variables, most importantly the listener's perspective, in order to maintain the deception. As our study described below shows, the better children are at sophisticated lying, the better their working memory. Most children by the age of three or four are capable of simple denial. Consider the following exchange that every parent has experienced:

"Did you eat the cookies?"

"No."

"Are you sure?"

"Yes!"

"Why do you have crumbs on your shirt?"

"I don't know."

All in all, this is transparently false, and their working memory couldn't deny that they ate the cookies and at the same time come up with a plausible explanation as to why they have crumbs on their shirt. At around six years of age, however, their growing working memory enables a theory of mind capable of developing a sophisticated fib designed to play on a parent's fears and emotions.

A friend of ours, Fiona, recently recollected a sophisticated lie she once told. Fiona told us that at age six, she decided to trim her own bangs one day. Looking at the resulting butcher job, she thought, "Uh-oh, I'm going to be in big trouble." A few minutes later, her mother came in and asked what happened. To avoid punishment, Fiona told her mom that a man had opened her bedroom window, come inside, chopped off her bangs, and then fled out the window.

When children tell sophisticated lies, they rely heavily on working memory, because in order to fabricate a suitable lie for the person listening to it, they have to imagine the person's mind (a mother's concern for the child's safety), as well as create an explanation that fits in with it (a man broke in and chopped off my hair). In Fiona's case, it worked. Her mom ran out of the house just to make sure nobody was lurking around nearby. When her mom returned, Fiona acted as if she was scared and got a big hug rather than the scolding she had originally anticipated.

In order to understand the relationship between working memory and Fiona's skill at sophisticated lying, we undertook a study of six- to seven-year-olds. First, we tested the children's working memory. Then we played a game where they had to answer some questions to win a prize. The questions were written on the front of cards, with the answers on the back in different colors alongside drawings of animals. After the children answered the questions, they were shown the answers on the back of the card.

For the last question, the children were asked about a nonexistent cartoon character: "What is the name of the boy in the cartoon *Spaceboy*?" Before they gave an answer, they were left alone in the room and were told not to look at the back of the card, which had the answer: Jim. Since there is no cartoon called *Spaceboy*, the children could have answered "Jim" only if they looked at the back of the card, where the name was written in green ink alongside a picture of a monkey.

A video camera captured all the action when the children were left alone. When we asked them to answer, those who peeked correctly said, "Jim." We then asked them if they peeked, and they all said "no." This is a simple denial that all children are capable of. In order to find out about sophisticated lying, we had to go deeper into the deception, so we asked two entrapment questions: "What color was the answer written in?" and "What picture is on the back?" The working memory of many of the children was not up to the task of realizing that in order to maintain the deception, they had to keep in mind the experimenter's perspective, and they answered correctly, unintentionally revealing that they had seen the back. Some children, however, had a working memory that allowed them to juggle all components of their lie, as well as to keep the experimenter's perspective in mind. They realized that if they didn't look, as they had claimed, they couldn't possibly have known the answer to the entrapment questions, so they gave wrong answers, like "red" and "lizard" instead of "green" and "monkey." When we compared how success-ful their lie was with their working memory, we found that those who avoided entrapment had the highest working memory.

The good news for parents is that they don't have to long tolerate deception for the sake of their child's working memory. By the time children go to school, lying drops significantly, as research by Kang Lee from the University of Toronto has shown. If children continue to lie on the playground, they will soon find that no one wants to play with them. But far from abandoning the skills of sophisticated lying, school children redirect them in order to navigate the complex social milieu into which they are thrust.

When discussing theory of mind, psychologists often stop at lying. But we propose a further stage of theory of mind that takes all the pre-vious skills and integrates them. We call this final stage *reinvention-mindedness*. Children and teenagers now use their working memory Conductors to imagine the perspectives of their peers and recast or showcase personal attributes appropriate to their social context. Reinvention-mindedness also adds the variable of modifying their own behavior and self-image, literally transforming themselves in order to fit in. We theorize that this transformation is working memory inten-sive and requires the inhibition and conscious alteration of established behavior. For example, a youngster might claim on Tuesday to dislike a pop band she loved on Monday.

Throughout childhood, adolescence, and the teenage years, reinvention-mindedness may manifest itself in conformation to a youth culture that can baffle parents—intentionally wearing jeans with holes, demonstrating apparent angst over the latest developments in a tween celebrity relationship, or emulating a Kardashian. But however silly these activities may seem to parents, they are no joke. They provide an important opportunity to develop the skill of reinvention and to pave the way for a far more practical purpose for theory of mind in everyday life. For example, reinvention-mindedness can help a teenager avoid conflict with their best friend by understanding their friend's point of view and altering the way they interact with this person accordingly. It can help them avoid getting in trouble at school by interpreting the teacher's nonverbal signals and altering their classroom demeanor in response. It can help them adapt to a new school by figuring out how to behave in an unfamiliar setting.

One of the most popular places for teenagers to experiment with their newfound skills is Facebook. Perhaps one reason that Facebook has so many users is because it is reinvention-mindedness writ large. If most users are honest, they would admit that what they post on Facebook, from pictures to updates, is not exactly the truth, but rather a version of it. To a large degree, a teenager's Facebook profile is a reinvented self, the ideal person they desire all the world to see. We wanted to see if the reinvention-mindedness exercised in Facebook had a benefit for working memory. The study, published in 2012 in *Computers & Education*, included over a hundred teenagers between fifteen and eighteen years old. Teenagers were selected because we wanted to find out if Facebook affected working memory at a time when individuals were entering this critical stage of theory of mind. We found that the longer the duration of Facebook membership, the better the working memory. Teenagers who had been members of Facebook for longer than a year had better test scores than peers who had been members for less than a year.

We believe that this may be related to the working memory effort required by the social media site. Appropriately responding to a friend's post about a new relationship, interpreting the emotional cues in a photograph, inhibiting irrelevant information (like a friend's post about what he had for a snack), or adding to what they know about a new boy band, is a cognitively demanding task. Facebook is a great place for teens to exercise their reinvention-mindedness, and working memory too. In chapter 10, we'll look at the working memory benefits for adults using Facebook.

As we mature, we develop our reinvention-mindedness to a remarkable degree and it can offer us a big advantage in life, helping us convince ourselves to excel and even enjoy a challenging job, change our automatic responses in an argument for the sake of improving a relationship with a significant other, or change how we spend money when our financial circumstances change. Indeed, reinvention-mindedness is something we should never outgrow, and if we do, we lose a valuable opportunity to exercise our Conductor. As we will see later in this chapter, when we retire and no longer need to adapt to the same degree that we did, our working memory begins to decline.

Working Memory Comes of Age

It is not until adulthood that working memory reaches full maturity. *Myelination*, a process crucial for healthy brain development, is also completed at this time. This process covers the brain's cells in a white protective sheath called *myelin*. Also known as white matter, myelin facilitates a faster transmission of electrical signals. Myelination starts at the back of the brain and slowly makes its way forward. The PFC, the home of working memory, is the last area to be reinforced with this myelin, and its arrival heralds the shift of working memory into high gear. Our own research shows that working memory continues to improve throughout our twenties and even into our thirties, when it finally peaks.

Our results were reinforced by an excellent review conducted by Silvia Bunge and Samantha Wright at the University of California in 2007. They described a study using an fMRI scanner to look at the differences in PFC activation according to age. The study focused on three age groups: kids in middle childhood (eight to twelve years old), teenagers (thirteen to seventeen years old), and young adults (eighteen to twenty-five years old). Each group had to complete a working memory task while in the brain scanner, and the researchers found that while the PFC, the home of working memory, was hard at work during this task in both teens and adults, it was remarkably inactive in the preteens.

In fact, the activation levels of the PFC increased with the age of the test participants. This supports our own study on working memory across the life span, which showed that the working memory of adults in their twenties and thirties can manage six pieces of information, while children's working memory can typically handle only two to three pieces of information. The increase in working memory coincides nicely with the increasing need to handle the multitasking and decision making that come with adulthood that we discussed in chapter 2. Think of it like getting promoted from a cubicle to the big corner office with an expansive desk that's large enough to hold all your important files.

Our forties mark the beginning of a decline in working memory, and as a consequence we can remember and work with fewer pieces of information. The reduction in the amount of information our Conductor can manage contributes to what is commonly known as midlife memory loss. You know: forgetting where you put your keys, neglecting to show up for the weekly marketing meeting at work, or momentarily drawing a blank on your neighbor's name when you run into her at the grocery store. One possible culprit behind this decline in working memory is a progressive loss of white matter in the brain, which begins in midlife. White matter is known to play an important role in working memory performance, so it makes sense that any loss of this brain tissue could affect working memory. Whatever the cause, the drop-off appears to occur gradually. In our study on working memory across the life span, we found that people in their forties can process an average of five pieces of information, just one fewer than they could when they were thirty.

Going from six to five pieces of information may not seem like much of a drop, but in fact, it represents a 20 percent decline in the amount of information your working memory can handle. It's like going from an A to a C in the classroom or moving from the CEO's expansive desk back to the cramped cubicle. And unfortunately, as your working memory weakens, the demands on it don't. In fact, your responsibilities may actually increase as you enter middle age: *you* get blamed if the accounts don't add up, *you* need to provide your teenagers with more careful guidance because their decisions now carry greater consequences, and *your* finances demand greater attention than when you were at the bottom of the salary scale.

In order to accomplish all these things, you need your Conductor to stay on top of them, for example, to recall that you need to finish the accounts meeting by 1:30 so that you can take your son to meet with a college counselor and then talk to your accountant about making changes to your pension plan. But your Conductor can direct only so much information before it loses control and things get dropped: keys, names, and those marketing meetings.

But it's not all bad news. Although our working memory declines, it compensates in order to keep performing at levels similar to a younger brain. Natasha Rajah and Mark D'Esposito reveal how in a review of existing brain-imaging research on working memory as we age. In one study, older adults show increased activation in the left side of the PFC while performing a working memory task, a pattern associated with more efficient retrieval of accumulated knowledge. In the workplace, this means that although younger employees may be able to work with more information, older employees are better able to exploit their experience in order to get the job done. At home, your working memory compensates by giving you improved access to your considerable knowledge to help you keep up with your increasingly intelligent teenager.

But what about later in life? Are we necessarily consigned to dwindling working memory strength with each passing year? Can working memory compensate for aging? Is there anything we can do to slow the decline?

The Twilight of Working Memory

In investigating what happens to working memory as we hit retirement age and beyond, we dug into the research and undertook some of our own. Much of the research on the aging brain is not specific to working memory, but in illuminating how our general cognitive skills change as we age, it sheds important light on the degree to which our working memory declines and also ways to keep it in the best shape we can.

Thanks to modern imaging techniques, researchers can actually see what happens inside the brain as we age, and you'll be happy to know that a growing body of imaging studies reveals that our neurons don't need to die out as we age. It appears that the brain changes that occur with advancing age are subtle. And even better, older brains appear to be able to use compensatory strategies to make up for declines that have taken place. For example, brain-imaging research has found that when older people perform cognitive tasks, their brains recruit more regions than those of younger people, and activation in those areas is more intense. What this means is that older brains can still perform the task; they just have to work harder and recruit more areas to get it done.

But if age-related memory loss isn't a given, how do we account for those mental glitches that seem to plague so many people past retirement age? Considering that there is expected to be a 50 percent increase in people aged 65 and over in the UK between 2010 and 2030, it's time to look for answers. We think they may lie in some of the life events that tend to come with the passing years.

Rethinking Retirement

Every weekday for forty-four years of his life, George woke up to a blaring, piercing, ringing alarm clock. He fought the urge to hit the snooze button and groaned as he placed his warm, bare feet on the cold floor. He trudged to the shower and turned on the hot water, which never got hot soon enough. He ate a slice of dry toast and drank muddy coffee to muster the energy to handle the accounts, manage the personnel, and fill in the correct forms. Now, over ten thousand days of work later, he is finally saying good-bye to the drudgery and hello to the warm sand. The mortgage is paid in full and the pension nicely fattened, so he is emigrating to Spain for a haze of sangria, sunshine, and afternoon naps.

His colleague, Kimberly, is the same age and has worked just as many days as George. But unlike George, she loves her work, enjoys interacting with her coworkers, and even gets a gleeful feeling of satisfaction out of completing those lengthy forms. She too has saved enough money to retire, but she is choosing to stay on the job. "Poor sap," George mutters to himself. But who is the sap, really?

If you're like the vast majority of Britons, you probably identify with George. You envision that once you reach the age of retirement, you'll hop off that crazy merry-go-round to enjoy the good life and relax, beer in hand and sand between toes. And, hey, can anyone blame you? Even if you enjoy what you do, what is the point of keeping at it if you can afford to stop?

A hundred years ago, George would never have been in the position to stop working. Large-scale retirement is a very recent invention. For thousands of years, it didn't matter how old you were; you kept working until you were unable to do so any more. It is only in the past hundred years or so that large numbers of humans have been retiring. Alicia Munnell, the director of the Center for Retirement Research at Boston College, shows that in twentieth-century America retirement has become the common place for the majority of the male population aged sixty-five and over. If you were sixty-five or older in 1800s America (and a man), you would likely have been working. We can't know the cognitive skills of working older people in centuries previous in terms of either an IQ or a working memory score, but the fact that they were still gainfully employed suggests that they did not have dementia. In fact, work may have been the secret to their long-lived intelligence.

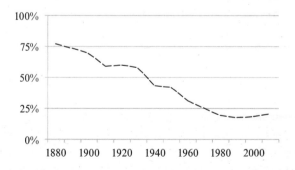

US Workforce Participation Rates of Men 65 and Older, 1880–2009.
With permission from Alicia Munnell and Steven Ruggles.

New research suggests a shocking reality: retirement may make you dumb. In 2010, Susann Rohwedder and Robert Willis studied the data of thousands of retirees from America and twelve European countries, including the UK, and discovered that retirement puts you at a cognitive disadvantage. Retirement marks not just a reduction of work, but a reduction in thinking that they call "mental retirement." They argue, "Workers engage in more mental exercise than retirees because work environments provide more cognitively challenging and stimulating environments than do non-work environments."

If you're retired or if you've ever gone on a long vacation, you probably know this to be true. Not having to impress potential clients, file reports, or conjure up new revenue streams allows you to switch off and relax. Relaxation is not necessarily a bad thing in and of itself, but the diminished expectations to perform at a certain level, the fewer challenges requiring quick thinking when others are counting on you, the fewer opportunities to use knowledge gained over years of working, the lack of using your wits to negotiate office politics, and not making an extra effort to climb the corporate ladder all diminish your long-term knowledge and critical thinking skills.

Rohwedder and Willis measured cognitive decline with a test that included remembering word lists, which required working memory to do them successfully.

The findings? The earlier you retire, the earlier you hasten cognitive decline. Rohwedder and Willis looked at the difference between the cognitive skills of those in their fifties and compared them with those in their sixties. They then looked at how many of the sixty-somethings were retired in comparison to those a decade younger. They found that the more likely the sixty-somethings were to be retired, the worse their cognitive skills were in comparison to the younger group.

The difference between countries is fascinating. France, for example, has long been the envy of the working stiffs of the West because of its early retirement age of sixty. But accompanying this supposed benefit is the greatest cognitive decline among those in their sixties of any country: 20 percent! This means that on average, French retirees are 20 percent less intelligent than their decade-younger counterparts.

This groundbreaking research shows that the later you retire, the smarter you remain. In the United States, where employees retire later than most of the Western world, the cognitive decline was the smallest: just 5 percent; in the UK, around 10 percent. In fact, in every comparison Rohwedder and Willis make, the United States—often followed by England—comes out at the top of the heap for cognitive skills of people who are nearing retirement age.

The science is clear: the longer retirement is delayed, the better for your cognition. Consider the amazing story of Dr. Fred Goldman, who at the age of one hundred was the oldest licensed physician practicing in the state of Ohio. Dr. Goldman has diagnosed patients and written prescriptions since 1935. Though he had cut back to a three-day work-week before he died in 2012, he loved what he did. He told a newspaper, "Work is life. I work on demand. If there's not much demand, there's not much work. Fortunately, the demand exists. I feel I can still be helpful to people. And, I can still do the job. So, there's no sense to consider retirement."

We couldn't agree more.

The Fading of Friends and Family

Another feature of later life that can diminish working memory is the decrease in our social interactions. As Joseph Coughlin, director of the AgeLab at MIT told the *New York Times*, "One of the greatest challenges or losses that we face as older adults, frankly, is not about our health, but it's actually about our social network deteriorating on us, because our friends get sick, our spouse passes away, friends pass away, or we move." Coughlin hits the nail on the head: the older we get, the fewer our friends and family. Cognitively speaking, this is a major blow. Just as retirement marks a cognitive decline, so does a shrinking social circle.

Relationships are working memory intensive. They certainly require a healthy dose of other-mindedness as well as reinvention-mindedness. With a significant other, your working memory has to keep your partner's desires, opinions, and feelings in mind at all times. And with each friend or group of companions, you must take on a slightly different persona and choose appropriate conversation topics. For example, with your book group friends, you talk about the latest novel and compare and contrast it with the book you read last month. When you're at your allotment, you may have a debate with fellow plot-holders about the best way of keeping slugs away from the courgettes. With your travel companions, you experience new languages, new cultures, and new foods. All these different social contexts give your Conductor an opportunity to play a different tune.

The fewer relationships you have, the fewer opportunities you have to engage your working memory. Less exercised than it was before, your Conductor can forget how to play. Let's say you used to have a golf buddy, Robert, who loved to go sea-fishing. As you played eighteen holes, he'd tell you about the ones that got away and the epic battles between man and fish. You never really knew that much about sea-fishing, but every time you had a conversation with him, you were able to speculate as to the meaning of much of the conversation and use your working memory to respond in kind. Now Robert is living in sheltered housing, and when you visit him, the conversation is never as energetic as it was on the golf course. Eventually you stop visiting Robert, but as an unexpected consequence, you have lost not only a friend but also an opportunity to use your working memory.

A growing body of evidence shows that the fewer social interactions you have after reaching retirement age, the more likely you are to experience cognitive decline.

In 2008, Karen Ertel and her colleagues at the Harvard School of Public Health found that when we reach retirement age, the fewer social interactions we have, the worse our ability to access our memory. They based their research on the Health and Retirement Survey, a survey of U.S. adults aged fifty or older. This is an important survey because of the large number of participants—over sixteen thousand adults—and the fact that they were representative of the population at large, making the survey very reliable.

Participants in the survey were given a delayed memory test over the phone. They heard ten common nouns and were then asked a series of unrelated questions. After five minutes, the researchers asked the adults to recall as many of the words as they could. Though not explicitly a working memory task, it relied on their working memory because they had to keep the words fresh in their mind and still focus on answering the questions accurately. The researchers used these responses to calculate a composite memory score and repeated the test four times over a six-year period. When giving the tests, they also took the opportunity to assess the quality of participants' social interactions by asking the following types of questions:

- Are you married?
- Do you volunteer your time?
- Do you speak with your neighbors?
- Do you keep in touch with your children?
- Do you talk to your parents?

Ertel and colleagues compared the results of the cognitive tests with the results of the social survey. What they found will encourage those of you who make a point of maintaining relationships with family and friends. The top 25 percent of adults with the highest scores for social integration performed much better on the cognitive tests over time compared to those with low scores for social integration.

Intriguingly, both groups started off with similar cognitive scores at the beginning of the study, but by the end of it, the differences in the social contacts had an impact on their cognitive abilities. Those who lived alone and were more isolated were more likely to suffer signs of memory decline associated with dementia. So one of the lessons of this research is that if we want to keep our cognitive abilities, including our working memory, in good shape as we age, we should continue to develop our social networks and pursue plenty of social activities.

Many other things can also help hold off working memory loss. Exercising working memory and practicing the working-memory-building exercises introduced in the earlier chapters shore up cognitive skills. You may also be surprised to discover that diet can contribute to keeping it in good shape, a topic we cover more fully in chapter 10. First, we introduce some provisional but important research that suggests keeping our working memory in good shape can help us cope with one of the afflictions of old age: pain.

Helping to Cope with Pain

Imagine that after a lifetime of hard work, you're no longer heading up your own company, but you are sitting on the board of a major corporation. Today is the day you have to decide whether to vote for or against acquiring a promising start-up company before your main competitor swoops in and snaps it up. Before the vote, you have to pore through its financials, but you wake up with a searing toothache, a nagging backache, or a bad knee that won't stop throbbing. How focused do you think you will be as you analyze the company's profit-and-loss statements? Will the pain throw you off your game?

Pain disrupts our working memory, as Bruce Dick and Saifudin Rashiq of the University of Alberta, Canada, suggest. They recruited twenty-four chronic pain sufferers and gave them an assessment known as *The Test of Everyday Attention*. This task revealed how pain affected their ability to focus. In one of the tasks, when participants heard a particular sound, they had to tap a particular image. Based on how well they did compared to the standard scores of a pain-free population, the participants were separated into three groups:

- Those whose attention was not affected by pain
- Those whose attention was mildly affected by pain
- Those whose attention was greatly affected by pain

Dick and Rashiq then gave all three groups of chronic pain sufferers a spatial working memory test, and when they analyzed the results, they found that the people who were most affected by chronic pain in the attention test were also those with the lowest working memory. They argued that this proved a link between pain and working memory. But everyone in the study was a chronic pain sufferer. So instead of proving that pain affects working memory, they had really shown only that people with attention problems also perform poorly on a working memory test. Pain might have been merely an incidental factor.

To see if pain makes a difference in how people use their working memory, someone would have to test an individual's ability when he or she was experiencing pain and when not. This is exactly what Christopher Sanchez of Arizona State University did in a study published in 2011. One of the problems Sanchez faced has plagued many pain researchers over the years: How do you inflict pain on people and still get the green light from the board of ethics?

Obviously Sanchez couldn't dole out hurt like a Grand Inquisitor—no waterboarding, no fire on the toes, no strikes with a thin cane. He needed to find something that would cause some discomfort but not too much. Imagine his surprise when he stumbled on the solution during his morning routine. As Sanchez recounted to us, "One morning after using Listerine, [I realized] it was challenging to count . . . the thirty or so seconds it recommends to use it." The pain from mouthwash made it hard to focus. Eureka! Make them swish mouthwash!

Sanchez gave forty college students a working memory test and retained the students who scored in the top and those who scored in the bottom. Next, he needed to make sure the mouthwash caused pain. He told the students to swish the mouthwash for forty-five seconds, then rate their pain on a scale from 1 to 10, with 1 being sitting in a comfortable chair and watching your favorite TV show, and 10 being burning your hand on a hot pan. Sanchez found that the high and low working memory groups both perceived the same level of pain for the mouthwash—around 4.

To make sure it was the mouthwash and not the swishing action that caused the pain, Sanchez also had the students swish regular water for forty-five seconds and rate their pain. The students rated the water swishing as a 1 on the pain scale. Sanchez had finally come up with an ethical way to test working memory with and without pain: have the students swish water to test their abilities pain free, and mouthwash to assess their skills with pain.

During a forty-five-second swish, the students had to memorize a list of twenty words, and on another occasion, they had to solve as many simple algebra problems as they could in the same period of time. They had to perform these tasks while swishing the painful mouthwash and the water. Sanchez found that the performance of those with a higher working memory was hardly affected by the pain, and they did almost as well when swishing the water. But those with a lower working memory were far more affected by the pain: their cognitive scores were 37 percent worse. If they got an A while pain free, they got a D with pain. As Sanchez proved, a good working memory helps you work past the pain, and a poor working memory means you can't take your mind off it.

But working memory can do more than help you grin and bear it; it can even help you ignore pain. If ever you find yourself wandering the misty streets of the Belgian city of Ghent and happen upon mild-mannered psychologist Valéry Legrain asking for experiment participants, run! In a 2011 paper, Legrain wanted to test a hunch that working memory tasks could distract from one's awareness of pain.

He gave his participants two tasks. The first was a pure attention task, requiring participants to push a button when they saw a specific color, like blue, on a screen. The second task put a working memory twist on the first task, and they were required to push a button when they saw a color that had previously appeared the screen before. Just before colors appeared on the screen, they were given either a mild electrical shock, similar to someone touching your arm with their finger, or a laser pulse to the back of the hand that simulated a pinprick to cause slight pain. Eighty percent of the time, participants received the mild shock, and 20 percent of the time, they got the painful pulse.

When Legrain looked at the results, he discovered that with the mild electrical shock, participants were able to do both tasks relatively easily; a touch on the arm didn't disrupt attention or working memory. But with the painful laser pulse, participants did worse on the attention task than they did on the working memory task. So pain can disrupt your attention, but working memory can distract you from the pain. Legrain's experiment suggests that when your working memory isn't engaged, you are more likely to pay attention to pain. However, when you are using your working memory, as the participants were with the second task, you aren't paying attention to the pain.

The obvious problem with Sanchez and Legrain's experiments is that they couldn't turn the dial up on the pain because of the ethical implications. Can you imagine the furor if Legrain turned the laser up to 10? Fair enough, but what everyone really wants to know, and what the experiments are unable to tell us, is if working memory can help with more acute pain. We expect that this is the case, but a definitive answer will have to come from additional research. For now, the best evidence suggests that when your Conductor is playing, it doesn't pay attention to the pain.

The Greatest Fear of All: Losing Your Mind

One of the biggest worries when you grow older is the looming threat of dementia. Will your magnificent mind betray you, robbing you of your memories, your personality, and ultimately your life? Nearly 40 million people around the world live with dementia. In the UK, around 800,000 people live with it and this number is expected to double by 2051. The older you get, the more likely you are to develop dementia: one in five people over the age of eighty in the UK have the symptoms. Some exciting research has produced results suggesting that a strong working memory may help to deter the onset of Alzheimer's, the most common form of dementia. Though these results are provisional and more work on the link is needed, we think the findings are so promising and important that we introduce them here.

Recent research suggests that for some people, the brain may show signs of Alzheimer's disease early in life. Alzheimer's disease begins by affecting key areas of the brain, shrinking it over time so it becomes harder to function. One area that is affected by shrinkage is the part of the brain associated with long-term memory, the hippocampus. The Alzheimer's brain also shows fewer synapses, and more plaque buildup and neurofibrillary tangles (twisted protein fibers in nerve cells) compared to a healthy brain.

One of the biggest unanswered questions about Alzheimer's is why, if nearly half of those over eighty-five have the disease, the other half don't. Why do some of us succumb to the disease while others manage to avoid it? Researchers have offered a couple of compelling theories.

1. *Cognitive reserve*: This theory argues that a good education creates a cognitive buffer that insulates you from the symptoms of the disease. Think of it like a retirement fund. The more money you have in the bank, the less likely you are going to struggle financially when you retire (not that you should, of course).

2. *Lifestyle*: In this theory, it's what you eat, where you work, your familial connections, and your other everyday habits that affect your risk for developing or sidestepping the disease.

Although both of these explanations are worth considering, they aren't entirely convincing because they don't directly address what we consider to be a key feature of Alzheimer's: a poor working memory. Alzheimer's disease is essentially a memory problem. Those who have it struggle to access different kinds of long-term memory, including these:

- Episodic memory: events, such as a great meal or a fun vacation.

- Semantic memory: facts, such as Paris is the capital of France

- Implicit memory: such as how to use a spoon to eat cereal

One of the reasons that they are unable to access these memories, is that their working memory, which searches through their long-term memory for information relevant to the task at hand (like remembering where the socks are kept or the names of family members) is severely undermined. The relationship between working memory and long-term memory is similar to that of a librarian and a library. Like a librarian, working memory allows you to search through the books, or information, stored in the library in order to accomplish a specific task.

With Alzheimer's, both elements are under attack: the librarian struggles to search through the stacks, and the worms are eating through the books. A shrinking working memory has a detrimental effect on your ability to access the books, to search through the library and find and apply what you need. And when the books deteriorate, it is much harder to read what remains. However, as we will see, working memory is such a dynamic and adaptive tool that if it remains strong, even if Alzheimer's begins to eat away at your neurons, it may in fact help to prevent you from experiencing the cognitive symptoms associated with the disease.

In 1986, Alan Baddeley and his colleagues presented evidence that those with dementia and Alzheimer's were particularly impaired in their working memory. This landmark study should have ushered in an era of scientific research on the relationship between working memory and Alzheimer's disease, but for some unknown reason, comparatively few people in the scientific community have followed up on their work.

Elizabeth Kensinger and her colleagues from MIT reinvigorated Baddeley's work by investigating whether patients with Alzheimer's disease also showed signs of working memory loss. She recruited twenty-two patients who had been diagnosed with Alzheimer's eighteen months before. As we've shown throughout this book, working memory can be affected by a wide variety of things, and in order to make sure that their results on the working memory tests were not influenced by other health problems, all the patients were screened to make sure that none of them had a history of alcoholism, major heart disease, cancer, or any other neurological problems.

Kensinger's team also recruited more than one hundred adults from the same age range who didn't show any signs of Alzheimer's to ensure that any results from the Alzheimer's patients would be the consequence of their disease. The researchers went to a great deal of trouble to ensure that there was no difference between the groups in age, education levels, and IQ.

Now they were ready to give both groups a working memory task. They used a reading span task where a sentence was presented on a computer screen, such as, "The boy ate four hamburgers for lunch." Participants read the sentence aloud and were then asked to answer a simple comprehension question about it: "What did the boy eat?" They had to follow this process for several sentences in a row and then remember the final word of each sentence. The researchers found that the patients with Alzheimer's performed much worse than the adults without the disease.

Kensinger's work undercuts the concept of *cognitive reserve*, because if patients were equal in their age, IQ, and education levels, they would likely have approximately the same level of cognitive reserve. But despite having the same IQ, one group is able to function in the world, and one can't remember the name of the cat they've had for twelve years. One explanation is that their poor working memory made it harder for them to access the language and knowledge they needed to perform well on the cognitive tests.

But what about the role of *lifestyle*? Do everyday habits and behaviors account for some people falling victim to the ravages of Alzheimer's disease and others maintaining their intellectual fortitude into their eighties, nineties, and beyond? We have shown how retirement, pain, and isolation can have a negative effect on working memory, but directly tying lifestyle to Alzheimer's is a much harder theory to test.

While it must have been a challenge for Kensinger to locate a group of Alzheimer's and non-Alzheimer's people who match in education, IQ, and health, it is even harder to find a similar group with exactly the same lifestyle. To do this, you'd have to find people who have essentially lived under the same conditions from youth into their very old age. Sounds impossible, right?

Fortunately for the science of Alzheimer's, such a group exists: the School Sisters of Notre Dame Congregation: a group of nuns who have been the subjects of one of the most famous and longest-running scientific research projects ever conducted. The groundbreaking "Nun Study" on aging and Alzheimer's disease has delivered a treasure trove of evidence that is giving scientists a better understanding of the effects of lifestyle on the risk of Alzheimer's disease.

The Nun Study is undoubtedly one of the most oft-cited studies, with media outlets, Alzheimer's organizations, and other researchers mining its data for clues about the disease. We too have been enthralled with the research, but we have a unique take on what it reveals about the risk for Alzheimer's. Before we share our view with you, let us tell you more about what this remarkable study shows us about lifestyle and the possibility of losing your mind.

Scientist David Snowdon spearheaded the Nun Study in 1986 when he recruited more than six hundred nuns, all of them born before 1917. As Snowdon pointed out, "Sisters in our study had the same reproductive and marital histories; had similar social activities and support; did not smoke or drink excessive amounts of alcohol; had similar occupations, income, and socioeconomic status; lived in the same houses; ate food prepared in the same kitchens; and had equal access to preventive and medical care services."

If lifestyle makes a difference, the nuns should then be relatively uniform in succumbing to Alzheimer's or not contracting it at all. But this wasn't the case. Some of them experienced devastating memory loss, while others retained their cognitive powers past the age of one hundred. In looking for clues as to why, Snowdon and his team peeked into the journals the nuns had been keeping faithfully since their earliest days as part of the convent—with their permission, of course. These journals provided an intriguing glimpse into the nuns' cognitive state when they were just in their twenties.

When the nuns first entered the convent, each wrote an autobiography. Snowdon, together with his colleague Susan Kemper at the University of Kansas, analyzed these writings for grammatical complexity in the sentences and idea density. Then they asked the same nuns to write another autobiography fifty-eight years later, when they were between seventy-five and eighty-seven years of age. Based on what they wrote and the grammatical complexity and idea density, the researchers grouped the nuns into high and low groups. Here is an example of the different writing styles:

Low: "I prefer teaching music to any other profession."

High: "Now I am wandering about in Dove's Lane waiting, yet only three more weeks, to follow in the footprints of my Spouse, bound to Him by the Holy Vows of Poverty, Chastity, and Obedience."

These language abilities are indicative of working memory ability: the more complex your thoughts are, the greater processing ability you have. Kemper, in particular, argues that working memory is an important cognitive skill necessary for writing. In her research, she found that poor working memory in healthy adults limits their ability to develop and use complex grammatical constructions, which can lead to language decline in later life. Indeed, one of the tests that the nuns were given was a delayed word recall. When Snowdon and Kemper looked at the nuns in the high and low writing groups, they found that those in the low group were up to fifteen times more likely to perform poorly on the delayed word recall task.

But this is not the end of the story. Some of the nuns arranged for their brains to be donated for research after their passing. This amazingly generous act allowed the team to understand the neuropathology of Alzheimer's. A number of the nuns' brains revealed an excessive number of neurofribillary tangles in the neocortex and hippocampus, the hallmark signs of Alzheimer's. When Snowdon and Kemper had a closer look at the language scores based on the nuns' early journals, they found that all of them expressed their ideas more simply compared to the sisters who did not show signs of the same amount of plaques and tangles in their brains.

As Kemper found that working memory is linked to linguistic ability in healthy adults, we suspect that low working memory in the nuns may raise the risk for developing Alzheimer's symptoms. On the other hand, groundbreaking new research shows that high working memory can protect you from the symptoms. For many years, Alzheimer's has been thought of as a cognitive death sentence. If you have it, the argument goes, it is irreversible and inevitably ends in senility. But the Nun Study suggests that not everyone whose brain is assaulted by Alzheimer's is destined to follow that path.

Juan Troncoso, director of the Brain Resource Center at Johns Hopkins University School of Medicine, unearthed a dramatic new twist in 2009. He started off by identifying nuns who had completed a battery of cognitive tests less than one year before they died. He also excluded nuns who had multiple brain diseases. Then he separated the nuns whose test results showed the cognitive symptoms of Alzheimer's disease from those whose test scores didn't show these signs.

Next, he performed an autopsy on the brains. When he looked at the brains where cognitive scores indicated Alzheimer's, he found the tangles and lesions in the brain tissue, as expected. But when he looked at the brains of those who had normal cognitive scores, something jumped out at him: almost half had brain lesions typically associated with Alzheimer's. This is like having a broken femur but being able to run, a remarkable outcome for a usually devastating disease. Troncoso calls this condition asymptomatic Alzheimer's disease (ASYMAD): literally Alzheimer's without the cognitive symptoms of it, because although the condition of their brains suggests they should have dementia, they somehow avoided it. Troncoso's discovery means that some who do are still able to function as if they didn't have the tangles.

Troncoso wanted to find out how this was possible, so he went in closer with the microscope so he could compare the brain cells of ASYMAD nuns with those who had full-blown Alzheimer's. It turns out that the ASYMAD nuns' hippocampus neuron cells were up to three times larger than those in the brains without any sign of Alzheimer's. Troncoso speculates that the increased size is possible evidence of neurons attempting to repair themselves, such as creating new circuits in order to compensate for the damage of Alzheimer-afflicted cells. It may be that by growing larger, the neurons are able to maintain cognitive function, despite the fact much of the brain is injured.

But what causes some brains to respond this way and others to submit to Alzheimer's? One exciting possibility is that the better one's working memory is, the more likely a person can withstand the cognitive ravages of the disease. Troncoso cites research that learning new things—a skill heavily reliant on working memory—can increase the size of neurons. Certainly the nuns who scored well on the cognitive battery had to have a good working memory to do so.

When Troncoso looked at the journals of the ASYMAD nuns written when they were in their early twenties, he found they had a higher score for idea density: they were able to pack more ideas in a short sentence while keeping it interesting. This suggests that an excellent working memory can help circumvent the cognitive symptoms of Alzheimer's later in life. In what is a positive finding for anyone worried about dementia, Troncoso believes that this reaction is far more common than previously presumed. It appears that many people with ASYMAD may in fact be leading normal lives without even knowing that their brains have been invaded by those potentially devastating tangles, or that by challenging themselves cognitively, they are warding off dementia.

What is more, the ASYMAD nuns' neurons were increasing in size well into their nineties and, in some of them, even after reaching the century mark. This shows that even at this late age, the brain can respond positively to the demands being placed on it.

Though this research is only suggestive, and much more work must be done to investigate how working memory might help to stave off the symptoms of Alzheimer's, we are hopeful that these results indicate that those with high working memory abilities are able to compensate for the damage to functioning done by the tangles associated with Alzheimer's. Thanks to Tracy's *Alloway Working Memory Assessment*, which offers scientists a standardized way to test working memory, it is only a matter of time before any links between working memory and Alzheimer's disease will be revealed.

In this chapter, we've seen how working memory develops and changes throughout our lifetime, reaching a peak in our thirties and then subtly diminishing. We've noted the role it plays in how we seem to evolve from being self-absorbed as youngsters to having a strong sense of other-mindedness to mastering reinvention-mindedness as adults, then retreating from work and social demands as we retire. We've shown how a strong working memory can help us cope with issues that come with old age and how it protects us from cognitive decline and perhaps even from the ravages of dementia. Next, we'll introduce the best findings about the advantages that working memory training can offer. In addition, we'll reveal important findings about how our diet affects our brainpower and the seven key things that we can do on a regular basis to best boost our working memory.

Working Memory Exercises

1. Try the Rouge Test (for Children Age 2)

For this test, hold your child facing you and take a cloth to wipe his nose. As you do this, wipe a little red lipstick (or rouge) on his nose. Then put a mirror in front of him and watch what he does. If he recognizes the image in the mirror as himself, he will try to touch his nose and wipe off the red mark.*

In terms of working memory, touching his nose implies that he is able to work with two pieces of information: the image in the mirror with the image that he has of himself in his mind.

2. Test Other-Mindedness with the M&Ms Task (for Children Age 5)

This test is designed to help you see how well a five-year-old is aware of what others are thinking:

1. Away from your child, carefully open a large package of M&Ms and replace the candies with a pencil. Reseal the package so it looks like new, using double-sided tape.
2. Show the child the bag of M&Ms and ask him to guess what is inside. He will probably say, "M&Ms."
3. Open the packet and show the child that you have actually put a pencil inside. To make sure that he remembers what you showed him, ask him what you put inside the M&Ms packet.
4. Now ask the child what his friend will guess is inside the packet if he is shown it.

---

* Dr. Jens Asendorf at Humboldt University in Germany devised a little twist on the rouge test. He wanted to make sure that a child would actually want to wipe the red dot off her face. So he introduced a doll to the child and asked the child to help clean up a red spot under its eye. After making sure that the child understood what she needed to do, Asendorf would then put the rouge on the child's face and put the doll in front of the mirror.

If the child answers "M&Ms," he is then able to use his working memory to suppress the urge to say "a pencil" and keep his friend's perspective in mind. If the child says "a pencil," he is not yet at the stage of development where he can put himself in someone else's shoes.

3. Take a Predictable-Time-Off Break (for Working Adults)

Turn off your BlackBerry to turn on your productivity. That's the message from Leslie Perlow at the Harvard Business School. Perlow got in touch with the Boston Consulting Group, an elite consulting firm, and asked some of its team members to turn off their BlackBerry in the evening once a week. They were to be incommunicado. No messages about the new slides for tomorrow's PowerPoint, no alert that Hannerty was out for blood after the printer paper fiasco, no ping about whose turn it was to get coffee in the morning.

At first, this predictable time off (PTO) was looked on with suspicion, but soon everyone started seeing benefits: workers were happier with their jobs and, more important for the company, productivity was up. We know why this is: constant messaging can be a drip, drip, drip effect for your working memory, always asking it to be on. By giving it a well-deserved break every so often, you can let it relax and recharge for more important things, like giving that presentation.

PTO Rules

- Turn the phone off in the evening at least once a week; the more often, the better.

- Let others know you won't be available. If you don't do this, you'll have some angry colleagues and clients!

- Relax. Take it as an opportunity to unplug, which means stay away from the computer! Go for a run, wrestle with your son, or let your daughter braid your hair as you tell her a story.

4. Get In Tune with the Beat (for Adults of All Ages)

Drummers may not be the most memorable members of the band, but they may be the smartest. Rhythm links to working memory skills, as Japanese psychologist Saturo Saito discovered. When he gave adults a list of numbers to remember and process, their skill in this working memory task was closely linked to how well they could remember a rhythmic sequence of tones. To boost working memory:

- Learn to play an instrument like the drums.
- When you listen to a song, pay attention to the beat, and see if you can play it with spoons on your legs, or pencils on a table, or index fingers on your desk.

5. Learn a Foreign Language (for Adults of All Ages)

If you want to enhance your *memoria del trabajo, mémoire de travail,* or *Arbeitsgedächtnis* (working memory), learn a new language. Research shows that bilinguals of all ages do better compared to monolinguals in a range of cognitive tasks, including working memory. Even better, bilingualism creates a kind of cognitive reserve that can buffer against the signs of dementia. A 2012 study showed that the cognitive functions of bilingual adults in the early stages of Alzheimer's were preserved for longer than those who spoke only one language.

- Sign up for a foreign language class at your local community college.
- Check out foreign language CDs from your local library.
- Take advantage of the Internet to read publications in foreign languages. One of our bilingual friends gets Facebook posts from *Paris Match* magazine to practice her French.

6. Don't Retire (for Older Adults)

Stop working = stop thinking. You may not like to hear it, but it is inevitable. The sooner you retire, the sooner you will struggle to put two and two together, the sooner your keys will end up in the ice cube tray, and the sooner you will put yourself at risk for dementia. Staying productive in your later years is key to keeping your working memory in tiptop shape. Conforming to the demands of a job or volunteer activity keeps your working memory on its toes, and that gives you the ability to spoil your grandchildren for a lot longer than you would if you were fully retired:

- If you like your job, keep at it regardless of your age.
- If you can't wait to leave your job, leave, but find another type of work you enjoy.
- Do volunteer work on a regular basis.
- Mentor young people in your former field of work.
- Take an active role in your community.

8

Working Memory Training 101

THE MOST EXCITING thing about your working memory is that ground-breaking research, from ourselves and others, shows that it can be improved. In the next several chapters, we'll look at a variety of ways you can give your working memory an advantage by training, engaging in certain everyday habits and strategies, and taking cues from exceptionally high-level working memory *super* performers. In this chapter, we explore the recent explosion of brain-training books, programs, and websites offering a variety of methods for sharpening mental acuity, including crossword puzzles, word searches and scrambles, logic problems, Sudoku, video games, and computer-based brain games.

Although all of these brain-training methods may offer some form of cognitive benefit, they don't necessarily sharpen your working memory, so we take a look at the best evidence for their effects and consider whether they generate any improvement specifically in working memory. Some of these products and methods hone in on one specific cognitive skill; others seek to enhance overall brain health; and a new category is geared specifically toward enhancing working memory. In evaluating how each affects working memory, if at all, we kept two key points in mind:

- What skills are you improving?
- How long will the improvement last?

What Skills Are You Improving?

When considering what specific skills are improved, we have to look at something psychologists refer to as the "transfer effect." Does playing a brain-training game just make you better at the game itself, or do you learn skills that you can transfer into other areas of your life? There are two kinds of transfer: *near* and *far*.

- *Near transfer*: This means that when you improve certain skills in a game, you also improve in closely related areas. Think of it this way—if you do leg lifts for two months and increase the strength in your legs, you will be able to squat a heavier weight. In the same way, if you keep playing a game that trains working memory, you will do better on a working memory test.

- *Far transfer*: This means that when you train specific skills, you also improve in other areas that are far beyond the skill you trained. For example, if you do leg lifts, you can also sprint much faster. When a working-memory-training program, like *Jungle Memory*, improves your grades, it is called far transfer.

Throughout this chapter, we discuss how some training programs have either near or far transfer effects.

The other key factor to consider is whether these improvements are short-lived or long-lasting. In some cases, the improvements may be the result simply of the novelty of using the training program and aren't lasting, but other training programs do seem to produce long-term improvements. With these considerations in mind, let's take a look at various training methods.

Sharpen Your Pencil for Puzzles

Doing crossword puzzles, logic problems, word searches, and Sudoku may not be on the cutting-edge of brain training, but it has been found to help keep you mentally sharp—and that's always a good thing. Sudoku, in particular, has been making headlines. Scientists are now assessing how beneficial it is, and the answer is looking good for Sudoku publishers. Jeremy Grabbe, from the State University of New York, set out to test this premise in 2012. He recruited two sets of people—one group in their twenties and another group in their sixties—and gave them Sudoku puzzles, as well as a working memory task, such as remembering numbers in backward order.

Grabbe found that people who did better on the Sudoku puzzles had 50 percent higher working memory scores than those who didn't do so well on Sudoku. This link was evident in both the younger group and the older group. But whether it's simply that people with good working memory perform better on Sudoku or that playing Sudoku improves working memory, we can't say, because Grabbe didn't directly investigate whether playing Sudoku puzzles over time will result in working memory improvements. Even so, knowing that there is a link between the two indicates that Sudoku could potentially serve as a useful working-memory-training tool.

Can Playing Video Games Really Help Working Memory?

Most of the news we hear about video games is downright depressing. Some teens and adults waste hours at the gaming console to the apparent detriment of their relationships, work or schoolwork, and emotional well-being. But video games aren't all bad. Researchers have found that playing video games may actually have some benefit for your brain, though there is no convincing evidence that they shore up your working memory. Researchers typically divide video games into three categories:

- Simple games, like *Tetris* and *Donkey Kong*

- General brain-training games
- Strategy games that require strategic thinking, planning, problem solving, and concentration in a complex virtual environment, like *Rise of Nations* or *Medal of Honor*, a perceptually demanding game that involves identifying multiple threats, locating supplies, and navigating enemy territory.

Simple Games

Some simple games provide near transfer effects—you also improve in closely related skills. For example, playing *Tetris*, a tile-arrangement puzzle that lets you move and rotate tiles as you match them, makes people do better in tasks that involve mentally rotating an object. Makes sense, right? In the Mario Brothers game *Donkey Kong*, the player must act quickly to make his character leap over holes and avoid falling into traps. This quick thinking in the game yields improvements in tests of reaction time. While it's great that these easy and fun games have some cognitive benefit, so far the evidence suggests that it is primarily near transfer effects.

General Brain-Training Games

General brain-training games have received quite a lot of research attention. With these computer-based programs, you can play a variety of games, including memory games, math problems, logic puzzles, word scrambles, and visual perception games. But does playing these online games boost cognitive skills, specifically working memory? This is the question posed by a number of researchers in both the United States and Europe.

To find the answer with regard to children, French psychologist Alain Lieury compared the benefits of a brain-training program by Nintendo with good old-fashioned paper-and-pencil quizzes, including deciphering coded messages, matching identical figures, or finding the differences between two images. In a large group of ten-year-olds, Lieury found that the computer-based program provided no more benefit for working memory than the paper-and-pencil games. In a follow-up study in 2010, he found that first and second graders' working memory scores did not improve after they played the brain-training program for six weeks. There was no far transfer effect to working memory.

In a 2010 study, American psychologist Phillip Ackerman recruited adults ranging from ages fifty to seventy-one and asked them to play brain-training games by Nintendo over four weeks. Although he didn't test specifically for working memory, he found that despite this extensive training, they showed no improvement in a range of cognitive tests, like completing sentences, verbal analogies, or timed tasks.

More recently Japanese researcher Rui Nouchi recruited adults in their sixties and seventies and asked them to play a brain-training program by Nintendo five times a week for four weeks. His 2012 study found that although the game-playing adults showed some improvements in cognitive tests, like managing motor skills, there was no gain in tests of working memory, which he examined by having them remember numbers in backward order. So overall, while you may enjoy playing various general brain-training games and you even get better at playing them, the evidence suggests that working memory does not improve as a result of playing these games.

Strategy Games

Strategy-based video games require ample amounts of planning, concentration, and problem solving, and emerging research suggests that they can improve cognitive skills in both younger and older adults. One study found that expert video gamers who played games like *Medal of Honor* or *Rise of Nations* had better attention, were faster at responding to moving objects, and could carry out mental rotation activities faster than non-players. If you've ever taken a cognitive test, you may be familiar with mental rotation problems where you look at a letter or shape, and then imagine rotating it on its axis to determine if the letter or shape next to it is the same or different.

Mental rotation task: In the first example, the *F* images are the same when rotated. In the second example, the letters are not the same when rotated.

In a 2012 trial, older adults were asked to play *World of Warcraft*, an online game in which players assume the role of a fantasy character and collaborate with other gamers to embark on quests, wage epic battles, and attempt to defeat monsters in a virtual world. The researchers chose this game because it is cognitively demanding: players are required to act within the specific skill set their fantasy character possesses, navigate to new locations within the virtual world using textual descriptions and visual maps, react quickly to constantly changing on-screen indicators, consider the health of their character, and selectively ignore on-screen information that might distract them from accomplishing their goal.

We have to admit that we think having the study participants play *World of Warcraft* was a somewhat ironic choice given the addictive problems some users experience, which we covered in chapter 4. The training group played for an hour a day for a number of weeks, while the control group did not play the game. Unfortunately, the researchers didn't test working memory directly, so we can't draw any conclusions about the effects of the game on it, but it is interesting that the people who played the video game did have better scores in the Stroop test, which is related to working memory skills. In this test, the name of a color, such as the word *blue*, is printed in a color, such as red, that is different from the one denoted by the name. Participants are asked to say the name of the color—in this case, "red" would be the correct answer—rather than read the word *blue*. Doing so requires the use of the working memory Conductor to keep instructions in mind and say the color rather than read the word. This suggests that there might also be positive working memory effects, and it would be valuable to test specifically for this.

So what does all this mean? In general, playing some video games or doing a general brain-training program can boost some cognitive skills, like reaction time and mental rotation. However, there is no evidence of direct improvement in working memory.

Working Memory Training

In contrast to the methods we have just looked at, the exercises and recommendations we have included throughout this book were designed on the basis of our research and the broader findings about working memory specifically to enhance your working memory.

Ross set up a company that provides *Jungle Memory*, a training program for children and teenagers. This computer-based program uses games to sharpen the Conductor in a variety of ways, including:

- A game that trains spatial skills

- Mental-processing games using words and letters

- A game that involves solving math problems

- Games that emphasize paying attention

The games become more difficult as students progress through the program, so their working memory is progressively challenged. Clinical trials demonstrate that *Jungle Memory* has both near and far transfer effects. As we will describe in more detail, students who trained regularly with *Jungle Memory* showed great improvements in their working memory (near transfer). And that's not all: their scores in tests of learning, like language and math, also improved (far transfer). A teacher who had been using *Jungle Memory* with her students informed us that a student who had been struggling with reading for years jumped three reading levels after training.

This story is not unique. Many teachers, parents, and school counselors have shared how children have made improvements in a variety of ways after training with the program. One teacher was thrilled that her students were not only improving their grades, but also paying more attention in class. One mom reported that her child was better able to remember things she had said several days earlier. Another teacher noticed a marked difference in students' ability to concentrate and complete tasks. And many have commented on a general increase in self-confidence and motivation to learn among youngsters.

The improvements as a result of training with *Jungle Memory* seem to last. Clinical trials so far have shown that these improvements last for the longer term—at least eight months later. At the end of this chapter, we'll tell you how you can get a free trial for *Jungle Memory* so your child can try it.

Tracy has carried out a number of clinical trials to examine the effects of *Jungle Memory* training. One of the most exciting pieces of evidence about the training is that it seems to have far transfer effects. Tracy conducted a trial of *Jungle Memory* with a group of students with learning difficulties. In order to ensure that working memory and grades were improving as a result of the *Jungle Memory* training, we also included a control group, which received tutoring classes in language and math, so that they would be motivated to do their best. Both groups were tested before and after training.

When Tracy tested the working memory, IQ, and academic attainment of both groups before they began their respective training, the groups performed equally. This was important to establish, as it would provide a solid basis for concluding that any improvements in the students test scores after training were in fact the result of the training and not due to the fact that they had started at different levels.

After eight weeks of *Jungle Memory* for one group and tutoring for another, Tracy tested them again. The differences between the two groups were dramatic. The *Jungle Memory* group jumped up almost 10 percent in their working memory ability compared to the tutoring group, which didn't show any working memory improvements. The working memory improvement is considered a near transfer effect because *Jungle Memory* is designed to train working memory.

But what about far transfer? Did *Jungle Memory* improve more than just working memory? Yes. The *Jungle Memory* group also improved in their language and math skills. For example, their spelling scores increased almost 10 standard score points, which is like going from a grade of C to a B, or from a B to an A. In contrast, the tutoring group did not perform much better after eight weeks.

To appreciate how dramatic the degree of improvement we saw from the *Jungle Memory* training—almost 10 points in tests of learning—consider that there has been a great deal of discussion about how substantial increases in IQ scores have been over the past fifty years, but the documented rise is only about 3 points per decade. Compare that to the dramatic increase in working memory we saw after just eight weeks of *Jungle Memory* training.

Tracy has since followed up this study with another one looking at whether *Jungle Memory* training can also improve working memory in students with dyslexia and autism. Here also she found exciting results: Students who trained regularly with *Jungle Memory* improved their working memory by five times more than those who trained only once a week. Their language and math skills improved considerably as well: they improved four times more in both a spelling test and a math test compared to those who trained only once a week.

The most exciting news came eight months later when Tracy retested these same students. She found that all the improvements they had achieved had been maintained—even though they had not been training during that period. This maintenance effect suggests that these students had made long-lasting gains to their working memory.

An important question for further research about the effects of the training is how effective it is for adults. As we described in chapter 7, the brain goes through many changes from childhood to adulthood, so training gains for adults may differ. So far, most of the research into the effectiveness of working memory training has been done with either schoolchildren or older adults. This is because working memory training has largely been aimed at those with pressing cognitive needs, such as students with learning disabilities or aging adults with cognitive decline. But there is one important study that offers promising evidence that the training has strong effects in adults also.

In 2008, Susanne Jaeggi, from the University of Michigan, published a paper demonstrating how working memory training could improve scores for adults on both a working memory test and a general intelligence test. The twenty-somethings in this trial practiced something known as the dual n-back task, which includes two elements: squares are presented in a number of possible locations, and letters are read aloud. The participants have to remember and pick out specific locations and letters based on their order in the sequence. This requires working memory because you have to keep track of and work with two separate kinds of information. It's the cognitive equivalent of flipping a pancake with one hand and making an omelet with the other: multitasking on steroids.

The participants practiced the n-back task for either eight, twelve, seventeen, or nineteen days. As they improved at it, they had to try increasingly difficult variations of the task so their working memory was constantly challenged. All four of these groups improved in the reasoning test after training. In fact, the study demonstrated that those who trained for longer showed the greatest improvements. Jaeggi's research also suggests that the benefits of the training had not only a near transfer effect but also a far transfer effect. The training task was entirely different from the reasoning test, but it helped the study participants do better on that test too.

It is important to note that not everyone is optimistic about the benefits of working memory training. Zach Shipstead and colleagues Thomas Redick and Randall Engle argue that there are a number of methodological issues that undermine the claims of working memory training: control groups tend not to engage in training; there are few objective measures of improvement; the working memory tests used aren't reliable. Jaeggi addressed these methodological issues in follow-up research where her control group engaged in non–working memory training (so that any benefit could be attributed directly to the working memory training). She also used objective measures of improvements, such as standardized tests. While in a recent study with college students modeled on Jaeggi's methodology, Redick and colleagues were unable to replicate her findings, Jaeggi was able to do so.

In Tracy's published trials with *Jungle Memory*, she has used control groups that engage in a task and a series of objective and standardized tests to measure improvement in working memory, as well as grades. In addition, she was able to replicate the benefits of *Jungle Memory* training in two separate clinical trials.

Based on growing research, including our own, we think that the advantages of WM training are clear. More research is under way to investigate the potential benefits for other groups, such as those with language difficulties or Down syndrome. Schools are also implementing *Jungle Memory* in their classrooms and seeing great improvements with their students. For example, a school that specializes in teaching dyslexic children in the UK recently ran their own in-house trials using *Jungle Memory* with their students. They found that students showed significant improvements in objective tests of reading.

Research on working memory training is ongoing and may help determine just how broad and long lasting its benefits are. But based on the evidence so far, we feel confident that working memory training is significantly beneficial and that *Jungle Memory* offers the trifecta of brain training: near transfer effects, far transfer effects, and improvements that last. If you think your child may benefit from working memory training, you can get a free trial of *Jungle Memory* by going to www.junglememory.com and typing the word *book* into the promotion box on the sign-up page.

As we said at the beginning of this chapter, actively training your working memory isn't the only way to strengthen it. Many routine habits and strategies can also boost working memory power, and we will explore these later. But first, in the following chapter, we introduce you to some stellar working memory performers and share the secrets of their mighty mental powers so you can learn from them how to enhance your own working memory.

9

Secrets of Working Memory Specialists

Some mental tasks appear so complex and require such a great deal of working memory that they may seem impossible at first glance. In years past, common wisdom suggested that people who could perform such mental feats were just born brilliant. We have to disagree with that assumption. After interviewing a number of apparent superhumans of the mind and reviewing the latest research on their mighty mental powers, it seems to us that the secrets of these working memory specialists lie not necessarily in genetics but more likely in their ability to figure out smarter ways to use their working memory Conductor: ways that you can use too.

In this chapter, we're going to introduce three powerful techniques—"code breakers," "bootstrapping," and "chunking"—that can help make even the most difficult mental feats possible.

- *Code breakers*: This technique involves coming up with a step-by-step plan, or algorithm, that is then transferred to your long-term memory. By housing the algorithm in your long-term memory, it gives your working memory Conductor fewer things to manage, allowing you to apply the code breaker on the fly so you can become a human calculator.

- *Bootstrapping*: This is the process of binding or joining verbal and visual information together using working memory and long-term memory. Bootstrapping can help you process names, conversation points, and useful details that you need to remember.

- *Chunking*: This memorization strategy involves breaking down information into subparts or "chunks" and then committing them to long-term memory. With chunks of information stored in long-term memory, your working memory Conductor can prioritize and manage data more efficiently.

In the following pages, we introduce you to working memory specialists who use these fundamental strategies to perform amazing mental achievements. These same techniques can help all of us in our everyday lives by freeing up our working memory Conductor when it is burdened with an inordinate volume of complex information. If we practice these methods, we can give our working memory the same advantages as the experts.

Code Breakers: Finding a Formula That Works

Pop quiz! What's 6 x 7? Easy, right? It's 42. What about 12 x 13? Hmm; that's not quite as simple. It's 156. How about 67 x 82? No fair using a calculator! It's 5,494. If you can still remember your times tables, there is a good chance you answered the first one correctly and perhaps even the second. If you missed that third math problem above, don't feel bad. That one stumps most people. But not Rudiger Gamm. A German math prodigy, Gamm has an extraordinary ability for mental calculation. Gamm's skill is based on what we call "code breakers." Code breakers are simple algorithms, or step-by-step procedures, to calculate the answer to a problem. Code breakers are stored in long-term memory and manipulated by working memory to solve a problem.

Because of his code-breaking algorithms, if you give Gamm a date, say, October 23, 1957, he can instantly calculate the day of the week on which it fell (it was a Wednesday, by the way). When he was asked on an Australian radio show to calculate the powers of 83, he was able to do so from the power of 2 (83^2, or 83 x 83 = 6,889) all the way to the power of 9 (83^9, or 83 x 83 x 83 x 83 x 83 x 83 x 83 x 83 x 83 = 186,940,255,267,540,400) without making a single mistake. Strikingly, Gamm is no Rain Man, possessing extraordinary abilities at the cost of his social skills. He is very much like you and me.

What we find most interesting and encouraging about Gamm is that he wasn't very good at math in school and had little interest in learning it. But after he left school, he became interested in an algorithm that allowed him to rapidly calculate in his head the day of the week from any date. For example, he could calculate that January 13, 1980, was a Sunday. That's when he realized that he already had the means within him to become a human calculator. Over time, he assembled a set of code breakers that he stored in his long-term memory, allowing him to use his working memory to apply them to challenging problems.

Gamm's code breakers are simple but powerful tools for lightening the load for working memory. He uses code breakers to separate the problem into distinct and manageable steps, and uses his working memory to hold just a few things in mind. One of his simple code breakers is a left-to-right algorithm, going from the far-left digit to the far-right digit and adding the results in between. It sounds complicated, but it isn't. Look at the steps he would take to solve this problem: 57 x 6 = ?

1. Multiply 50 by 6 (300).
2. Hold this answer in his working memory.
3. Multiply 7 by 6 (42).
4. Add both numbers together (300 + 42 = 342).

Contrast this with the way most of us are taught to do such calculations, stacking the numbers on top of each other:

$$490$$
$$\underline{\times\ 142}$$

If you are working on paper, stacking is a good way to calculate because you can write down part of your answer along the way and do single-digit multiplication and addition. However, if you try doing it in your head, you must carry numbers as well as hold all the numbers together at the end in order to add them, a very challenging job for working memory. Gamm's code-breaker is much easier. You have to keep only three things in mind: the numbers in the problem (490 x 142), your place in the problem (I've already multiplied 400 x 100, so now I need to do 400 x 40, and so on), and the overall sum of the preceding steps.

Gamm makes great use of what we call the Working Memory–Long Term Memory (WM-LTM) Loop. The WM-LTM Loop is the process of using your working memory to manipulate information stored in your long-term memory. To build up his long-term memory for math, Gamm practiced and practiced calculations for four hours a day so that he could commit a vast store of solutions in his long-term memory, as well as a number of code breakers that are shortcuts for solving longer problems. It was like memorizing his times tables, but on a far larger scale. Because you know that 6 x 6 is 36, you don't have to use your working memory to add 6 + 6 + 6 + 6 + 6 + 6 = 36. Similarly, for Gamm, by having a larger set of automatic answers and code breakers, it meant his working memory Conductor had fewer things to manage. When tackling problems, Gamm always sorts through his long-term memory to find answers that he may already know as well as the most efficient code breaker, which allows him to use his working memory to hold the intermediary solutions.

Working Memory–Long Term Memory (WM-LTM) Loop

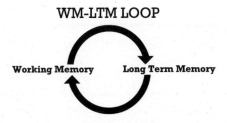

WM-LTM LOOP

Working Memory   Long Term Memory

Some fascinating research done by Mauro Pesenti from the Université Catholique de Louvain in Belgium revealed what is happening in the brain that makes the way Gamm performs his calculations so much more effective than the way most of us would go about the task. Pesenti used PET scans to discover differences in the ways nonexpert mental calculators go about the task versus Gamm's approach. When Pesenti scanned Gamm's brain as he performed calculations, the scans clearly showed that Gamm was tapping into his long-term memory. The right parahippocampal gyrus in his brain lit up, which is an area involved in what is known as episodic memory, or long-term memory for your experiences. But, crucially, he also activated his PFC, showing that code breakers alone were insufficient to answer the problem, and he needed to use his working memory to find the appropriate code breaker and manipulate it.

Pesenti also gave PET scans to the nonexperts while they performed a range of calculations, from simple ones that rely on memorization of the times tables up to more difficult ones that engage working memory. For simple multiplication problems like 3 x 8, 2 x 6, or 5 x 6, the participants were accessing the left parietal lobe and premotor circuit, areas of the brain associated with numerical knowledge. In other words, they had memorized the answers and were simply accessing them. No working memory was required. As the problems became harder, like 32 x 14, the nonexperts began to engage working memory in order to calculate the answers because they hadn't memorized them. They had to break the problems up into multistep calculations, which required them to use their working memory Conductor to manage it all.

Up to a point, they were able to answer these questions with a pretty decent success rate, around 82 percent, but as the numbers to be multiplied got larger, like 76 x 68, they needed a code breaker but didn't have one on hand like Gamm. The calculation became so hard that they spent all of their time trying to work out the intermediary calculations using their intraparietal sulcus, the brain's calculator, and they rarely engaged their working memory. This was probably because they were struggling so much just to calculate that they never arrived at the intermediary answers to place in their working memory. As Gamm's story shows, however, with practice and the right code breakers, nonexperts may be able to dramatically improve their results.

Of course nonexperts don't go to the same lengths as Gamm because everyday life doesn't require them to calculate 83 to the power of 9. But everyone can benefit from a code breaker—a familiar, step-by-step method for solving a math problem. With the advent of any number of calculating devices, we seem to have lost the ability to do quick mental math.

This mental math deficit can affect you negatively in many ways. For example, when buying a car, refinancing a mortgage, or offering an opinion about projections at a board meeting, it isn't always convenient or socially appropriate to consult your smartphone calculator. This can often result in bad financial decisions. By daring to drop the calculator and pick up a code breaker, you can become a math master and possibly improve your circumstances.

Consider Mary and Mark, two low-paid interns at a media company. Their boss wants them to do more work but doesn't want to pay them extra for it. Mary has code breakers; Mark has a smartphone. Mary quickly uses one of her code breakers to calculate on the spot that the boss is asking her to do 35 percent more work than she is currently doing and asks for more pay. Here's how the negotiation goes:

> Mary: *"If you want me to do 35 percent more work,*
> *then pay me 35 percent more in wages."*
> Boss: *"How about 15 percent?"*
> Mary: *"I can't do it for less than 20 percent."*

They agree on 20 percent, and now Mary is not only a tad less broke, but she is also on the boss's radar as a clever employee. Mark, when asked to do more work, simply agrees without protest. He wants to keep his job and doesn't want to be seen taking out a calculator to see how much extra work he is agreeing to do. Who would you rather be? If you would like to learn the advantage of code breakers for mental math, there are a number of books on the subject, including *Rapid Math Tricks and Tips* and *Mind Games: Amazing Mental Arithmetic Made Easy*.

Bootstrapping, or the Art of Remembering Anything

In 2002, Dominic O'Brien won the Guinness World Record title for remembering a random sequence of 54 packs of playing cards. The rules for the title were simple: O'Brien was allowed a single sighting of each card—2,808 in total—and then had to recall all of them in the order shown. He was able to achieve this remarkable feat using a very simple working memory strategy psychologists call "bootstrapping." Bootstrapping is the process of binding or joining verbal and visual information together using working memory and long-term memory. Bootstrapping turned O'Brien, a guy whose schoolteacher once said that he "would not amount to much," into a memory champion.

When O'Brien described his school years to us, he said he was often distracted by visual information, which made it hard for him to focus on what the teacher was saying. Little did he know at the time, but his penchant for visual information would eventually form the cornerstone for his remarkable memory feats. It wasn't until he hit age thirty that O'Brien decided to dedicate himself to training his bootstrapping skills in a concerted effort to reach the highest levels of memory feats. This is yet another indication that superhumans of the mind aren't born that way.

A few years ago, Tracy got the chance to work with O'Brien, teaming up with him in an effort to give secondary school students strategies to enhance their working memories when competing in the U.K. Schools Memory Championships. She saw firsthand how he uses bootstrapping by inventing a story in his working memory that binds together familiar characters with a familiar journey. O'Brien's bootstrapping strategy, which he calls the Journey Method, is a modern twist on the ancient Roman "loci method," said to be derived from a real-life Greek tragedy. The story is that the Greek poet Simonides of Ceos stepped outside of a banquet hall where he had just recited a poem, and the hall collapsed behind him. Everyone inside had been crushed and the bodies were unrecognizable, but Simonides was able to identify the victims because he associated each of the guests with where they had been sitting. In a similar way, O'Brien, by bringing together familiar characters with a familiar journey, is able to tap into the power of the WM-LTM Loop to recall that vast amount of information.

He does this in two stages:

1. He comes up with a cast of familiar characters representing each card in a deck. For example, O'Brien associates the Seven of Hearts with James Bond. The King of Clubs is Jack Nicklaus, the king of golf (clubs).

2. He uses a story to bind the exact sequence of the card/characters with a journey that he is very familiar with: walking his favorite golf course.

Both of these bootstrapping steps involve working memory because they are linking together two pieces of information. Once they have been brought together, he sends them to his long-term memory. During a memory competition, if O'Brien sees the Seven of Hearts followed by the King of Clubs, he imagines James Bond (remember, the Seven of Hearts) getting a lesson from the Jack Nicklaus (remember, the King of Clubs). He then moves this story to his long-term memory. After he's done this for a full deck of cards, he reviews the journey, and, eventually, after six decks he'll review the complete journey with the six decks again.

A fascinating study done by Eleanor Maguire revealed what is going on in O'Brien's brain during this process. The researchers asked O'Brien and a number of other memory experts to memorize sequences of numbers, faces, and snowflakes; as they did so, fMRI scans detected their brain activity. The brain images showed activation in the superior parietal cortex, which is associated with manipulating and managing information in working memory. They also indicated that two areas of the brain involved in long-term knowledge were activated: the hippocampus and the retrosplenial cortex. Both of these areas are associated with the memory of routes taken—such as our regular commute to work—and the ability to navigate. These results verify that O'Brien is accessing the WM-LTM Loop with his method.

When he was memorizing the fifty-four decks for the Guinness World Record title, he created fifty-four separate journeys. He was allowed to view the order of the cards only once and had twelve hours to review and rehearse the cards in the correct sequence. He was able to recall all but 4 of the 2,808 cards correctly. Watching O'Brien in action is impressive, but we were even more amazed to discover that he could still remember the cards in the right sequence two weeks later with 95 percent accuracy without any review.

An important additional point about this method of shifting information from working memory to long-term memory is that it also greatly helps in coping with distractions as we're getting information. Think of all of the distractions from constant emails at work. We have to use our Conductor to filter these out, making it harder to process the information we are supposed to focus on. In order to measure how well working memory can filter these out, psychologists ask participants to perform a working memory task and a distraction task at the same time. In the working memory task, the participants repeat a set of numbers in backward order (if they are given 1,2,3, they have to repeat 3,2,1). At the same time, they repeat a random string of letters, like JCDBZA, as a distraction task. While most adults can usually repeat five numbers in backward order, when they are doing the distraction task they can remember only two or three numbers.

O'Brien's bootstrapping allows him to cope with distractions. On one occasion he appeared on a live television show and was given six decks to memorize in forty-five minutes. In addition to the hot studio lights and the film crew and cameras, O'Brien had to contend with sitting next to live performances of women dancing and interviews being conducted during the forty-five-minute time period. But he was able to stay focused, and he enthralled the television audience with the right answer every time.

How can you apply O'Brien's bootstrapping technique in the real world? By using your working memory to bind verbal and visual information together, bootstrapping can help you process names, conversation points, and useful details. This can be extremely helpful in the business arena. For example, let's say you're at a business conference and a potential client, Jim Padder, tells you that his company is in the process of redesigning its logo from its signature red to yellow. You need to remember to relay that information to your own sales team back home so they make sure to use yellow in their PowerPoint sales presentation with Jim next week rather than the red that they have now. You are an inveterate yellow legal pad user, and, using your working memory, you bootstrap "Padder" with your yellow legal pad. Padder is now "Yellow Padder," and you remember to inform the sales team.

When bootstrapping, keep in mind that visual information can include many things: what a person looks like, what they're wearing, or even their emotional expressions during your conversation. When you take a note of these many verbal and visual facets, use your working memory Conductor to link the information with something familiar from your long-term memory. Whether you are someone who prefers to remember faces or someone who never forgets a name, remind yourself to bootstrap this information.

Chunking: Recognizing Relationships and the Bright Idea of Working Backward

The third strategy that working memory specialists employ is chunking, and it has been used to tremendous effect in the world of chess. The late computer scientist and psychologist Herbert Simon of Carnegie Mellon University began publishing studies on chess in the 1950s. In one seminal study from 1973, Simon looked at differences between the way chess experts and beginner players view a chessboard. They presented experts and beginners with a chessboard with pieces in positions taken from regular games. The participants had five seconds to look at the board and then had to try to recall the chess positions.

As expected, the experts were much better at remembering the chess positions than the beginners. However, when the chess pieces were randomly arranged on the board, both the beginners and the experts remembered similar amounts. This study established that the key to expert players' superior recall was that they store patterns from chess games as chunks in their long-term memory.

Simon collaborated with Swiss psychologist and chess International Master Fernand Gobet to provide more insight into how chess players make use of this chunking process. They suggest that expert chess players memorize chess patterns and then chunk three or four patterns together. A typical chess Grandmaster, who usually has at least ten years of experience, has accumulated hundreds of thousand of chunks. There is strong evidence to suggest that working memory allows them to manipulate these chunks. A study that scanned the brains of chess players suggests that expert players tap into the power of the WM-LTM Loop.

Neuroscientist Onjgen Amidzic from Switzerland has played chess professionally for over fifteen years and has dedicated his research to understanding how the brains of experts such as chess Grandmasters function. When he compared the brain activity of amateur and professional chess players during matches against a computer, he found that amateurs use the temporal lobe, which is associated with analyzing rules and unusual moves during the game. But the chess experts showed more activity in the frontal and parietal cortices, which include the PFC and are linked with working memory skills. Whereas the amateurs were struggling to make sense of the patterns, the Grandmasters were so familiar with them that they could quickly retrieve the relevant chess chunks from their long-term memory and plan their moves. Amateurs didn't have enough familiarity with the chess chunks in order to use their working memory to manipulate them like a Grandmaster.

We gained further insights from chess Grandmaster Susan Polgar. It is no small feat to be a Grandmaster and extremely rare for a female. In 2012, only twenty-seven of the world's 1,367 Grandmasters were women, or about 2 percent. Polgar entered the *Guinness World Records* in 2005 by playing the largest number of chess games simultaneously. Over seventeen hours, Polgar played 326 chess games at the same time with players whose expertise ranged from novices to experienced players, including chess masters. Walking up and down a line of chessboards, she made each of her moves in less than ten seconds and set a record for winning 97 percent of the games. You can imagine our excitement when she agreed to talk with us about how she accomplishes such feats.

Like Rudiger Gamm and Dominic O'Brien, Polgar's remarkable achievements are the result of hard work, not genetics. Her father, a Hungarian psychologist named Laszlo, fiercely believed that geniuses are made and not born. He even wrote a book called *Bring Up Genius*, and he wanted to apply his theories to his three daughters. So he intensively home-schooled them in chess. Rooms were filled with diagrams of games, moves, and boards. One of Polgar's first public games was in a Budapest chess club when she was just four years old. A club regular laughed when he was challenged to a game, but he wasn't laughing when she decimated him. The rest is history. One of Polgar's advantages is the distinct way that she thinks about chess. Polgar proves that some chunks are better than others. Whereas many experts and even Grandmasters chunk the *locations* of pieces on the board, Polgar has trained herself to chunk the *relationships* between chess pieces. By way of simple explanation, she describes a relationship known as a *fork*—where a single piece attacks multiple pieces at the same time. For example, a knight can attack the king, queen, and rook at the same time. When the king is being attacked, he is in "check" and must always get out of the way. But this leaves the queen or rook open for capture.

Fork: *The knight moves in an L shape and
is simultaneously attacking all three pieces.*

Many chess players see things differently. Instead of looking for a
fork relationship between pieces, they see four separate pieces in different positions on the board. If they try to memorize the exact locations
of these pieces in a variety of game situations, they end up creating an
unnecessarily large store of chunks. Moreover, if the pieces end up in
a way they don't recognize, they are lost. But by focusing on the fork
relationship, Polgar doesn't have to memorize the exact location of four
pieces, she has to remember only the underlying relationship, which
allows her to do much more with her chunk than others can when they
are remembering locations.

By knowing the relationship, Polgar can apply it in a huge variety
of settings, even if the exact positions of the pieces don't correspond
to something she has played previously. Of course, a fork is a relatively
simple relationship, and Susan's winning relationship chunks are more
complex, involving numerous pieces and move sequences, but the
beauty of her relationship chunking is that what works for a Grandmaster can be scaled down for a novice.

The other distinctive feature of the way Polgar plays that she
described to us is that she starts from the outcome she wants, checkmate, and works her way backward to the current state of play on the
board. Working backward in this way demands engagement of working
memory, but Polgar suggests it gives the working memory Conductor
fewer possible moves to consider.

Chunking, Part 2: Keeping It Simple and Starting from the Endpoint

Another working memory specialist we interviewed who uses the chunking method is Feross Aboukhadijeh. He may look like an ordinary student in the Stanford computer science program, but *New York Magazine* has already tagged this superprogrammer as one of the Steve Jobs and Mark Zuckerbergs of the future. A recent claim to fame is YouTube Instant (ytinstant.com), a website that instantly plays videos as you type letters into the search bar. He bet his roommate that he could build a real-time search engine for YouTube videos in less than an hour. He was wrong. It took him three hours, probably because he was watching a movie at the same time.

That night, he posted a link to his new site on Facebook and went to bed. When he woke up, he had fourteen missed calls, ten text messages on his phone, and a request for an interview with the *Washington Post*. Fourteen hours after he posted the site, the CEO of YouTube, Chad Hurley, offered him a job, which he turned down. Millions of users later and working on his degree at Stanford, Feross has politely declined job offers to program for top companies, save one, Facebook, for which he has coded as an intern alongside Mark Zuckerberg. As he told us, he wants to be his own CEO.

Feross is a great example of how the seemingly esoteric skills of the specialists in this chapter can help us use our working memory to our advantage in the real world. As a child, he reprogrammed the microwave's child lock so that his mother couldn't use it. He built his first website at age eleven. By the time he was in high school, he went to a bookstore, bought a book on making a website, and, without any formal training, figured out how to put a website online. The result, freetheflash. com, was a video-sharing site, a conceptual precursor to YouTube. The code underlying the site wasn't pretty, but it worked and quickly became popular, achieving 600,000 visitors and 3 million page views. How did he achieve all this? In his own words: "practice, practice, practice." With all his practice programming, Feross has learned to work smarter, and it turns out that one of the ways he does it is by chunking.

Let's take an inside peek at how he does it. It all starts with a computer program, which at its foundation is an idea brought to life by chunks of code: instructions that tell the computer to do certain things. Though each program is different, all are created by combining chunks of code. Many of the same chunks are used in numerous programs. The combined chunks of code for any particular program can run to thousands of lines long, and a larger program, like Microsoft Word, may be millions of lines long. It simply isn't possible to store all these lines in long-term memory.

So how does Feross do it? Rather than focusing on remembering whole programs or even sections of them, he focuses on manipulating and combining the familiar chunks of code to write a program, like a chess player linking chess chunks to win a game. Let's say he needs to write a password program for email. One chunk would check the password entered in the box against the correct password. Another chunk would allow you access to your email when you entered it in correctly, and another would block you when you don't. Together these chunks form a password system. If improperly assembled, the program might block you when you enter the correct password or allow you access when you enter the wrong one. But by being familiar with the separate chunks, you get a secure password program.

Furthermore, like Polgar's chess chunks, some programming chunks are better than others. Feross was able to create ytinstant.com so quickly because rather than focusing on the details, his chunks allowed him to keep the big picture in mind. Remember, Polgar's chess chunks are comprised of the *relationships* between pieces—chunks that are far simpler than those based on the exact locations of pieces on a board. Similarly, Feross's programming chunks are all about what he calls "managing complexity." This means he opts for simplicity wherever possible.

To illustrate this, he describes two kinds of levels in programming: high level and low level. High-level programming can be described like an easy-to-read article, where the programmer, a writer of sorts, sets out what the program does. Sometimes writers have to go into more complex detail but must resist doing so because it would disrupt the flow of the article. Writers solve this problem by using footnotes or endnotes, which give the necessary detail at the bottom of the page or the end of the article. Super programmers like Feross manage complexity by using lower level of programming similar to the way writers use footnotes. So if they want to write a "footnote" for squaring a number, they don't need to detail the full operation ($x^2=x*x$) in the higher level, they just write *sq* (for square) and define what *sq* means in the lower level of the program.

As we know, the greater the amount of information, the more likely your Conductor will be overwhelmed. By using simple chunks like *sq* and elaborating on the "footnotes" once the program is sketched out, Feross keeps his Conductor in control and can keep sight of the end goal. In fact, Feross can automatically tell how good a programmer is by how simple their chunks are. Lesser programmers tend to put footnote material in the main text. If a lot of what should be in the lower level is included in the higher level, it means they aren't managing their complexity well, and as a consequence programmers can get lost in the details. If Feross had tried to keep track of all the footnotes when he was writing ytinstant, it would have taken him a lot longer than three hours. But by simplifying, his working memory was able to focus on innovative programming.

Simplifying is only part of what makes Feross such a lean, mean coding machine. Another one of his "superprogramming" secrets is using the technique of starting with the endpoint, which Polgar described to us. Just as Polgar starts at checkmate and works backward, Feross starts with the result he wants and then works backward step by step to figure out how to get there. He describes his technique like a builder who works in reverse, starting with the roof and ending with the foundation.

He illustrates how it works using the example of a spell check program. For Feross the "roof" he is starting with is the end result of a good spell check program: incorrectly spelled words being highlighted. To get to this point, he needs beams to support the roof: a code that will run through every word in the document to identify the incorrectly spelled words. Next, he needs walls to prop up the beams: a list of correctly spelled words. Lastly, he lays the foundation: a set of rules governing when words are determined to be incorrect. Now that he knows the overall design of the house, he can begin to write the code for highlighting incorrect words and then move on to the step below once he has finished. By building his house backward, he limits the possibilities that his working memory has to consider, and he knows how to write the code appropriately for each step. His working memory makes sure the house is solidly built.

What can we learn from working memory specialists like Gamm, O'Brien, Polgar, and Feross? We can all benefit from the techniques they use—code breakers, bootstrapping, and chunking—in our everyday lives to help cope with the endless flood of information bombarding us. For example, you can use Gamm's techniques when you need to multiply numbers quickly and don't have access to a calculator. You can borrow O'Brien's bootstrapping method when you need to remember a lot of information. And when you need to come up with a schedule to meet a deadline, create a new product, or achieve a career goal, you can start at the end and work backward like Polgar and Feross.

One of the things we find most exciting about these techniques is that they aren't difficult to learn. All you have to do is practice. Make it a point to put these techniques to use every day, and you'll likely enhance working memory and feel less overwhelmed by information overload. Here are a number of exercises to help you make code breakers, bootstrapping, and chunking feel like second nature.

Working Memory Exercises

1. Become a Human Multiplier

Rudiger Gamm's algorithm or rule for multiplication is to multiply across the numbers, from left to right, adding up the results in between.

Example 1: Double-Digit/Single-Digit Multiplication

Using Gamm's technique, 53 × 6 would be solved this way:

$$50 \times 6 = 300$$
$$3 \times 6 = 18$$
$$300 + 18 = 318$$

When you do this type of calculation in your head, you activate your working memory when keeping your place in the problem and holding the interim answers in your head before adding them together.

Exercise 1

Repeat the same steps above to solve the following problems (answers appear at the end of the chapter):

$$78 \times 4 = ?$$
$$33 \times 5 = ?$$
$$25 \times 8 = ?$$
$$45 \times 3 = ?$$

Example 2: Double/Double-Digit Multiplication

With two double-digit numbers, the trick is to hold only the running total in mind rather than all the results from the previous multiplication steps. This frees up your working memory Conductor to pay attention to where you are in the problem, which becomes increasingly important when you multiply more numbers.

Using Gamm's technique, 35 x 56 would be solved this way:

$$
\begin{array}{rcl}
30 \times 50 & = & 1{,}500 \\
30 \times 6 & = & 180 \\
1{,}500 + 180 & = & 1{,}680 \text{ (keep only 1,680 in mind)} \\
5 \times 50 & = & 250 \\
1{,}680 + 250 & = & 1{,}930 \text{ (keep only 1,930 in mind)} \\
5 \times 6 & = & 30 \\
1{,}930 + 30 & = & 1{,}960
\end{array}
$$

Exercise 2

Repeat the same steps above to solve the following problems (answers appear at the end of the chapter):

$$
\begin{array}{rcl}
23 \times 34 & = & ? \\
12 \times 24 & = & ? \\
17 \times 55 & = & ? \\
64 \times 70 & = & ?
\end{array}
$$

2. Take a Mental Journey When You Need
to Memorize a Series of Things

Memory champion Dominic O'Brien's abilities are rooted in an ancient technique, the loci method. Here's how you can use loci method to remember a laundry list of items:

Step 1: Link random information to something meaningful to you. Say you are new to a company that casts metal weights for workout equipment, and you need to remember the product numbers 32, 62, 95, 13, 30, and 25 in that order. Use your working memory to link these random numbers with meaningful information stored in your hippocampus—for example:

— 32 is Michael Jordan's old number, so that number becomes Michael Jordan.

— 62 reminds you of your friend Terry's height—he's 6 foot 2 inches—so 62 becomes Terry.

— 95 is a very old age to live to, so 95 becomes an old man.

— 13 reminds you of the movie *Friday the 13th*, so 13 becomes Jason.

— 30 sounds like Bertie, a friend's dog you used to play with, so 30 becomes Bertie.

— 25 reminds you of a quarter, so 25 becomes a quarter.

Step 2: Place your "characters" in a familiar place. Choose a familiar location or route, such as a favorite hiking trail where you know every bend, your drive to work, or even the rooms of your house. Using your house as an example, you put:

Jordan on the porch
Terry behind the front door
The old man in the kitchen
Jason in the bathroom

Bertie in the backyard
The quarter in the couch cushions

Step 3: Create a story. Use your working memory to manipulate the information into an outlandish and memorable narrative.

For example:

Jordan knocked on the door.
Terry invites him in with a high five.
They go to the kitchen where an old man is making a cup
     of tea.
A guy in a hockey mask jumps out of the bathroom and
     waves a knife around.
Bertie barks from the backyard and scares him off.
You are so grateful you fish out a quarter from the cushions.

Or, in other words, 32, 62, 95, 13, 30, 25.

3. Keep It Simple, Smarty!

Superprogrammer Feross Aboukhadijeh says that simplifying where he can frees up his mental power to innovate. In terms of working memory, simplicity allows your Conductor to focus on what is really important. The end result is a quicker and more productive use of your time and efforts.

Most world-changing technologies started out as ideas of just a few, albeit imaginative, words—Google: unlimited web search; iPod: unlimited music; Gutenberg (printing) press: unlimited words; motorcars: horseless carriage.

Think of a goal you want to achieve, a product you want to create, or an idea you want to develop—and capture it in just two or three words. Do this on a regular basis to train your brain to zero in on a clear, concise, and spot-on concept. Your idea may not be a new technology. It may be something more personal, such as in the areas of career advancement ("marketing director"); living space ("less furniture"); or personal health ("weight loss").

4. Start at the End

Like Polgar who begins her chess games at checkmate and works backward to achieve it and Feross who envisions the end product before he ever writes a single line of code, you too would be wise to start with your end goal in mind and work your way backward. Let's say you are hired to an entry-level position at a technology firm that gives in-house employees first crack at job openings. You receive your first notice of job openings, and two of them sound interesting. But should you go for the sales position or the marketing job? It's simple. Start where you want to end up. If you want to become a vice president, figure out what path leads there. Your company has historically promoted a sales manager to the vice president position. So the decision is easy. Go for the salesperson job, not the marketing position.

On a piece of paper, write down your ultimate goal. Then write down the steps that will get you there in top-down order. Using the example above, you would write:

Vice-president
Sales manager
Salesperson
Entry-level job

5. Make Connections That Stick

Working memory makes information stick. Get new contacts to use their working memory to remember you when you introduce yourself or tell them what you do.

What Is Your Name?

A simple way to get someone to remember your name is to spell it backward on your name tag, or take your tag off and introduce yourself by spelling your name backward. For example, "Spelled backward, my name is y-c-a-r-t" (Tracy).

If you are hosting a conference and want everyone to be as memorable as possible, try a coffee break or greeting session where people substitute numbers, symbols, or pictures (or anything else suitable) that correspond to letters of the alphabet. "Hi, my name is: 18-15-19-19" (or Ross). This particular example will probably work better with mathematicians and accountants, but the idea is to get people to "codebreak" someone's name. The working memory demands will ensure that it will be productive for all.

What Do You Do for a Living?

The easiest way to engage someone else's working memory when answering the above question is to ask them to solve the riddle of your job. An example of that, which was found circulating on the web, is the following:

> I dig out tiny caves, and store gold and silver in them. I also build bridges of silver and make crowns of gold. They are the smallest you could imagine. Sooner or later everybody needs my help, yet many people are afraid to let me help them.
>
> Who am I?
> A dentist.

By inviting people to use their working memory when remembering you, you will ensure that you are never forgotten.

6. Remember Other People's Names

Before you try these methods to remember people's names, think about whether it is easier for you to process visual or verbal information. Use whichever is easier for you to bootstrap a contact to your long-term memory. The key is to make an effort processing the information and binding it together with something that you already know.

For visual processors: When you meet someone, focus on what that person is wearing, what she looks like, or how she is wearing her hair. Then take that image and bind it to something you already know. For example, you meet a man named Robert and he's wearing a red tie so you think "red Robert." Or you meet Maureen and she's wearing a green necklace and *green* rhymes with *Maureen*, so you say to yourself "green Maureen."

For verbal processors: Pay attention to the conversation and find links with events or memories that happened to you. Here are a few examples of how it works. His name is Phil and he likes to fish, and you have a fish tank in your office. Brian told a joke about a duck, and you just bought a new feather pillow. You meet Jordan, and remember that it's the same name as one of your university friends.

Answers to the Math Problems

$$78 \times 4 = 312$$
$$33 \times 5 = 165$$
$$25 \times 8 = 200$$
$$45 \times 3 = 135$$
$$23 \times 34 = 782$$
$$12 \times 24 = 288$$
$$17 \times 55 = 935$$
$$64 \times 70 = 4,480$$

10

Feed Your Brain, Fuel Your Working Memory

WORKING MEMORY TRAINING can be a great tool to maximize your working memory an advantage, but it certainly isn't the only one. In fact, some of the most effective working memory-boosting tools may be your fork, spoon, and knife. That's right, the foods you choose to put in your mouth have a profound effect on your working memory. Your eating habits can either fire it up or make it slow and sluggish. Just how powerful is food? Ask Elliot's parents.

They reported to the BBC that their nine-year-old son, Elliot, was struggling in school. He really didn't like reading and camped out on the couch watching TV for hours rather than do his homework. It definitely wasn't looking like a bright academic future was in the cards. But this all changed when Elliot took part in a scientific study. As a participant in this trial, Elliott was asked to make one simple change to his diet: he had to start taking a particular food supplement every day.

By the end of the trial, this one new habit made a remarkable difference for Elliot. Rather than putting his mind on autopilot in front of the TV, he devoured Harry Potter books and even started going to the library after school. His parents couldn't believe the dramatic change in their son. By all measures, a simple food supplement (we'll tell you what it was below) had made Elliot more attentive and more focused—signs of an improved working memory.

What can food do for your working memory? A lot. In this chapter, you'll discover foods that enhance working memory, eating habits that boost your cognitive skills, and more. Bon appétit!

Focus on Foods That Fuel Working Memory

Your working memory is a function of your brain, and if your brain isn't working at its best, your working memory won't be either. Food provides the building blocks of your brain, so what you feed your brain feeds your working memory. In recent years, there has been a flood of media coverage of foods that bolster overall brain health. But we wanted to dig deeper to find the foods that specifically enhance working memory. We've filtered through all the latest research and zeroed in on the main building blocks for working memory, dividing them into three categories based on their effect on the brain:

- *Sustainers*: These foods help prevent your working memory from deteriorating.
- *Boosters and protectors*: These foods encourage neuron growth and increase blood flow in the brain, which boosts working memory. They also protect against neuron inflammation and cell aging, which are associated with cognitive decline.
- *Sparkers*: These foods make it easier for electrical signals to pass between neurons. The faster a signal can get from one neuron to the next without encumbrance, the clearer and better your working memory is going to be.

If you want to enhance your working memory, stock up on the following sustainers, boosters and protectors, and sparkers.

Sustainers

Dairy

We've all heard that milk does a body good, and from the latest research, it looks as if it may do your working memory good too. A number of studies have shown that the less dairy there is in a person's diet, the more likely he or she is to suffer cognitive decline. In 2012, an international team of researchers from Maine and Australia looked at the effect of dairy consumption (milk, yogurt, cheese, and even ice cream) on cognition. They gave more than nine hundred people between the ages of twenty-three and ninety-eight a series of cognitive tests, including a working memory one. The people who drank at least one glass of milk per day had a sharper working memory than those who didn't drink milk on a daily basis.

In fact, the highest scores in each of the eight measures of the cognitive tests were associated with those who had the highest daily dairy consumption. Note that the study measured the frequency of dairy intake rather than exact amounts (for example, two glasses rather than 8 ounces of milk), so it doesn't offer clear guidelines on exactly how much dairy to consume.

What about reduced-fat versus whole-fat dairy products? Does that make a difference for your working memory? The jury is still out. In the study above, consumption of whole-fat dairy products was not linked with poor cognitive performance. A 2012 study in the journal *Appetite* from one of these same Australian researchers specifically tested the effect of reduced-fat dairy intake on cognitive performance and found that consuming a diet rich in reduced-fat dairy may improve working memory.

The full-fat versus low-fat issue gets confusing because many studies have shown that consuming a diet high in saturated fat is associated with memory loss and cognitive decline. And whole-fat milk, cream, ice cream, and yogurt contain more saturated fat than reduced-fat varieties. This has led many experts to demonize whole-fat dairy products as brain drainers. But we aren't necessarily convinced that this is the case.

After all, when you look at the nutrition labels on cartons of milk, the differences in the amount of saturated fat between whole milk and low-fat milk aren't all that substantial, especially if you're drinking only one cup.

Type of milk	Saturated fat content per cup
Whole milk	5 grams
2 percent milk	3 grams

Going carefully through the data, we realized that the key words in most studies regarding saturated fat and poor cognitive performance are *high intake*. They don't say that saturated fat in and of itself is detrimental to mental acuity, but consuming too much of it is. While a small scoop of ice cream could help your working memory, a tub will probably hurt it. So don't worry so much about higher fat milk products, just make sure that you have them in moderation, like a little cream in your coffee, or a few portions of cheese.

Red Meat

Red meat has gotten a bad rap in recent years, but it has been shown to have benefits for working memory. Red meat contains two working memory-friendly nutrients: carnitine and vitamin B-12. Carnitine helps your body burn fat, and it is also associated with speeding up signals between neurons. The human body naturally produces carnitine in the liver and kidneys, though there is evidence to suggest that the older you get, the more you benefit from consuming it.

In one study with rats, carnitine was found to improve performance on tasks that required the use of their working memory. When doctors looked at the benefits of carnitine for centenarians, they found that it reduced their mental fatigue. Vitamin B-12 is also important because if you don't get enough of it, your brain will shrink, a symptom associated with diseases like Alzheimer's that are known to impair working memory.

The problem is that when you hear the words *red meat*, you probably think first about beef, by far the most popular red meat. But many cuts of beef are marbled with saturated fat. What's the key to getting carnitine and B-12 without too much fat? You should consider lean cuts of beef, including sirloin tip, top sirloin, and top round and bottom round. Keep an eye on portions too. We've traveled around the world and are well aware that when you order a steak in Paris, Singapore, or Guatemala, you get a serving about the size of the palm of your hand. In America, it seems that when you order a steak, you get everything but the horns and hooves on your plate. As with full-fat dairy, a little goes a long way.

One other red meat is worth mentioning because it is high in carnitine and also has more B-12 than beef, but is extremely lean. That is venison, or deer meat. Of course, hunting down venison may not be easy. It is usually found only in butcher shops or specialty markets, so you may not find it in your local grocery store. If you can't track down venison in your area, check online retailers or make friends with a local hunter so you can get wild, fresh, hormone-free, steroid-free, antibiotic-free meat.

Boosters and Protectors

Boosters and protectors are mainly plant-based foods, including fruits and vegetables, that are rich in flavonoids, photochemicals that act as powerful antioxidants. There are thousands of flavonoids, and they give vegetables and fruits much of their color—they put the blue in blueberries and the red in grapes, for example.

In a 2009 review of studies investigating the benefits of flavonoids, the researchers found that they can enhance working memory and also protect against memory deficits associated with the normal aging process. What is it about flavonoids that make them so wonderful for working memory?

- They can cross the blood-brain barrier, which protects your brain from infection by sealing it off from the bad guys like dangerous pathogens. But flavonoids can bypass this barrier. If the blood-brain barrier is like the bonnet of a car, flavonoids are like the mechanics that can open the bonnet, take a look, and fix the engine.

- One of the ways they fix the engine is by improving circulation in the brain, allowing it to get the blood it needs when you are performing a complex mental task. If you were an athlete and unable to get blood to your muscles, you wouldn't last long on the field. In the same way, your brain needs blood when thinking, and flavonoids help it move through your brain.

- They reduce oxidative stress, which prematurely ages and can even kill your neurons. Neuronal cell death is a major contributing factor to dementia.

- They modulate neuroinflammation, a natural response to brain injury and disease that, if unchecked, can lead to progressive damage to the neurons. Flavonoids may pull neuroinflammation back before it gets out of hand.

- They stimulate neuronal regeneration even in adulthood. Your brain is made up of neurons, and if too many are damaged or die, that's going to affect your working memory. By regenerating your neurons, flavonoids help your whole brain achieve its potential, including, of course, your working memory.

Here are some great sources of flavonoids:

- Berries: elderberries (these are off the charts in flavonoid content), blueberries, blackberries, cranberries, black raspberries (for highest flavonoid content, opt for raw, unfrozen berries)

- Herbs and spices: capers, dill weed, parsley, sage, thyme

- Dark chocolate, at least 70 percent cocoa (tastes great too)

- Vegetables: collard greens, kale, spinach

- Black-eyed peas

- Green tea, black tea

- Plums (raw)

- Red wine (cabernet and syrah are very high), dessert wines. You can also try blueberry, blackberry, and cranberry wines.

Sparkers

Sparkers are the foods that make it easier for electrical signals to pass between neurons. The faster a signal can get from one neuron to the next without encumbrance, the clearer and better your working memory is going to be. To move from neuron to neuron, the signal has to pass through the cell walls of each neuron, and cell walls accommodate this transmission by either opening or closing little tunnels in the walls. These cell walls are made of fat, and the more flexible the fat, the easier it is for cell walls to open and close as required.

The most flexible fats for the brain are the omega-3 fatty acids, DHA, and EPA. When your brain is stocked up on these fats, the tunnels can open and close with ease, and the signals can flow between neurons like they're in the carpool lane. This means enhanced performance for your working memory.

Remember Elliot, the nine-year-old who moved from the couch to the library and from video games to tomes? It was an omega-3 fatty acid supplement that made all the difference for him. Scientific evidence points to omega-3 fatty acids as working memory enhancers. Even if you're a healthy young buck and sharp as a whip, your working memory will benefit from omega-3. A 2012 study gave omega-3 to healthy young adults (ages 18–25) over a period of six months. They found that their working improved significantly by the end of the six months. On the other hand, a deficiency of omega-3s can cause your working memory to suffer. For example, in a 2012 study of three thousand participants, researchers from UCLA discovered that adults with lower levels of DHA performed worse on tasks requiring working memory than those who had higher levels of DHA.

Our prehistoric ancestors may have also hugely benefited from the omega-3 found in oily fish. Fossils of Neandertals, who died out in prehistory, show no evidence of marine protein in their bone collagen. The remains of prehistoric humans, however, show evidence of fish protein in their collagen: up to 50 percent of their diet was made up of marine animals. Some researchers suggest that the beginning of the consumption of fish coincides with the emergence of art and culture in prehistoric humans, activities that are heavily reliant on working memory (more on this in the chapter 13).

Some of the best sources of DHA and EPA are oily fish like salmon, tuna, trout, mackerel, and sardines. You can also get it from venison and other lean red meats, as well as from DHA-enriched eggs. Plant-based sources include walnuts, flax seeds, and green leafy vegetables. DHA and EPA are also widely available in supplement form and in oils, such as cod liver oil and flaxseed oil. Be aware, however, that animal-based foods and supplements provide more benefit for the brain than plant-based ones.

Foods Containing DHA or EPA

- Oily fish: mackerel, salmon, sardines, trout, tuna
- Venison and lean meats
- DHA-enriched eggs

Make It a Habit: Whip Up Working Memory Meals

Ross is a bona-fide foodie who loves using his working memory to create and improvise in the kitchen, much to the delight of Tracy and our two sons. Here for the first time, he is sharing the recipes for two of his favorite meals that incorporate some of the foods that sustain, boost, protect, and spark working memory. Portions are for one. Use your working memory to expand these recipes as you like. And note that Ross tends to cook using a pinch of this and a dab of that, so when you see these terms in the recipes, just add those ingredients to taste—there's no right or wrong amount.

Meal 1: Venison with Black-Eyed Peas

Venison typically has a slightly gamey flavor. If you're a newbie when it comes to eating venison, opt for roe deer, which has a milder flavor. The trick to cooking wild game is to cook it with things that can be found in the forest that it came from.

Venison

> 1 venison steak or several medallions from the filet, thawed (total serving size: about the size of the palm of your hand)
> 2 splashes olive oil
> pinch flaked sea salt
> pinch ground pepper
> 6–7 juniper berries, crushed flat with spoon or mortar and pestle
> 5–6 blueberries or blackberries
> 1 clove garlic
> 1 sprig thyme
> a dab of whole-grain mustard (Maille has a lovely flavor)
> 1–2 generous sloshes port wine

1. Splash olive oil on venison and season with salt, pepper, and crushed juniper berries.
2. Set aside to marinate.
3. Preheat a pan (steel, if you have one) on a low temperature setting for 5 minutes or so.
4. Splash olive oil in pan and place marinated venison in pan.
5. Place berries, garlic, thyme, and dab of mustard around venison (not under it).
6. Cook 3 minutes or so until the meat is brown on bottom, then turn over. While cooking, jostle berries and garlic so they don't burn.
7. Cook 3 more minutes, or until brown.
8. Remove venison and set aside.
9. Pour in port and deglaze the pan, crushing berries, garlic, mustard, and thyme with a wooden spoon. To deglaze, pour liquid in

the pan and use a wooden spoon to remove the residue from the bottom of the pan so it all dissolves. This adds flavor to the sauce.
10. Slice venison thinly. Pour port sauce through a sieve over the top of the venison. Serve.

Black-Eyed Peas

1 splash olive oil
*Optional: 2–3 small cubes of bacon (adds great
    flavor, just make sure they are small)*
½ onion
½ red pepper, chopped
small pinch flaked sea salt
small pinch black pepper
½ cup black-eyed peas, soaked overnight and
    boiled until soft (retain water)
Optional: 1 slosh of port wine

1. Splash olive oil in small, preheated pot.
2. Add bacon cubes and cook until brown.
3. Add onion, red pepper, salt, and pepper and cook until onions are translucent.
4. Add black-eyed peas with some of their liquid, and maybe a slosh of port if you desire.
5. Reduce liquor until black-eyed peas are glazed. Serve.

Dessert

Selection of cheeses, such as Stilton, Beaufort,
    and Brie (one small slice of each)

Meal 2: Salmon and Steamed Kale

Salmon

    1 salmon fillet (4–5 oz.)
    2 splashes olive oil
    small pinch flaked sea salt
    small pinch ground black pepper
    1 tablespoon dill, chopped
    1 dab whole-grain mustard
    ½ lemon plus ¼ lemon
    2 handfuls kale, chopped
    1 tablespoon capers

1. Preheat pan on low heat.
2. Splash olive oil on salmon and rub in salt, pepper, dill, and mustard.
3. Place in preheated pan and squeeze ½ lemon on salmon. Cover with a plate or a large lid.
4. Cook for a few minutes on each side.
5. Take the salmon out of pan and squeeze ¼ lemon on it.
6. Let it cool for a few minutes so it will absorb the lemon.
7. While salmon is cooling, steam chopped kale in a pot for a few minutes; dress with olive oil.
8. Top salmon with capers and serve with dressed kale.

Dessert: Berries with Dark Chocolate Sauce

    2 heaping tablespoons fresh blackberries
    2 heaping tablespoons fresh blueberries
    2 heaping tablespoons fresh raspberries
      or
    4–6 heaping tablespoons of any berries you can get
    about 1.5 oz. dark chocolate (Lindt is Ross's favorite)
    2 tablespoons heavy cream

1. Put cream and chocolate bar in a pot over low heat and melt while whisking constantly.
2. Pour sauce over berries and serve.

Wine suggestion: For both meals, choose a cabernet, syrah, blueberry, or blackberry wine. If you really must have a white wine with fish, go ahead, but don't fool yourself into thinking it is doing much for your working memory!

2. Curb Consumption and Take a Periodic Break from Food

It's not just what you eat that affects your working memory, it's how much you eat. A growing body of research reveals that obesity, which is often caused by overeating, is associated with memory loss, cognitive dysfunction, and a poor working memory. At the opposite end of the spectrum, evidence suggests that eating less can have big health benefits, including improved working memory. Two strategies in particular have shown remarkable results:

- Calorie restriction (CR): Eating fewer calories while maintaining adequate nutrition

- Intermittent fasting (IF): Alternating between periods of fasting—consuming nothing but water—and eating

CR has its roots in decades of studies showing that rodents, mice, and rhesus monkeys on restricted diets perform better on cognitive tasks than their free-eating peers. Exactly how eating less protects working memory function is still up for debate. Mark Mattson of John Hopkins University speculates that such diets create a kind of immunity against brain degeneration. Eating less produces a mild stress response in our brain neurons. In response to this stressor, we develop a resistance to more serious stressors associated with the aging process. As part of this stress response, the body releases an important protein, brain-derived neurotropic factor (BDNF), which has a protective effect on neurons and encourages new neuron growth. Some studies show that having lower BDNF levels in the brain is associated with lower working memory.

Mattson also found that eating less may save you from the cognitive ravages of a brain disease. In a study, Mattson subjected rats to a degenerative brain disease associated with memory loss. Then he put some of those rats on an IF diet, giving them access to food on alternate days only. The other rats were allowed to eat unlimited amounts of chow. The rats were given working memory tests periodically as they aged. With age, the all-you-can-eat rats started showing signs of cognitive dysfunction. But the IF rats showed no signs of working memory impairment; they were able to sidestep the mental losses.

If you think you are too old to see the benefits of such a diet, you're wrong. One experiment on elderly rats showed actual improvements in working memory tasks as a result of following an IF diet. This gives us hope that it's never too late to start feeding—or perhaps *not* feeding— your working memory for peak performance.

But here's the question everyone wants to know. It may work on rats, but what about humans? After all, if you are going to regularly restrict your diet or periodically stop eating altogether, how do you know it will have a positive effect for your cognition? Scientists are currently exploring how CR may be beneficial to humans by using human participants in the experiments. One team of researchers reported in a 2009 issue of *Proceedings of the National Academy of Sciences* that elderly participants who restricted their diet by 30 percent for three months increased their verbal memory scores, while participants who did not restrict calories showed no improvement in verbal memory.

The first long-term study on CR in humans, the CALERIE Trial of Human Caloric Restriction from researchers at Tufts University in Boston, is just beginning to reveal some of its findings. In this trial, participants cut 10 to 30 percent of their daily calories for six months. In 2011, the researchers published some of their initial results, showing that CR showed positive changes in some measures associated with aging. We don't know if the CALERIE trial will measure working memory scores in future papers, but we certainly hope so. Based on the research using rats and humans, there is good reason to expect that limiting your food intake will benefit your cognition. In fact, we believe that this research is so promising that we are willing to not put our food where our mouth is, and fast every week.

Make It a Habit: Eat less.

We have one crucial recommendation about trying CR or IF: *check with your doctor before starting any type of reduced-calorie diet or fast.*

If you're interested in CR, you can learn more about it from the CR Society International (www.crsociety.org). Most of the scientific research on IF is based on alternate-day fasting, but there may also be benefits in less frequent fasting. Here's how we do it. Ross fasts for up to sixty continuous hours a week and Tracy fasts for thirty-six continuous hours a week (drinking water and the occasional espresso). You may initially think that this is impossible, but we assure you, you get used to it and can perform your daily activities without impairment. In fact, we run about 6 miles a day when fasting, though we don't push for a top time. Best tip? Avoid delicious smells. However, this is not always possible, and circumstances recently conspired to place Ross directly across from a contented Tracy tucking into a steak about forty-eight hours into his fast. Ross breaks his fast with a berry smoothie, some salmon, and steamed kale.

3. Take a Whiff of Rosemary or Peppermint

Shakespeare was on to something when he had Ophelia say to Laertes, "There's rosemary, that's for remembrance, pray you love, remember." The memory-enhancing properties of rosemary were extolled by the ancient Greeks; scholars in fact wore wreaths of rosemary to help them remember during their exams. Today, thanks to British psychologist Mark Moss, we know that rosemary is great not just for cooking but also for your working memory.

In a 2003 study, Moss randomly assigned a group of adults to one of three groups: a rosemary group, a lavender group, and a control group. None of the participants were told that they would be asked to smell any essential oils. All three groups were seated in test cubicles as they took a series of cognitive tests, including working memory tests. For both the rosemary and lavender groups, four drops of pure essential oils were placed in a device that diffused the scent. The device was placed out of sight and was switched on five minutes before the participant entered the testing room.

In the working memory task, participants were shown five numbers at a rate of one number per second. Then they were shown thirty different numbers and had to respond with a "yes" or "no" if the numbers matched the original five numbers. They did this three times, with different number sets each time.

Moss found that the rosemary group performed much better in the working memory tasks compared to the control group. However, lavender had the opposite effect: the participants in this group did even worse than the controls. Moss suggested that rosemary has an arousing effect that can improve working memory performance, while lavender has a sedative effect.

How can a scent affect your working memory? Active compounds present in the aromas may be absorbed through the mucous membranes in the nose or lungs. And because these compounds are tiny, they can travel across the blood–brain barrier and affect brain activity. One particularly important neurotransmitter, acetylcholine, plays a key role in maintaining attention. Moss speculated that inhaling the rosemary tincture prevents the breakdown of acetylcholine, which allows you to focus your attention for longer.

Moss ran a similar study comparing ylang-ylang and peppermint oils using the same procedure as we have described. In this trial, the people who got a whiff of the peppermint group had higher working memory scores compared to the ylang-ylang group.

So when you need to stay focused but feel tired or are thinking slowly, dab a little rosemary or peppermint oil on a tissue (not directly on the skin) to keep near you.

4. Do It or Ditch It? The Real Scoop on
Caffeine, Candy, and Cocktails

It seems as if almost every day, we come across conflicting views on caffeine. It may make you alert, but it can also raise your cholesterol. The same goes for alcohol—one day it's lauded for its health benefits, and the next day it's going to put you on the fast track to dementia. And sugar? Sugar has taken a real beating lately, with some calling it a poison that is literally killing us. What's the real story on these foods? Do they affect working memory, and if so, how?

A Cuppa Joe or Just Say No?

Coffee: it's the blessed liqueur of hyperactive programmers, the fuel of eighteenth-century coffeehouse culture, and the salvation of two authors with two young boys, full-time jobs, and a looming deadline for a book on working memory. We love coffee. Ross loves it so much that he was willing to spend a sizable portion of our book advance on a $4,000 precision Swiss espresso machine known as the Cremina. Fortunately, a saner head (Tracy's) prevailed, and the magical machine was not purchased. Why do we love coffee so much? Aside from its intoxicating aroma and rich flavor, the fact that a cup of brew can boost alertness and help us zero in on the positive (chapter 3, "Exercise 2") doesn't hurt either.

Despite this, and our own anecdotal experience, as well as the received knowledge of hundreds of years, a recent study has shown that caffeine is not an unequivocal blessing to working memory. If a task requires just light working memory involvement, caffeine can boost performance. However, if a task requires a heavy working memory involvement, then caffeine won't give you the perk you were hoping for, and it may even impair your performance. A heavy working memory load means that you are already over-aroused as a result of anxiety or stress. Consuming caffeine will only add to the stress and anxiety and ultimately diminish your performance.

Do it or ditch it? Do it, but save the joe for the easy jobs.

What does this mean for the average Joe in need of a cup of joe? If the job at hand is somewhat familiar and requires only a cursory manipulation of information—like making a few minor changes to an existing presentation for a new audience—then caffeine will make it easier. But if you're putting together new information for a once-in-a-lifetime, career-defining presentation, avoid that cup until you finish.

Put a Cap on the Nightcap?

The question of whether alcohol consumption affects working memory isn't easy to answer. Research showing that binge drinking and alcoholism cause a drain on working memory appears to be irrefutable. But it's in terms of moderate drinking that the conclusions get a little cloudy. Some research shows that it's detrimental, while other findings show no effect on working memory.

Scott Saults and Nelson Cowan at the University of Missouri set out to find out why the results were so variable. They recruited healthy adults who were moderate social drinkers, and had not been in treatment for substance abuse problems or arrested for any alcohol-related offenses. They gave some participants a vodka tonic and others a placebo (a highly diluted tonic). Then they were given two different types of working memory tasks: in one version, all the information was presented at the same time, and in the other version, they were presented with the information one piece at a time.

The researchers found that alcohol consumption impaired working memory when information is taken in piece by piece. In contrast, alcohol consumption did not impair performance when all the information was presented at the same time. Saults and Cowan suggest that alcohol creates a kind of myopia where it reduces our ability to use working memory to multitask. This means that we find it hard to focus on tasks where we have to divide our attention between two or more things. So if we don't have all the information available at the same time and we have to keep something active and add it to a new piece of information, a vodka tonic won't help.

Do it or ditch it? Do it, but if you need to multitask, skip the glass of booze.

If you've got some serious multitasking to do, avoid drinking. But rest assured that from the research to date, it appears that moderate drinking isn't likely to damage your working memory. In our opinion, the flavonoid content in red, blackberry, or blueberry wine makes these the best option if you choose to drink. Just remember there can be too much of a good thing, so stick to light or moderate drinking, and whatever you do, don't drive.

A Spoonful of Sugar or a Spoonful of Poison?

Sugar always gets a bad rap, but calling it a "poison" may be a little over the top. Without sugar, you wouldn't be able to think at all. Your brain runs on glucose (a sugar), and the more you think, the more it uses. In fact, a recent review of studies on the effect of glucose has also shown that working memory gets a boost when you have a sugar boost. British psychologist Michael Smith reported that ingesting something sugary (and not a sugar substitute like aspartame) can boost working memory. However, this works only when the task is difficult. When the tasks were easy, glucose didn't improve working memory at all. A difficult task quickly depletes the supply of glucose to the brain, more so than an easy task. So a quick sugar burst can bring your working memory performance back to optimum levels.

This doesn't mean that you should chow down as many candy bars as you can. An excess of sugar can be very bad for your overall health. And sugary junk food like doughnuts often comes with other health busters like transfats.

Do it or ditch it? Do it, but don't overdo it. Most people get enough glucose as it is, and many get far too much (think type 2 diabetes). If you think you may benefit from a little bit more of it when feeling mentally sluggish, check with your doctor first. You can get your glucose a number of ways, through starchy foods like potatoes, through fruit including cantaloupe or watermelon, or from glucose tablets. If you are getting your glucose through food, your body takes time to digest it so that it is readily available for your brain to use.

11

Seven Habits to Supercharge Working Memory . . . and a Few to Avoid

TRAINING AND EATING the right way are great for your working memory. Several ordinary routines can also bolster your working memory powers. We highly recommend that you make them daily habits that show a direct impact on working memory.

Habit 1: Give Your Working Memory a Rest

While you are blissfully snoozing the night away, your working memory is recharging, similar to the recharging of your cell phone overnight. And just as if you forget to charge your phone, it may stop working when you need it most. In order to be sure your working memory will kick in when you need it, you need adequate sleep. A wealth of studies on sleep and working memory have shown that a lack of sleep can make it much harder for your Conductor to make music—regardless of your age.

How Much Sleep Do You Need?

Age	Hours
Toddlers (1–3)	12–14
Preschoolers (3–5)	11–13
Kids (5–12)	10–11
Teens	8.5–9.25
Adults	7–9
Seniors	7–9

Kids

Sleep is especially critical for young children, who need their z's for their developing working memory. It is believed that much of the brain maturation process takes place during sleep. In addition, research shows that when youngsters don't get the sleep they need, their working memory pays the price and their classroom performance suffers.

Teens

Teens are better able than younger kids to compensate for sleep deprivation before it starts affecting their working memory functioning. For example, Mary Carskadon at Brown University found that teenagers were able to perform a working memory task successfully with just four hours of sleep. But when the stakes were increased to tasks that required more effort, their performance suffered, especially if they had stayed up all night.

If you've ever been the parent of a teenager, you know how hard it can be to get teens to go to bed early and what a struggle it can be to get them out of bed in the morning. But this doesn't mean your teen is lazy or purposely disobedient. Studies have found that at the onset of puberty, teenagers develop a delayed sleep pattern known as a two-hour sleep-wake phase. This simply means that due to their body's changing needs, they need to go to sleep later at night and need more sleep in the morning. They still need about the same amount of sleep as when they were tweens, but they need it at different times.

Not convinced that your teen isn't just being lazy in the mornings? Consider this. In a recent study, Judith Owens and colleagues at the Hasbro Children's Hospital in Rhode Island worked with a high school to delay the start time to allow students to get extra sleep in the morning. Did it make a difference? Did it ever! The teenagers were more alert and reported feeling less irritated during the day. Their mental health also improved—fewer students reported feeling depressed—and fewer students skipped class. The study was considered a success by the school and the students, and the late start for the school is now permanent. So the next time you're having trouble rousting your teenagers out of bed, remember that their late-night, late-morning sleeping pattern is recharging their working memory.

Adults

One of the most important functions of working memory is quickly accessing information stored in your hippocampus (your brain's library), and sleep is a crucial link in the chain between working memory and the hippocampus. If you want to emblazon something on your hippocampus, sleep on it—literally. A good night's rest can improve the retention of what you're learning, according to a 2012 study by Jessica Payne at the University of Notre Dame. Payne's team gave participants word pairs to remember either in the morning or at night and they tested them twelve hours later. The folks who studied the words at night, then went to sleep, and were tested in the morning remembered the word pairs better than those who learned the words in the morning and were tested at night. Even more interesting was that after twenty-four hours, when all participants had slept and been awake, the memory performance for those who learned the words at night had improved even more. Payne suggested that sleep can stabilize the information we send to our memory stores and make it more permanent.

A lack of sleep, and especially a string of sleepless nights, doesn't do your working memory any favors. A review of studies on sleep deprivation and cognitive function in the journal *SLEEP* showed that long-term sleep deprivation resulted in problems performing the simplest of cognitive tasks. If you've ever fumbled with your car keys while opening the front door or buttoned your shirt wrong after several days of insomnia, you know what we're talking about. But surprisingly, this same review found that people who had trouble with the simplest tasks could still muster their working memory to cooperate on more complex tasks. How can that be?

When you experience sleep deprivation, your brain goes into conservation mode and shuts down some of the more basic cognitive mechanisms. According to sleep researcher Paul Whitney at Washington University, working memory steps in to compensate for the poor functioning of these basic processes and helps us perform more complex tasks when we are fatigued.

But before you burn the midnight oil without worrying about your working memory, there is a catch. In 2010, Lisa Chuah and a team of researchers at Duke-NUS Medical School in Singapore found that the ability of working memory to compensate has its limits. They gave a group of adults a working memory task that required them to remember certain photos while ignoring distracting photos that suggested negative emotions—like people getting punched or mugged. The adults did the task under two conditions: when they were well rested and when they were sleep deprived. They found that when participants were well rested, they were able to use better their working memory to remember the right pictures and ignore the distracting ones, but when they were sleep deprived, they struggled with the task. In the real world, this means that when you don't catch your z's, your Conductor can struggle to help you focus on what you are supposed to.

During testing, when the participants were well rested and when sleep deprived, the scientists performed brain scans. By scanning while subjects were well rested, the scientists could see what their brain patterns looked like when working memory functioned normally, and then compare these patterns with sleep-deprived patterns. When the sleep-deprived adults saw the negative emotional pictures, there was an increase of brain activity in the amygdala and a decrease of activity in the PFC. There was also less interaction between these two brain areas when the adults were distracted by these photos. This pattern suggests that sleep deprivation not only makes us more likely to react emotionally but also makes it harder for our Conductor to control our emotions. If you've ever found yourself more likely to snap when presented with a challenging or emotional situation after working into the wee hours of the morning, you have this brain pattern to blame. If you find yourself struggling to control your emotions, turn off the computer or TV at night and take the remedy of rest for your frayed nerves.

Older Adults

The notion that if you're a older adult, you don't need as much sleep as you did in your thirties, forties, and fifties is a myth. You still need the same seven to nine hours of rest, but you may not be getting those hours due to problems falling asleep or staying asleep. The good news is that some research is showing that a lack of sleep may not be as much of a brain drain for the older crowd. One study comparing the impact of sleep deprivation on working memory found that older adults were able to recover much better than their younger counterparts. A group of young adults aged nineteen to thirty-eight performed worse on tasks that required working memory as a result of sleep deprivation compared to when they had adequate sleep, but the adults aged fifty-nine and up performed just as well with or without adequate sleep. Lead investigator Sean Drummond suggests that older adults who are healthy are more resilient and can fend off stressors such as sleep loss.

Quantity Versus Quality

Most of the advice you see on sleep and its effect on working memory focuses on the number of hours of shut-eye you should get. But when it comes to working memory, the quality of sleep also makes a difference. Evva Aronen and colleagues at the University of Helsinki in Finland looked at this issue in a group of six- to thirteen-year-olds over three days. They measured both the quantity of sleep and quality of sleep, including periods of light sleep and deep sleep.

In order to measure the sleep quality, participants were given sensors to wear on their wrist that recorded their movements on a minute-by-minute basis. In addition to recording their sleep patterns, the students also completed verbal and visual working memory tests. Aronen and the team found that those who took longer to fall into deep sleep and spent the least amount of time in deep sleep made more errors in the working memory tasks.

Make It a Habit: Sleep Smarter

The bottom line is that you should make sleep a priority in your life rather than burning the candle at both ends and aim for seven to nine hours of quality sleep at night. Here are a few tips on how to do it.

- Create a sleep schedule, and stick to it seven days a week. Schedule time for your sleep the way you would schedule a meeting. Be on time and be prepared: that means pajamas on, face washed, and teeth brushed.

- Turn off the TV an hour before your sleep time.

- Turn off your computer, cell phone, tablet, and gaming console an hour before your sleep time.

- Unplug anything in your bedroom with standby lights.

- Skip the coffee and alcohol after dinner. Coffee disrupts sleep and alcohol can prevent you from getting that restorative deep sleep your working memory needs.

Habit 2: Clear Clutter to Clear the Cobwebs in Your Working Memory

When we lived in Edinburgh, we owned a two-bedroom Victorian apartment with a panoramic view of Edinburgh, including a medieval castle that was hauntingly lit in the evening with torch light. Sometimes the gold light from a setting sun reflected off the windows of other buildings, turning the whole city into El Dorado. The cost of this stunning view was a stunning lack of space. Knickknacks wrestled for shelf space, an inordinate amount of specialized cooking tools spilled out of kitchen drawers, and mountains of books threatened to avalanche. Our bursting closet was packed in such a manner that whatever you happened to need was inevitably the least accessible. On one occasion, Ross had to go to the emergency room because of a possible hernia sustained when trying to excavate a suitcase.

Worse, the clutter was beginning to affect us all. Our older son didn't have much space in his bedroom and that contributed to making him irritable. We both lost important documents in the mess, and of course, it was always the other person's fault.

We desperately wanted to move to a bigger place, but the realtor took one look around and told us our Victorian apartment wouldn't sell unless we removed most of the stuff. So we gave the place a good cleaning. By virtue of necessity, the only things that stayed were those we used all the time. This had two benefits: (1) we now had space to live in, and (2) if we wanted something, we knew exactly where it was. We thought we would miss all that stuff. But the opposite happened: we felt unburdened. We were much happier, and our relationship experienced far less friction. By getting rid of stuff, everyone got along much better. We found that the extra space also meant that we could now use our working memory much more effectively, such as when researching for this book, making dinner, paying the bills, and planning a trip.

This got us thinking about the relationship between clutter and working memory. There is little hard science on the topic, but based on everything we know about working memory and the striking difference in our own experience of living in a cluttered and then clutter-free environment, we have a hunch that the more stuff littering your living and work space, the greater the demand your living space inflicts on your working memory in all sorts of daily ways. If your working memory is fully engaged just trying to find an important piece of paper you need— "Honey, where did you put that paper with the account details?" "I don't know. Didn't you put it away?"—you have less bandwidth to devote to the task itself.

We suggest that if you want to be as productive as possible, have as few books, folders, pens, and scribbled notes littering both your physical work space and your mental work space. This goes for the clutter on your computer too. When your files are randomly scattered, retrieving what you need is a good deal harder. You spend much too much time hunting down files. And typically, as you search for any given file, you come across others that sidetrack you from the task at hand. An hour or so later, you realize you never finished the project you set out to accomplish.

Make It a Habit: When in Doubt, Throw It Out

To keep clutter from taking over, follow these suggestions.

- If you buy something new, you must throw out, donate, or otherwise get rid of something you already own. Buy a new pair of shoes? An old pair has to go.

- Play the "cherish it or chuck it" game. Once a week or once a month, depending on the level of your clutter, evaluate ten "treasures" in your home and ask yourself if you really cherish them. If you don't, chuck it. Try another version called "use it or lose it" with practical items. If you haven't used it in the last thirty days, lose it.

- Schedule a few minutes—really, that's all it takes—to straighten up each day. Do this on your computer too, sorting emails into folders or into the trash and otherwise cleaning it up.

De-cluttering and "organizing" has become big business. Just look at the number of big-box retailers, such as The Container Store, that have popped up around the country selling goods that promise to help you clear the clutter. Some four thousand "de-clutter experts" claim membership in the National Association of Professional Organizers. Do some quick searching on Google and you can find clutter blogs (*Clutter-DietBlog*, *CleaningUpTheClutter*, *Unclutterer*), books (*The Clutter Diet*, *Unclutter Your Life in One Week*), and more. In all, the de-cluttering industry is estimated to be nearing $1 billion a year in business. So if you feel you might need a little guidance, help is close at hand.

Habit 3: Move It, Naturally!

As you recall, running—and especially barefoot running—is a phenomenal way to spark your working memory power. But barefoot running certainly isn't the only type of exercise that can boost working memory. We would like to introduce you to a revolutionary approach to working out that gets your body moving the way it was intended to move: MovNat.

MovNat gets you outside—a working memory booster in itself—and moving your body in a natural, efficient manner. MovNat is the original workout; the workout our prehistoric ancestors had to do every day in order to survive—jumping, running, climbing, throwing, crawling, and balancing in a random, natural environment.

The idea is to go on a walk or run in a random, unpredictable environment—over branches, under bushes, up a tree, and around boulders. That's MovNat. And there's a groundswell of belief that this type of movement is more beneficial than any gym workout. MovNat founder Erwan Le Corre describes gyms as zoos—unnatural environments entirely unsuited to the animals they contain. A human in a gym is like a caged lion, a fish in a bowl, a hungry bear staring across a moat at some guy named Bob eating a chili dog.

We wanted to see the effects of unleashing the human animal on working memory. So Ross headed out to a park with a MovNat group for a workout. For seven hours, he learned to balance, walk, and crawl on railings like a cat, crawl on the ground on all fours, roll, carry heavy and awkward objects, spin on bars like a gymnast, and climb up poles. And he got a workout. Let's just put it this way. The last time the muscles in his feet felt this sore, they had run thirty-three miles at one time. At every stage, to do the movement efficiently, he had to be very aware of his body and calculate where to place it. When he lost that mindfulness and focus, he fell over.

Before the MovNat workshop began, Ross gave all participants a working memory test: remembering numbers in backward order. On average, the participants, between eighteen and forty-nine years old, could successfully remember about four numbers in backward order. As the day's workout progressed, Ross tested them again, at lunchtime, with a different set of numbers. This time they could remember five numbers in backward order. By the end of the day, despite being tired and muddy after training for so many hours, they were now able to remember about six numbers in backward order, or 50 percent more than they were able to in the morning.

Make It a Habit: Unleash the Animal

The first thing that Ross learned is that his body already knew what to do. Here are a few things Ross's body relearned:

Mindfulness: This one is easy. Pay attention to what your body is doing, and pay attention to how you are moving. To get a sense of the difference this makes, get close to the ground, close your eyes, and move in ways that you don't usually. Pay attention to the differences in how your body feels.

Balance: Balance is a process, and according to MovNat, when you are in an environment you don't control, "balancing is the act of continually losing and regaining balance." To balance, you have to be imbalanced at points. Be careful, though, and take baby steps with this one. Start by walking on the edge of a curb, and work up slowly to more difficult tasks, like balancing on a railing.

Walking: This one you can do with little danger. Go off the trail; step over logs, crouch, move sideways. Whatever you do with this, get off the beaten path.

Crawl on all fours: Get down and dirty with this one. Crawl on your belly, crawl with your knees on the ground, and crawl with your knees off the ground.

All of these skills and more—like climbing, running, jumping, throwing, and catching—will help improve your working memory. If you'd like to find out more about MovNat, and want to learn the movements right the first time, go to movnat.com.

Habit 4: Get Creative

Tracy was recently at a dinner in Copenhagen for a conference on working memory, and the conversation turned to how creativity engages working memory. An art teacher described how she gave her students three paint colors—red, green, and white—and asked them to paint a seaside portrait. It wasn't long before one bright student, Taylor, came up and asked her for blue paint. "I can't paint the ocean without blue," Taylor explained. The art teacher nodded in understanding but said, "Yes, but you have three colors. Paint with those." After trying to explain it to the teacher a few more times, Taylor dejectedly went back to her seat. But before long, she had painted a brilliant seascape with an amazing combination of the three colors. This teacher knew that by giving her students such limitations, she would encourage them to be their most creative. This is also a good way to encourage your Conductor to work with what you have.

We know this thanks to research from Andreas Fink at the University of Graz in Austria. He performed brain scans on people as he gave them problems that they had to solve creatively, for example, asking them to think about an everyday object and come up with unusual uses for it, such as using a tin can as a mirror. The scans showed that as they were coming up with creative uses, the areas of the brain associated with working memory were strongly activated.

Make It a Habit: Pull a MacGyver

Remember MacGyver? The TV character who could turn table salt and a candy bar into a bomb or transform a rattan chair and a brassiere into a hang glider? One way to keep your working memory in shape is to regularly unleash your inner MacGyver. Take an everyday object and use your working memory to conjure up at least three unconventional uses for it. A fork, for example, can be refashioned into a fish hook, a paint scraper, or a lever for opening stubborn jam jars. See what uses you can devise for an old wine bottle, a piece of string, or any other common object at hand, like a stapler. Of course, you don't actually have to MacGyver them; just imagining doing so will do the trick, and it might be safer. (Ross collaborated with a friend on the construction of a potato launcher from a piece of pipe, hydrogen gas, and a milk carton. Unfortunately, they forgot to glue it all together, and the device exploded when launched.)

Habit 5: Doodle

Have you ever been caught doodling during a class or a meeting? Well, take heart that what you were doing might have helped you better understand the information. Whenever you are trying to make sense of new information, like growth forecasts, you need your working memory, and the problem is that in a long class or meeting, your working memory can be worn down, especially if the presentation is boring, even if the information is important. Eventually you will tune out, and the information will sail over your head. But new research shows that doodling can help you remember information by recruiting your working memory.

British psychologist Jackie Andrade asked volunteers to listen to a boring conversation but told them they didn't have to remember any of the information. Half of the volunteers were asked to doodle, and the other half weren't. At the end of the taped message, Andrade confessed to the participants that she had deceived them and that they actually had to recall not only the names of the people mentioned, but the places as well. Andrade found that the doodlers remembered more names and places compared to those in the control group.

This "doodling effect" is probably due to keeping your working memory from drifting away. Doodling may keep your working memory at a minimal "arousal" state, so that you still pay attention instead of daydreaming. It is also great because it doesn't actually compete for working memory resources—doodling doesn't require much focus or effort—so you can still focus on the task at hand.

Make It a Habit: Doodle While You Work

If you want to encourage information retention at your meetings, make sure that everyone has a pencil and some paper and encourage them to doodle while others are speaking. Though it may seem rude, it is a way to increase productivity for the cost of a few sheets of paper. And if you ever find yourself dozing or daydreaming during a meeting, lecture, or class, grab a pencil and paper and start doodling.

Habit 6: Like Facebook

Facebook is omnipresent. Even if you don't have a Facebook account (like Ross), you know someone who does (like Tracy). When things become big and successful, they inevitably find detractors, and Facebook is no exception, with one study suggesting that Facebook can be harder to give up than smoking. That's certainly possible, but in moderation, Facebook can be great for your working memory.

In chapter 7, we talked about how longer Facebook membership is associated with higher working memory in teenagers. In a different study published in 2012, we asked almost three hundred adults how often they engaged in a range of different activities on Facebook, such as updating their own status, checking their friends' status updates, and chatting online. We found that one Facebook activity in particular led to higher working memory scores: checking friends' status updates. This makes sense because when you check a friend's status updates, you are using your working memory to delete the prior information you held in your hippocampus about what he or she had been up to and replacing it with new information. This effect is not exclusive to Facebook, of course. By checking in with friends by phone, you are engaging your working memory in the same way.

Make It a Habit: Keep in Touch

As long as you aren't losing hours a day to Facebook, go ahead and regularly see what your friends are up to. If you don't have an account and don't want to get one, still make sure that you are connecting regularly with people.

Habit 7: Go Outside

If you're feeling sluggish, head for the great outdoors. And no, we don't mean that you have to pack up the car and drive to the nearest national park for a vacation. Just go outside and find some trees and grass because communing with nature recharges working memory. Marc Berman and colleagues put nature to the test in 2008, and they found positive benefits. They asked thirty-eight adults to come into a lab and put them through over half an hour of cognitive testing, including a working memory test: remembering numbers in backward order. They also checked their mood by asking them to rate how well different adjectives, like *cheerful, enthusiastic,* and *bashful,* applied to them. After all this testing, the researchers asked two groups of participants to take an hour-long walk. One group walked in a park, while the other walked downtown. The walk through the park was lined with trees and secluded from traffic and people. In contrast, the downtown walk was largely on traffic-heavy streets that were lined with buildings. After returning from their respective walks, the participants retook the working memory test and again answered the same mood questionnaire. All of the participants returned the following week and carried out the same testing-walk-testing procedure. The only difference was that this time, they walked in the other location—the park walkers hoofed it downtown, and the downtown walkers strolled through the park.

The researchers found that when people walked through the park, their working memory scores were almost 20 percent higher. When they walked downtown it only improved by 5 percent. They suggest that nature has a restorative effect on working memory and even a short exposure in a single instance can make a difference.

Make It a Habit: Get Outside in Nature

When you need an instant working memory boost, go outside to a nearby park for a quick walk. This is a great practice to keep in mind if you're about to take a big test, make an important presentation, or solve a tricky problem at work.

Are Bad Habits Bad for Working Memory?

We all know about the many dangers of smoking and doing drugs. But what is their effect on working memory?

Is Nicotine Killing Your Working Memory?

In 2010, Stephen J. Heishman and a team of researchers at the National Institute on Drug Abuse in Maryland performed an analysis of a number of studies examining the relationship of nicotine to working memory, reviewing close to fifty articles on the effect of nicotine on cognitive skills. These studies, conducted from 1994 to 2008, compared the performance of nonsmokers (never smokers and former smokers) with smokers. The majority of the studies used the n-back task to measure working memory. The pattern was clear: when nonsmokers were given a nicotine gum, patch, or nasal spray, the nicotine burst did not harm their working memory scores. Nor, it is important to note, did nicotine improve them. But there's more to the story.

When the researchers looked at how fast the participants responded in the working memory tasks, both smokers and nonsmokers were much faster in responding after a burst of nicotine. And it wasn't just the gum, patch, and spray that did the trick. Even smoking a cigarette improved their reaction time. But before you petition your local education authority for free Nicorette to be handed out with lunch, note that the research-ers speculate that nicotine doesn't improve your working memory but rather your motor skills. In other words, you respond faster because your fingers are moving faster, not because your working memory is working better.

Weeding Out the Truth on Weed

Carl Hart from the New York State Psychiatric Institute gave fans of weed a boost when he reported in 2001 that research volunteers who had smoked an average of twenty-four marijuana cigarettes per week did not show any impairments in performing tests that involved work-ing memory. But don't make your brownies "magic" just yet—the story is not over.

Alecia Schweinsburg from the University of California recruited teenagers who were abusers of marijuana and alcohol and compared them with teenagers who were not abusing either substance. When she and her colleagues had these students perform a working mem-ory task, they found that both groups performed very similarly, just as in the Hart study. But the researchers also took brain scans while the teenagers were busy responding to the working memory task. And this revealed something very interesting: the marijuana-using teenagers had to work harder to achieve the same results on the working mem-ory task. Their PFC was working overtime to get to the same point as their peers. Furthermore, for marijuana users the part of the brain dedicated to monitoring information—the anterior cingulate cortex— showed less activation compared to the control group. The researchers suggest that the teenagers had to shift their PFC into overdrive in order to compensate for the demands of the task. We speculate that in a situ-ation with increasing demands on their attention, these students will struggle to recruit the cognitive resources required to execute the task effectively.

Opium: Mind Expanding or a Working Memory Disaster?

Much has been said about how Samuel Taylor Coleridge's opium use helped him write wildly creative poems, such as "Kubla Khan." But when a team of Harvard Medical School researchers investigated how opium use affects the brain, comparing the brain volume of long-term opiate users with those of participants who had not used opium, they found that opiate users had less gray matter density in their PFCs.

The cognitive effects of opiate use on working memory were illuminated by some additional research by University of Cambridge scientists. They gave opiate users and those who didn't take any drugs a series of cognitive tasks that required working memory. The opiate users made more impulsive decisions and did not do well in tasks that required them to discriminate and plan strategies. According to the researchers, the opiate users showed "pronounced neuropsychological impairment."

Instant Working Memory Boosters

Many of the working-memory training programs, foods, and habits we have introduced so far enhance working memory on a long-term basis. But what if you have a big test, presentation, or interview coming up? What can you do to enhance your working memory when it's crunch time? Here are some recommendations that can give working memory an instant boost.

The Weeks and Night Before the Event

- Avoid transfats prior to the test and eat salmon with a lot of parsley instead.

- Don't eat pizza the night before the test.

- Put an "out-of-office" message on your BlackBerry the week before so you can focus on studying.

- Get at least seven to nine hours of sleep a night in the week before the test.
- De-clutter your bag, and get all your things ready the night before so you know where everything is.

The Day of the Event

- Spend some time outdoors.
- Go for a barefoot run.
- Close your eyes and balance on one foot.
- Have a cup of green tea (or coffee).
- Eat some fresh blueberries and dried fruit.
- Have a whiff of some rosemary or peppermint oil.
- If you can't think of an answer immediately or you find your attention waning, doodle, or quietly tap your leg to a beat in your head.

PART III

The Future and Past
of Working Memory

12

Designing the World for Working Memory

JUST THE OTHER DAY, Ross was driving our older son to school and got stuck in a terrible traffic jam. Ross fumbled with the GPS system to find an alternate route while also attempting to ignore a stream of his son's incessant questions from the backseat—*Why is the sky blue? Where do clouds come from? Why do dogs have tails, and we don't?*—and when he looked up, he had to slam on the brakes to avoid hitting the car in front of him. His Conductor had so many things to control, that it had dropped the information about how close he was to the car in front of him, and he almost got into an accident. When he arrived home, he told Tracy, "Somebody ought to make a car that lets you just say what you need, like 'warmer' or 'find alternate route to school' and do it for you." That would be a great way to free up the Conductor and prevent accidents.

Almost every day we find ourselves complaining about things that overload our Conductor—figuring out our taxes, choosing health insurance for our family, trying to tune out our colleagues' annoying conversations about last night's episode of *The Real Housewives of Beverly Hills*. What if we could do something about these distractions?

The Advantage of Cognitive Design

The world is filled with technologies, architecture, and transportation systems seemingly designed to confound our working memory, to get the peace and quiet we need to think, and to make it hard to get from A to B. In this chapter, we imagine what the world would look like if it were designed to support our working memory.

This chapter examines what we call *cognitive design,* to invent a term. Feng Shui for the brain. Cognitive design is organized around the principle of designing structures from the macro—like airports and roads—to the micro—like buildings, schools, and our homes—in ways that give our working memory the advantage. The central question of cognitive design is "does it help or hinder our working memory?" Here we imagine what the world would be like if civil engineers, city planners, architects, principals, teachers, and homeowners thought more about how we think when constructing their roads, buildings, classrooms and homes. We call this world Wutopia, and we have a lot of fun thinking about what things would be like there.

Improving Transportation

During a hectic year jetting all over Europe and Asia promoting the science of working memory, we became exhausted with travel. Each airport, train terminal, and subway was a monument to confusion and obfuscation. Walking through them was like walking through an archaeological site where various stages of poor planning have accumulated, one on top of the other, on top of the other, on top of the other. Current public transportation designs overwork working memory and cause stress.

The stress in travel is all about the navigational choices: *How do I get to the gate? Do I take the tram? How do I find terminal 4?* You know that if you make the wrong choice, you may miss your flight, train, or bus, which causes anxiety. It all adds up to travel being a colossal drag on your working memory.

If Working Memory Ruled the World . . .

The designers of airports, train terminals, and subways would minimize our navigation choices. Simplicity and clarity are the key features here. The fewer bends and corners, branches, terminals, and platforms, the better. Imagine how easy it would be if at any airport, you could just walk in almost a straight line from the parking garage to check-in, to security, to your gate. The straighter the line, the fewer the choices. In Wutopia, airports would be shaped like a flower with elongated terminals that fan out like petals from the top half of a central disk. Connected to it would be a rectangular area in the place of a flower stem, for ticketing and baggage claim, and at the very bottom, like a pot, a parking structure.

In this design, getting from check-in to arrivals requires no more than one or two turns, and hence no more than a single decision as to where to go.

Wutopian Airport

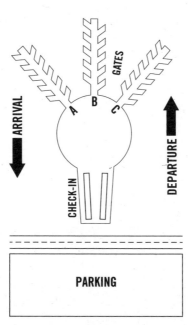

City Planning

Have you ever had your GPS go on the blink and have to figure out on the fly how to get to, say, the intersection of San Marco and Philips? We have. Just the other night, we were meeting some friends for dinner in an area of town we weren't familiar with. When the GPS battery ran out halfway there, we had no clue how to find the intersection of San Marco and Philips. The problem is that street names in most cities are entirely random, with no discernable logic. Knowing that we were on San Marco, for example, didn't tell us how close we were to Philips, or even if we were going the right way. Only when the sign for Philips came into view too late and then quickly retreated in the rearview mirror did we realize where it was.

If Working Memory Ruled the World . . .

City planners would name streets using a grid system with numbers or names in alphabetical order. In fact, in the early days of city planning, this practice was fairly common, and grids account for large parts of some of America's founding cities, such as Manhattan, Chicago, and Washington, D.C.

Wutopian Road Map

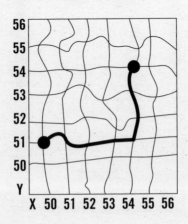

In Wutopia, all streets would be given numerical positions on x- and y-axes. So if you needed to give directions, only two numbers would be needed, say 6 and 3, to indicate the intersection. The first number would always refer to the x-axis, and the second to the y-axis. So, if you are on 50 and 51, to get to 54 and 54, you'd know you needed to go over four streets and up three.

Reconstructing Classrooms and Teaching

In the United States, most classrooms are a riot of visual distraction: colorful books crammed in cases, walls patchworked with fluorescent maps of the world, an alphabet with two-foot-high letters, flags, number lines, holiday decorations, and more. The problem is that many young children can manage no more than two pieces of information in their working memory. If classrooms are jammed with hundreds of pieces of information and kids pay attention to just one of them, they've reduced the power of their Conductor by half.

If Working Memory Ruled the World . . .

Schools applying the principle of cognitive design would minimize visual distractions. In Wutopia, classroom walls would be bare. Remember, of course, that Wutopia is an *ideal* world, and a real-world teacher may prefer to minimize decorations, rather than banish them altogether.

Some teaching techniques would also change. In the United Kingdom, learning by repetition, memorization, or drilling is often considered an outdated learning technique. It has become the hallmark of bad teaching. Educators fear that rote learning will kill children's desire to learn and will quash their creativity. But if a child doesn't have a foundation of some knowledge, what can he or she create? Mozart is the example par excellence of genius and creativity, but no one mentions that he spent hours and hours practicing scales and learning how to compose.

Rote learning in the 3Rs—reading, writing, and arithmetic—can be beneficial. Our Conductor needs the raw materials in order to put them together in a creative way. For example, learning the alphabet by looking at a letter and then repeating after the teacher, "A, A, A, A," "B, B, B, B" allows youngsters to build their language foundation. It's the same with math. Mastering counting and writing the numbers 1 through 100 lays the groundwork for solving math problems.

In Wutopian language classes, preschoolers would memorize their ABCs, and over the course of the year, they would build up to learning common word sounds, both speaking them and writing them. Then they could use their working memory to bring together sounds into words. For example, they would learn the sounds /sk/ /ip/ /in/ /sl/, and with these basics, they would be able to spell the words *skip* or *skin* the first time they were asked to do so. In order to understand the meaning of words, children would learn a list of word roots and use their working memory to help them unlock the meanings from those building blocks.

In math, schools would base their procedure on how the brain solves a math problem. The way this works is that first the problem is held in working memory. Then the long-term memory of numbers is called on to recognize the numbers in the problem. Those numbers are next sent to the intraparietal sulcus, which performs the calculation, and finally the answer is sent back to working memory.

Simple Addition

To maximize the ability to perform their procedure, kindergartners would be taught to memorize their numbers first and lock them safely into long-term memory. At some point in the year, they would be able to use their working memory to hold a problem in their head, recognize the numbers (long-term memory), and go up and down the number line in their mind to find the correct answer, hold it in mind (working memory), and write it down. As students got older, they would memorize code breakers to store in long-term memory, which would greatly facilitate the solution of more complex problems.

R, R, R, PE

PE is as important as the three Rs. A growing body of research shows that physical activity offers a wealth of cognitive benefits and perhaps an improvement in school performance. Despite the vaunted sporting legacy of the Olympic games, U.K. schools have been cutting back on physical education in favor of increased classroom time. According to Ofsted, the education watchdog, even when children are ostensibly engaged in exercise, instructors talk too much and don't let the children engage in strenuous activity. This is likely bad for working memory, because it means that it rarely gets a break from classroom demands. Ultimately, students become less productive even though they are spending more time at their desks. Research has shown that working memory is best used in short bursts—no more than fifteen minutes—on a single task. Any more than that, and the effort can become unproductive and inefficient. A 2009 study published in the journal *Pediatrics* found that a daily break of fifteen minutes or more may improve learning, social development, and health. And the American Academy of Pediatrics says free unstructured play is critical for healthy cognitive, emotional, and social development.

When kids take breaks, it's best to do the exact opposite of classroom learning, to recharge working memory with outdoor play. This also teaches children how to shift their attention quickly. That message isn't sinking in, though. Since 2001, 20 percent of the school systems have reduced recess time, slashing an average of fifty minutes per week.

If Working Memory Ruled the World . . .

In Wutopia, children would be given regular breaks; in particular, breaks for physical activity or outdoor play.

Teachers would aim to spend around fifteen minutes on a lesson before shifting to another subject, and children would be given regular, short outdoor breaks. Schools would increase the amount of time dedicated to physical education, and elementary schools would offer more free, unstructured play.

Revamping the Office

You would think that modern office space would make it a snap for employees to do their jobs. But many office environments, including those at some of the biggest companies, may tax our working memory in a number of subtle and not-so-subtle ways, and that decreases productivity, job satisfaction, and ultimately the bottom line.

Consider office design. Most firms occupy space in square or rectangular buildings with vast internal spaces filled with desks and partitions. Initially designed with lofty ideals about fostering teamwork, communication, and group meetings, open-plan offices offer an abundance of distractions instead: ringing phones, annoying chatter, loud keyboards, absent-minded clicking of pens, and noisy photocopiers. Taken together, this din can distract the Conductor, which undermines our productivity.

We would venture to say that the open-plan office has done more to advance the cause of office idleness and mindless chatter than the latest episode of *American Idol*. In fact, research shows that when employees think they have low privacy, they are unable to successfully complete a complex task involving attention and inhibition. When we are overstimulated in a distracting environment, it becomes harder for our Conductor to inhibit irrelevant information and focus on the task at hand.

The solution seems to be to give everyone a private office, but if everyone is locked away from the hustle and bustle, businesses will miss out on the collaboration that sparks some of the best company ideas. The fine line is between privacy and interaction.

Office layouts aren't our only beef with today's work spaces. Did you know that a work environment that is too warm causes a drain on working memory? Or that a heavy reliance on paper files contributes to clutter, can make it hard to find what you need when you need it, and can make it hard to distribute information efficiently? Paper in an office clogs the transmission of information between departments. Of course, there are also almost constant tech hassles, such as souped-up software programs that are too complex, difficulties sharing digital information, and constant email, not to mention phone interruptions.

Break times should reset and recharge working memory, but they don't. When employees spend their breaks in front of their computer screens checking Facebook, reading the news, or spending their hard-earned paycheck with a little online shopping, their working memory never really gets a break.

If Working Memory Ruled the World . . .

Cognitive architects would spend more time thinking about the way people think, and offices would do a better job of enhancing working memory skills. The argument for the open plan is that it allows people to meet easily with others, and there may be some truth in that: perhaps it's a good idea to have some open space where people work together on projects. But there is also a need for privacy. Our solution? A mix of closed-door spaces with open meeting areas. But please, do away with the cubicles and build some real walls so that everybody in accounting isn't forced to overhear Bob's bragging about his weekend adventures at the Tilted Kilt gentleman's club.

Office designers would pay close attention to the best temperature for peak performance. Research from the Helsinki University of Technology shows that an office temperature of 72 degrees is associated with the highest productivity. Performance starts to wane when the temperature exceeds 75 degrees.

An office space would feature an open area where small groups of people could engage in discussions and work on team projects, with attached sections to house private offices with sliding glass doors. In our ideal design, hallways would extend away from the inner circle, connecting to other circles off which there would be additional buds with offices.

This fractalized building mimics the way working memory acts as the hub bringing together a variety of cognitive skills.

Some companies realize the value of physical activity and set up treadmills in an on-site gymnasium or offer on-site yoga classes. We take our play a little more seriously and would love to see companies encourage people to learn a new sport and physically challenge themselves—basically to do the opposite of sitting in front of a screen. This new perspective would be hugely advantageous for creativity as some of the best ideas come when running on a trail or clinging to a climbing wall.

Wutopian Office Campus

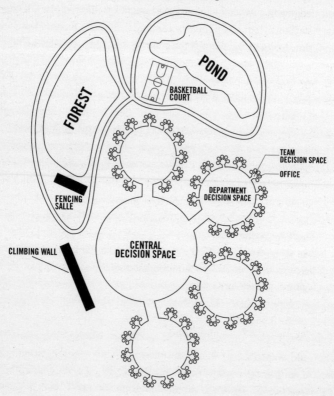

De-cluttering Our Homes

As a society, we are accumulators. So crowded with the evidence of our poor purchasing decisions and our inability to let go, many garages can no longer fulfill their original function as the place to park a car. As we noted in chapter 11, the more stuff you have, the more your attention is divided and the easier it is to become frustrated. If we don't use this stuff, why do we feel compelled to keep it?

Perhaps we are unwilling to chuck unused stuff because it means acknowledging that we should never have bought it in the first place. If your home is starting to look like it could be featured on *Britain's Biggest Hoarders*, then it's time to dig in and identify the crap. Yes, we said it, *crap*, meaning:

1. Anything you don't use.
2. Almost everything that's in a pile on your coffee table, desk, or nightstand.
3. The clothes your wife pretends to wear when you try to throw them out.
4. The toys your children pretend to play with when you try to throw them out.
5. Ninety-nine percent of what you have in your garage.
6. Absolutely, positively, *not* your books lovingly collected from used bookstores. Specifically, crap is not a full set of the 1971 edition of the *Oxford English Dictionary* that you consult only during fierce Scrabble battles with family members in order to prove the legitimacy of obscure words.

If Working Memory Ruled the World . . .

You would want to cognitively design your home, making it simple, minimal, and, most important, stripped of clutter. In order to enforce clutter-free living, the space would be relatively small, which would incentivize us to use the space we have far more efficiently. Efficiency is a principle that Hong Kong architect Gary Chang has taken to heart. He has turned a tiny 344-square-foot apartment into twenty-four rooms!

The key to his design is a sliding wall system, which means that at any one time, you are focused on only a single room function. The bed folds into the wall, the kitchen is behind the TV, and the guest bed is above the bathtub.

Efficiency of space is also a principle at work in the new microhome trends, that is, homes for a fraction of the price (and space): small functional kitchens, beds on the roof, small areas to heat. You can't accumulate there. You have to make choices about what you keep.

The Wutopian home would be designed according to a concept similar to that of architect Chang's sliding doors so that whatever you were doing was the focus of the space. But we've got an important tweak on Chang's sliding doors that borrows from hydraulic stagecraft: you know, where stage sets rise from flat floors.

Wutopian Home Design

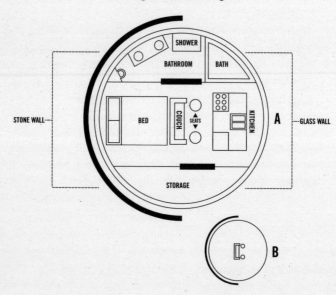

Plan A shows all features ascended. Plan B shows
only couch and seats ascended.

In Wutopia, couches rise from the floor, beds descend, kitchen worktops and stovetops appear where there was only a floor before. As a result, whatever task you are doing—cooking a meal, sleeping, reading a book, getting office work done—is the single focus in the space and the single focus of your working memory Conductor. The glass front gives you a great view, whether perched on a mountaintop or nestled in a garden. The figure on page 256 shows a schematic drawing of what such a home might look like.

From Wutopia to Reality

We use Wutopia as a place to rest our mind, to create, to build something up. But unless we take what we learn (and some of what we imagine) and give it life outside Wutopia, it won't have much of an impact. Much of the inspiration behind this book was to take what we know and give it to a wider audience. Now that you know about the advantages working memory provides, what are you going to do about it? You can start by applying some of the things we've discussed to your own life. You can get enough sleep, add some berries to your diet, get control of your finances, and remove the clutter that is cluttering your mind. If a friend asks you what is so different, you may want to tell them. Wutopia can be more than a state of mind.

13

The Dawn of
Working Memory

THE DAWN OF MAN, the opening scene of the movie *2001: A Space Odyssey*, is one of the most memorable in movie history. A group of hominin, or what you might think of as ape-men, deep in the evolutionary past scrape a meager existence out of a brutal land. As they forage for food, one is killed by a leopard, and they are later driven from their water hole by another group. Fearful of the night, the group huddles together, and they awaken to an alien black monolith standing in front of them. The monolith changes everything.

At first, they are terrified, but curiosity overrides their fear, and they dare to touch it. Soon after, one of them picks up a thick femur from a pile of bones and experiments with it, using it as a tool to smash a sun-bleached skull. The newly realized technology allows him to hunt a tapir by smashing its skull and bring meat back to the group, whose members in turn learn how to use the technology to kill and drive their competitors from the water hole. In triumph, the bone weapon is flung into the air, and the image on screen cuts to an orbiting satellite.

Cryptic and ambiguous, this scene has generated decades of heated debate about its meaning. Director Stanley Kubrick intentionally resisted giving a clear explanation so viewers could come up with their own interpretations. Our interpretation is simple: the monolith represents the unlocking of an unparalleled working memory.

The Missing Intellectual Link

A shocking and profound improvement in working memory transformed the fortunes of Kubrick's hominin and our real-life evolutionary ancestors. Before the dawn of working memory, Kubrick's hominin may have walked past piles and piles of bones, but never did it occur to him that they could be used to accomplish specific tasks. He may have even picked up a bone before the arrival of the monolith and thrown it or smashed something with it. But it is only after the appearance of the monolith that he is able to link things together: the action of smashing with the bone and crushing the tapir's skull, smashing with the bone and driving off his competitors.

This process is what psychologists refer to as "conjunctive binding," when more than one piece of information, sometimes disparate, is joined together to create a novel concept.

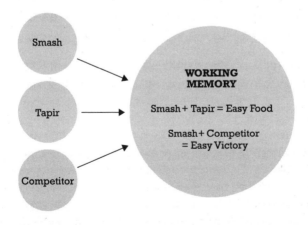

Conjunctive Binding

Conjunctive binding, which gave us the ability to adapt and survive, requires working memory. It helped us with language (sound + object = word), cooking (meat + fire = cooked meat), hunting (stick + flesh = food), and clothing (fur + hominin = warm hominin). If it were possible to scan the brain of Kubrick's hominin before he touched the monolith, we would likely see activation dominated by the amygdala (fear) and the hippocampus (memories of episodes in his life, such as where to forage or find water or his memories of being overcome by other groups). If we were to scan his brain after he touched the monolith and at the moment he realized he could kill a tapir, we would see his hippocampus activate with his knowledge of the tapir and the smashing of the skull with the femur, and his PFC fire when combining both of them together. Back in the real world, our working memory has improved to such a degree that it can easily manipulate multiple pieces of information. And it is our superior working memory that gives us an evolutionary advantage over other species.

We would be remiss if we didn't admit that our viewpoint that better working memory is what sets us apart from other mammals has its detractors. Tetsuro Matsuzawa of Kyoto University, Japan, is one of them. In an experiment that made headlines around the world, he administered what he called a working memory test to college students and a group of five-year-old chimpanzees. During the experiment, both the chimps and the students were shown numbers from 1 to 9 on a touchscreen computer monitor. Then the numbers were replaced with blank squares and the participant had to touch the correct square for each number. Which group do you think scored higher? If you said the college students came out on top, you would be wrong.

How on earth could chimps outclass highly educated humans? Chimps have an amazing photographic memory—an ability to quickly look at a scene and retain an accurate image of it. They use this ability in the wild to quickly assess any potential dangers. Some may argue that Matsuzawa's chimps were performing more of a short-term memory task rather than a working memory task. But even if the chimps were using their working memory to process the information, their photographic memory made it that much easier to perform the task.

Humans excel at more complex processing and in this regard we have a clear edge over chimps. Look at our ability to use conjunctive binding in innovative and incredibly useful ways. Chimps simply don't innovate in the same way that humans can. Indeed, chimps have yet to conduct an experiment to test the working memory of humans.

The Quest for Our Working Memory Monolith

There was no alien black stone (that's science fiction), but *something* unlocked our working memory. The fact that we are smarter than a similar species begs the question: What was *our* "monolith"? What sparked our unparalleled ability to innovate? These are questions that some of the world's best and brightest scientists have been trying to solve. In scientific circles, they're known as paleoneurologists and paleogeneticists, but we prefer to think of them as a sort of "CSI: Paleo" crew.

Think of a CSI-type situation: a forensic detective sees the footprints at a crime scene shortly after a crime has been committed and can make assumptions about the weight and height of the attacker, the direction in which he or she was moving, and so on. But what if forensics arrived at the crime scene a day or even a month later? Rain has now washed away the evidence, and other people have trampled over the crime scene. It would be difficult to recover any hard evidence, and the crime may languish forgotten at the bottom of the cold-case file.

With a chasm of time separating them from their subjects, the CSI: Paleo crew investigates the coldest of cold cases: the mystery of human evolution and the dawn of our unique cognitive skills. Some detectives point to structural changes in the brain as the possible monolith, while others search for clues to the monolith within our genes. Here's a lineup of the main monolith suspects and the relentless CSI: Paleo detectives who have hunted them down.

Monolith Suspect: Structural Changes in the Brain

Meet paleoneurologist Emiliano Bruner, a CSI: Paleo detective who has spent years tracking the structural changes in the prehistoric brain. Of course, the actual gray matter of our cave-dwelling cousins no longer exists, so Bruner studies skulls to determine what the brain looked like. His fascinating work lends credence to the idea that the evolutionary growth of a certain part of the brain enabled us to use our working memory more efficiently.

In 2010 Bruner and his team performed a number of analyses, comparing the proportion of the brain to the body of Neandertals and modern humans. Surprisingly, in modern humans there was a significant increase in the size of the parietal lobe, an area that is associated with manipulating information in working memory. Bruner suggests that the expansion of the parietal lobe provides a "space" for conceptual thinking. Could these structural changes in the brain be the monolith that unlocked a superior working memory?

Monolith Suspect: FOXP2 Gene

One of the prime genetic suspects in the mystery of the human monolith is Forkhead box P2 (FOXP2), a gene associated with speech, a skill that implicates working memory.

FOXP2's existence was investigated by Oxford University's Anthony Monaco. He had been working with a family with severe speech and language difficulties, including dyslexic tendencies, difficulty processing sentences, poor spelling, and poor grammar—all problems associated with an undermined working memory. The interesting thing about this family was that unlike most language disorders that involve a complex interplay between genetic factors, their language disorder, which spanned three generations, was the result of a defective FOXP2. Because the family's FOXP2 was not working like it should, they had language problems, suggesting that the gene is critical for language.

In 2002, CSI: Paleo detective Svante Pääbo, a paleogeneticist who cut his teeth by cloning the DNA of an Egyptian mummy, suggested that FOXP2 could be the key that gave modern humans the edge over our Neandertal cousins. In a high-profile paper published in *Nature*, Pääbo reported that FOXP2 is a "highly conserved" DNA sequence.

This means that FOXP2 survived because it performs a crucial function: if it didn't matter, it wouldn't stick around for long.

Pääbo and his colleagues searched for evidence of what is known in paleogenetic circles as a "selective sweep" in the FOXP2 gene. A selective sweep is a mutation that makes those who possess it much fitter than those who don't. In other words, Pääbo was trying to find out whether a beneficial mutation of this gene had occurred in early humans, basically flipping a switch that provided an immediate advantage. They speculated that FOXP2 carried a twofold benefit:

- It gave humans the advantage of modern language.
- It lay the foundation for the development of communication and human society as we know it.

Pääbo's work was supported by the findings of yet another CSI: Paleo detective, paleoanthropologist Richard Klein at Stanford University. He too suggested that the late appearance of FOXP2 provided the foundation for complex language and signaled the change necessary for modern humans to expand into Asia and Europe. All signs seemed to be pointing to FOXP2 as our monolith.

But then, in a surprising twist of events just a few years later, Pääbo himself challenged the idea that FOXP2 gave modern humans a cognitive edge. Based on evidence from bones excavated from a cave in northern Spain, he discovered that Neandertals had a similar version of FOXP2 as modern humans. This finding throws a monkey wrench into how scientists previously thought of Neandertals.

If they possessed at least one key genetic component important for language, does this mean that Neandertals could speak like modern humans? Not necessarily. Scientists like Sonja Vernes at the Max Planck Institute for Psycholinguistics have found that FOXP2 seems to act like a switch for other language-related genes. Just because Neandertals had a key switch in place, it doesn't mean all the lights were there to be switched on. FOXP2 is a good potential suspect, but we need to look at the rest of the lineup.

Monolith Suspect: ASPM and Microcephalin Genes

Bruce Lahn, a geneticist from the University of Chicago, has been credited for investigating the mutation of two genes—microcephalin (MCPH1) and abnormal spindle-like microcephaly associated (ASPM)—and their possible contribution to cognitive evolution. This CSI: Paleo detective speculates that the genetic mutation of these two genes regulated brain size, which has prompted some to wonder if the genes make our brains bigger and better.

The timing of these genetic mutations seemed to coincide with key events in early human culture. According to Lahn, the MCPH1 variant arose approximately thirty-seven thousand years ago, about the same time art and symbolism first appeared in caves in Europe. The ASPM variant occurred about five-thousand eight-hundred years ago, which some researchers speculate coincided with the explosion of cities and written language. Excitement among Paleo detectives reached a fevered pitch, as they hoped that the new mutations of ASPM and MCPH1 could explain the monolith factor.

But here again, the cold-case nature of paleogenetics froze the excitement when Timothy Bates of the University of Edinburgh decided to thoroughly investigate whether the new mutations were linked to intelligence. Bates's participants underwent genetic testing and took IQ and working memory tests. The results showed no association between the new versions of ASPM or MCPH1 with any of the IQ or working memory scores. In short, ASPM and MCPH1 did not give us superior intelligence. They were just another dead end in the pursuit of the monolith.

As Lahn himself explains the nature of genetic research: "Is it a few mutations in a few genes, a lot of mutations in a few genes, or a lot of mutations in a lot of genes? The answer appears to be a lot of mutations in a lot of genes."

In spite of the challenges of tracking down ancient genes, the intrepid CSI: Paleo detectives press on. In 2010, Pääbo finished sequencing an initial draft of over 60 percent of the Neandertal genome from over 1 billion DNA fragments found in Neandertal bones. In 2013, his team mapped the entire DNA of a Neandertal from a toe bone, and they put the entire genome online for free download (http://cdna.eva.mpg.de/neandertal/altai/bam, if you're interested). As the genetic makeup of our evolutionary cousins comes into focus more clearly, allowing us to compare ourselves with them, we may finally discover the monolith that unlocked our remarkable working memory.

The Archaeology of Working Memory

Though we have yet to zero in on our monolith, we clearly see evidence of a quantum leap in working memory power in the tens of thousands of years of the archaeological record. To show you what we mean, let's journey back some thousands of years in time and observe two Neandertals, Prat and his mate, Gurk. Prat and Gurk live in a cave with other Neandertals. Prat is like the MVP of his clan because he can make better spearheads than anyone else in his group using a long-standing process called the Levallois technique.

Prat must first hunt down a stone that is large enough and has a specific shape. When he finds one of these stones, called a core, Prat grunts, "Burg!" He uses a rudimentary working memory to conjunctively bind a sound ("Burg") and the object (a rock). Then Prat begins chipping away at the core—a process called *knapping*—with great precision until it resembles a tortoise shell, and a large flake of rock can be removed with a hard strike. The resulting flake is sharp and thin, excellent for piercing the flesh of an animal when hafted to the end of a spear.

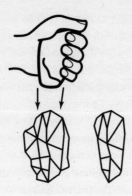

Knapping: The image on the left is a prepared core being struck, and the image on the right shows the resulting flake.

Prat is so good at this technique that he once made nine flakes from a single core—the most ever found in history. If they had a *Guinness Book* of prehistoric world records, Prat's proud face would be pictured with his nine flakes. The process requires a steady hand and some forward planning. To do it successfully, he has to use his working memory to hold in mind two pieces of information:

1. What an ideally prepared core looks like.
2. A calculation of how to make the core he is working on look like that ideal.

To let everyone know that Prat is the group's most skilled toolmaker, Gurk fashions some ornamental shell beads for him to wear. Only the best spearhead producers get to wear them. Gurk herself has earned a place of respect in the group after giving birth to yet another live baby. She swells with pride whenever she hears the others utter the sound "Durg" to her, which means strong babies. Both the physical (bead) and the verbal (spoken word) symbols require working memory to bring two things together—the beads and the status, the sound and the thing to which it refers.

The problem for our Neandertal friends is that there is almost no evidence to suggest that they ever progressed beyond beads, simple spearheads, and "burg" and "durg." In fact, no Neandertal artifacts are complex enough to suggest that they would have needed a working memory capable of handling much more than two pieces of information, about the equivalent of a five-year-old.

If there were a prehistoric TV show called *Are You Smarter Than a Neandertal?* an early modern human contestant would beat the Neandertal every time by a huge margin. And if you pitted a present-day eight-year-old against the brightest Neandertal, the twenty-first-century kid would walk away with the prize, hands down.

While the apex of Neandertal technology was a pointy rock, early modern human technology exploded with seemingly unlimited potential. Let's take a peek now at the lives of two of our early modern human ancestors, Snare Maker and her mate, Fish Finder (note the greater verbal complexity of their names).

Living a nomadic lifestyle during the Upper Paleolithic period, which began around forty thousand years ago, Snare Maker and Fish Finder are always looking for ways to do things better and more efficiently. As they move from one European cave to another, they bring with them a huge variety of precise stone tools developed seemingly to work in specific situations—thin stone blades perhaps for cutting hair, robustly edged stones perhaps for crushing bone to get to the tasty marrow, blades with edges that curve slightly upward possibly for filleting meat, and blades with edges that curve downward possibly for foraging plants.

Specialization implies a constant cognitive engagement with the natural surroundings, visualizing and manipulating resources like stone, wood, and bone with working memory in order to come up with ideal designs for particular tasks. Human tool specialization also suggests advanced planning. Think of a Swiss Army knife: you may not need to use its tools at the moment, but you know to take it with you on a camping trip because you just might need that small saw, cutting blade, or can opener when you arrive at camp.

Brain imaging of modern humans confirms that forward planning requires activation of the PFC. In a Carnegie Mellon University study using fMRI brain scans, researchers found that when participants undertook a planning task, they were using their PFC.

The planning task used in this study is known as the Tower of Hanoi task. It involves a stand with three rods and colorful disks of different sizes. The goal is to move the disks from the peg on one end to the peg on the opposite end. But there are a few rules: you can move only one disk at a time, and you can't place a bigger disk on top of a smaller disk. Although it sounds simple, this task requires considerable planning to get from one end to the other without breaking any of the rules.

Snare Maker and Fish Finder use the same type of planning for foraging and hunting: some specialized tools would work, and some wouldn't. They would each use their working memory to plan their task in the present. Snare Maker would ask herself, "What am I going to gather today? Berries? Nuts? Roots? The berries aren't in season and the nuts I got yesterday were bad, so I'll dig for roots and take this blade that curves downward with me."

Fish Finder would ask himself, "What should I hunt today? Salmon? Mammoth? Fox? Ibex? Squirrel? I saw some ibex nearby yesterday, so ibex it is." Then he would think about the tools he would need. His thought process would go something like this: "If I'm going to hunt ibex, I don't need a heavy mammoth spear, but I do need a light throwing spear for killing, and I'll need a large blade for dressing, and tinder for cooking."

Snare Maker would also have to call on her working memory if she were going to set traps to catch prey. To be successful, she would have to hold four pieces of information in mind—twice as many as the working memory of those Neandertals Prat and Gurk could handle:

1. The game she was trapping so she wouldn't set a fox trap for a boar
2. A knowledge of the terrain to plan the best place to set the traps

3. An understanding of percentages to calculate her chances of success and how many traps to place
4. A temporal calculation so she could plan to leave the trap and return at an appropriate time

With a working memory able to manage far more information than our Neandertal cousins, early modern humans gained the evolutionary advantage. We have to thank two academics who have done the ground-breaking work in this area: Thomas Wynn and Frederick L. Coolidge of the University of Colorado. Most academics tend to be specialists, but a rare few are interdisciplinarians. It is these Indiana Joneses, who, without whip or fedora, set out to expand the frontiers of knowledge and bring together the insights of more than one field to found an entirely new perspective. Wynn and Coolidge are such adventurers.

In 2000, Coolidge, a psychologist, was researching executive function—higher-level processing skills closely connected to working memory. Wynn, an archaeologist, was researching the mental processes needed for making prehistoric tools. When Coolidge popped by his office, the combination was kismet. Coolidge had always had an interest in archaeology and Wynn in cognition due to the nature of his work. Together they became cognitive archaeologists. In their book *The Rise of Homo Sapiens: The Evolution of Modern Thinking,* they point to enhanced working memory (EWM) as the evolutionary spark that moved us from throwing a bone in the air to launching satellites.

Enhanced is an important adjective. Wynn and Coolidge do not argue that working memory didn't exist before humans made the cognitive leap—remember our Neandertals, Gurk and Prat, who could hold two pieces of information in mind—but that working memory was improved to such a level as to spark technological, social, and cultural innovations.

We can get a glimpse at that innovation in action by looking at how hunter-gatherer tribes like those in Papua New Guinea, practice Stone Age technology. A hunter's quiver may be filled with many arrows, each to be used in a specific situation—one for killing small animals, one for larger prey, and one with big barbs for purportedly killing a person. Modern-day Stone Age tribes also use an assortment of ropes, bone knives, scrapers, and stone and wooden axes in complex industries. Consider how one tribe processes the sago palm. Each tribe member is assigned a specific task: Men use stone axes and ropes to chop down the palms; women use wooden axes to scrape the valuable pith, which is crushed; and a drainage system is used to extract the starch from the pith.

Their methods aren't really all that different from the production processes used in the most modern factories in Indonesia. Granted, much of today's processes are automated, but the methodology is strikingly similar. Putting together a multistep process and assigning roles for those carrying out those steps demands enhanced working memory. You have to first invent the process, adapt it to particular circumstances, and then figure out who performs each role the best. If you don't do this accurately, people starve.

Meet the Flintstones, Your Modern Stone Age Family

When most of us think about our Stone Age ancestors, we cling to a romantic image of noble savages living in perfect harmony with nature and using nothing more than brute strength and luck to avoid starvation. But this picture needs serious revision. In fact, the way life was depicted on *The Flintstones* might actually be closer to reality in some respects.

Remember Fred, Wilma, Barney, Betty, Pebbles, and Bamm-Bamm? Fred worked as a crane operator at the local quarry. Fred and his next-door neighbor, Barney, strengthened their bond as friends as members of the Loyal Order of Water Buffalos Lodge. And they all constantly sought out innovative ways to make their lives easier. Wilma used a baby woolly mammoth as a vacuum cleaner. Fred used a bird as a car horn. And the family employed the services of a giant woolly mammoth to spray water from its trunk to serve as a shower.

Okay, so early modern humans weren't driving stone cars or vacuuming with mammoths, but perhaps their lives weren't so different from those depicted in Bedrock. Thanks to their enhanced working memory, our ancestors like Snare Maker and Fish Finder didn't just live off the land; they managed and exploited the land and the water around them to suit their needs. They did so with their specialized tools, Stone Age machines, cleverly engineered devices, and sophisticated techniques. With their own version of industrialization, early modern humans weren't just scraping by; they were thriving.

For example, Fish Finder and the other men in his group may have participated in industrial-scale fishing. A rod, line, and hook are great for a single fisherman, but Fish Finder and his clan knew that if they wanted to feed their whole group, they would need something bigger. What they possibly created is something akin to a fish weir, a complex machine that uses the river current and precisely designed obstructions like poles or netting, allowing fishermen standing on platforms in the river to scoop up the confined fish. Imagine Fish Finder and his buddies carting away dozens of fish and laughing at poor Prat, one of the few remaining Neandertals, limping back to the cave from an unsuccessful mammoth hunt.

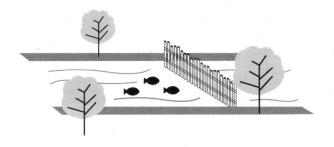

Fish weir: The fish are caught in the trap
as they swim downstream.

Inventing and adapting this fishing technology was no simple task. It required careful calculation and visual spatial manipulation using the working memory to make crucial design decisions. The possible fish weir suggests that Fish Finder and other early modern humans weren't thinking on a small scale; they were thinking on an industrial scale.

One of the more exciting pieces of evidence of advance planning indicative of enhanced working memory is the desert kite, which Wynn and Coolidge cite in their work. Here's how they are believed to have worked. Fish Finder and the other men in his group would create long walls of stone arranged in a V pattern to funnel and trap herds of gazelles. Fish Finder may have found inspiration in natural gorges, which restricted the movement of herds, and replicated their confining properties in areas where the herds were known to gather. Of course, after trapping a large herd, they would have killed the entire herd, which would have far exceeded what they could eat in one sitting. Perhaps Snare Maker and the other women would have been charged with cutting away the meat and preserving it for later use, when game was hard to find.

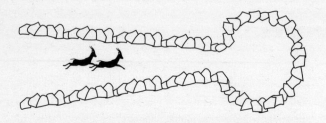

Desert kite: The animals are herded into a narrowing trap and are caught in the corral at the end.

This suggests that their working memory was strong enough to give them the ability to inhibit their desire to gorge on a limited supply of food. If you've ever brought home a bag of miniature-sized Snickers with the intention of storing them in the kitchen cupboard for a few days until you can hand them out for Halloween, you know just how hard it can be to stop yourself from ripping open the bag and eating every last one of them.

Snare Maker and the other early modern humans can thank their enhanced working memory for giving them the intellectual capacity to manage the resources around them. And it helped them do even more. Perhaps it was Snare Maker—a Stone Age Steve Jobs—who developed a bone tool with precise scratches that functioned as a rudimentary computer. In order to work with larger amounts of information than she could reasonably keep in her working memory, Snare Maker—or some other inventive early modern human like her—created algorithmic or calculating devices with repetitive scratches in bones.

One of the ways in which they might have worked is that each scratch represented a number that they could have kept their fingernail on to hold their place in counting. Perhaps using this primitive computer, Snare Maker would have been able to keep track of an inventory of fish or gazelles. We may never know exactly what she used it for, but it is abundantly clear that she needed an enhanced working memory to create it.

Unleashing Creativity

Snare Maker and Fish Finder aren't just land managers and specialized toolmakers. They also happen to be your average Upper Paleolithic culture lovers. Indeed, their experiences with prehistoric art and culture bear a striking resemblance to our own.

In our society, going to the cinema, watching TV, reading books, and listening to new music allow us to connect with one another, to form a view of our world, and to understand—or at least contemplate—our place in that world. It doesn't matter if you're attempting to deconstruct the deeper meaning of Damien Hirst's pickled animals—a dead tiger shark in a tank of formaldehyde named *The Kingdom* that sold for about £9.6 million—or following the escapades of the characters in *The Only Way Is Essex*. Culture and entertainment are what give you something to talk about around the water cooler.

For Snare Maker and Fish Finder, cave drawings, statues, and musical instruments are some of the most compelling artifacts suggesting that, just like us, early modern humans took time to interpret their surroundings, to see the "big picture," to ask about their role in the world around them, to reflect, and to imagine the self. All of these thought processes require enhanced working memory.

Music is an example. We like to think that Fish Finder, Snare Maker, and the others in their group might have sat around an evening fire listening to the sweet sounds of a bone flute, similar to the ones found in the Hohle Fels Cave in Germany that are believed to be about forty thousand years old. We'll probably never know whether the music was the main attraction of the night, more of a backdrop for storytelling, or perhaps some kind of a call to action. And we can't say if their musical tastes ran more toward the flute sounds in Canned Heat's "Going Up the Country," Jethro Tull's "Nothing Is Easy," or Mozart's "Flute Concerto No. 1."

What we do know is that whoever created such a musical instrument had to follow a highly complex process. Here's what one of Fish Finder's friends would have had to do:

1. Hold the concept of an ideal flute in mind throughout the entire process
2. Find bones that are just the right shape
3. Make calculations to know where to drill the holes
4. Make calculations to know where to form the mouthpiece

Flute making in this fashion requires the calculation, concentration, and judgment of working memory, or the tones will be off. But did early modern humans really have an ear for music? Would they even notice if a flute were out of tune? Apparently so. Experts have determined that the tones from similar bone flutes are indeed quite harmonic, which is good news for our prehistoric friends who listened to them.

In today's world, we often look at modern pieces of artwork and struggle to understand what they mean. Trying to determine what a thirty-two-thousand-year-old statue means is virtually impossible. But that hasn't stopped archaeologists from spending years puzzling about the significance of *Lion Man,* a statuette with the head of a lion and the body of a man carved from mammoth ivory. We certainly can't tell you what it means, but we are certain that it is a startling example of enhanced working memory.

The artist would have used working memory to judge the symmetrical relationships and three-dimensional proportions of the arms, head, and face during the sculpting process. But to come up with the concept behind the artifact, the artist had to combine the head of a lion and the shape of a man using his or her working memory. This was a sophisticated form of conjunctive binding that used analogical reasoning to create an imaginary creature from two real things, one of the earliest examples of such thinking.

Artwork that points to the awakening of imagination, of the self, and the awareness of others has been found in the Chauvet Cave, Snare Maker and Fish Finder's equivalent of a movie theater. Located in southern France, the cave houses the oldest examples of prehistoric paintings and engravings. A landslide thousands of years ago blocked the cave's entrance and froze it in time, preserving the art for us. Discovered in 1994, it was immediately sealed off so that scientists could examine the pristine environment.

In 2011 when the German director Werner Herzog made a three-dimensional documentary on Chauvet, *Cave of Forgotten Dreams,* we gained a glimpse of the inventive, cinematic imaginations of the ancient artists. In creating some of their works, the artists combined the three-dimensional surface of an undulate cave wall with images of animals that had extra limbs, such as a bison with eight legs. It almost appears as if the limbs are painted one on top of the other, and in 2012, Paleolithic researchers Marc Azéma and Florent Rivère identified this technique as "superimposition." When combined with a flickering torch, the dancing flame illuminates some legs and hides others, and makes the bison appear to gallop, an effect that Herzog describes as "proto-cinema." Furthermore, Azéma and Rivère argue that Paleolithic artists also developed graphical narrative. They draw attention to a painting in the Chauvet Cave where a hunting narrative runs from left to right, from lions stalking their prey, to rushing a herd of bison. Such visual and narrative sophistication suggests a fierce intelligence capable of combining multiple elements in order to tell a story.

Chauvet Cave art: Eight-Legged Bison. As a flickering torch was passed over the drawing, it would illuminate different legs, giving the perception of cinematic movement. *Reproduced with permission from Marc Azéma and Gilles Tosello*

Just imagine the excitement Fish Finder and Snare Maker must have felt in that cave as the light from their torches danced across the walls, making the images practically come to life. But more than that, they would have shared a unified menagerie of animals: bison, rhinos, lions, birds, horses, and bears. Was this fixation on the animal world a compendium of dangerous animals, animals that held some spiritual significance, a part of shamanistic practices, or something yet to be revealed?

Regardless of the meaning, Chauvet Cave holds clues about the working memory power of early humans. The world represented on the walls is not random or arbitrary. Instead, it reflects an intentional and selective process that required the use of working memory to hold in mind the possible animals and then choose what and what *not* to represent. For example, there are no trees, no rivers, no spears, no hills depicted. Perhaps more intriguingly, there are no humans. We may never know the exact meaning of these images, but we can easily see how they would have fascinated our cave-dwelling ancestors.

So how can we know what early humans like Fish Finder and Snare Maker thought about their place in this world? Joëlle Robert-Lamblin, an art historian, argues that the artists define the human relationship with animals by depicting them. For example, the animals are not portrayed as menacing or threatening, which suggests that early modern humans were not frightened by them—it wasn't a prehistoric version of *Jaws*.

The walls also show intentional and carefully placed red handprints close to images of animals, suggesting a conscious awareness of a connection between themselves and animals. Of course, this begs the question: To what degree were the artists self-aware, a state of mind that is a defining characteristic of working memory?

As you recall, working memory is the cognitive location of our consciousness. It's where we give attention to our self, where we decide, and where we act. Aside from the handprints—a declaration of identity—there are some semi-human depictions, including a figure with a bison head and the legs and genitalia of a woman. Similar to the concept of the *Lion Man,* this fantastical creature required an artist to bring together two separate concepts in his or her working memory. These semi-human creations just might be the prehistoric version of a sci-fi creature—*Attack of the She-Bison*, anyone?

The artwork on the Chauvet walls also provides clear evidence of an awareness of each other, another key sign of working memory at work. This takes shape in apparently erotic images, including pubic triangles and vulvas. Cultural artifacts found at other European sites include anatomically correct phalluses and figurines of voluptuous nude women. Though clearly driven by brain regions other than the PFC, only working memory could have allowed for the symbolic reduction of human anatomy to sexual organs and the conceptualization of woman as an exclusively sexual figurine.

Innovative special effects, fantastical creations, erotic imagery and figurines: these works reveal that our ancestors like Fish Finder and Snare Maker possessed cultural tastes that ran the gamut from high art to titillation.

Perhaps the coldest of all cold criminal cases is the disappearance of the Neandertals. For decades, archaeological detectives have been pointing to early modern humans as the perpetrators. As the theory goes, through their superior intelligence, early modern humans out-competed Neandertals and drove them into extinction by a superior exploitation of resources. Some even accuse humans of eating them! But a new lead suggests that humans just might have an airtight alibi.

According to groundbreaking research led by Love Dalén at Uppsala University in Sweden, early modern humans, those with enhanced working memory, simply weren't at the scene of the crime. Dalén's research, published in 2012, compared the DNA of chronologically recent Neandertal remains found in Spain with older European and Asian Neandertal remains. He found that the older samples had much greater genetic variation, suggestive of a larger population. The more recent Neandertals, however, had a severely limited variation in their DNA, indicative of a tiny population on their last legs.

Dalén argues that it was likely changes in climate, *not humans,* that killed them off. Humans simply weren't in Europe when they died, he argues. Most of the Neandertals had died out around fifty thousand years ago, and the stragglers hung on for another ten thousand years. They died out around the time early modern humans, coming from Africa, began to colonize Europe. Our interaction with them would have been limited, effectively ruling out the theory that humans committed prehistoric genocide.

The art in the Chauvet Cave paints a clear portrait of early modern humans, and it isn't one of mass murderers. It reveals humans who were using their enhanced working memory to begin to conceive of themselves, to become aware of their place in the world, and to form cultural threads that would eventually serve to unify groups together in strong bonds that were about more than just how to get the next meal.

Though working memory is not exclusively responsible for the trajectory from throwing bones to launching satellites, it is deeply implicated in it. Working memory in large part made civilization possible. It is the ultimate evolutionary tool that has allowed us to make everything from a bone flute to a Stradivarius violin, from the *Lion Man* to Michelangelo's *David,* from a bone "computer" to Google. It helped cave people like Snare Maker and Fish Finder have group meetings around a fire and modern humans to invent democracy. Working memory will continue to evolve in the digital age and beyond.

We may not know exactly what that future will look like—perhaps some version of Wutopia (hey, we can dream, can't we?)—but we do know that it will be our working memory that will help us flourish in that world. It won't matter what technological tools will be at our disposal—whether it's a fish weir or a cyborg. As long as we have a good working memory, we will be able to make the best use of them. In fact, working memory is the greatest tool we will ever have. And in the future, it will be those who take full advantage of their working memory who will not just survive, but thrive. Will you be one of them?

WORKING MEMORY
QUICK HITS MANUAL

THROUGHOUT THIS BOOK, we've introduced exercises geared toward improving how you use your working memory, to make sure that you get the most out of it. To make it easier for you to take advantage of these strategies, here is a quick hits manual that pulls many of them together in one place. To help you find the exercises that fit your greatest needs, we've organized them according to three basic principles: *simplification*, *manipulation*, and *support*.

- *Simplification*: The tips and tactics here help you limit the number of unnecessary things that your working memory Conductor has to work with so you can focus on the most important things.
- *Manipulation*: These exercises enhance your ability to actively work with information.
- *Support*: Strategies in this section provide support and care for your working memory so it can operate optimally.

Simplification Exercises

Simplification is the reduction of complexity wherever possible. By simplifying, we limit the number of unnecessary things that our working memory Conductor has to work with so that we can give our attention to the things that matter. By simplifying, our working memory can deliver better results, make us happier, more productive, and more effective. These exercises are geared toward taking out the mental trash that all too often clutters our working memory.

Simplify Your Life at Home, at Work, or at School

This following exercise can be applied to every area of your life.

- Write down every daily activity that uses your working memory. Remember, working memory is the conscious processing of information, so if you have to think about it, remember it, or work with it, it should be on this list. Be prepared, this could be a very long list.
- Order the list from most important to least important.

  —Lop off as many of the least important items as you possibly can and don't do them for an entire week.

  At the end of the week, assess your clarity of thought, memory, productivity, moods, and frustration levels. If you see improvements by eliminating these tasks, then consider removing them permanently from your to-do list. You could also relegate them to a once-a-week or once-a-month schedule so they don't distract you on a daily basis.
- Knock a few more things off that list and repeat.

At home, you can help your children learn this valuable lesson by having them write out a to-do list and prioritize it. In the workplace, employers and managers can boost productivity by clearly communicating to employees which projects take priority and by encouraging workers to dedicate the majority of their time to the most important tasks. In schools, teachers can weed out the things that don't make as much of a contribution to improved learning and improved grades (cursive writing anyone?).

Take a Break: Predictable Time Off

For adults: BlackBerries and mobile email delivery devices help you keep in touch, but they can also bleed your working memory and your job productivity if they are always on. Disconnecting from time to time can give your working memory a much-needed break. Some ground rules:

- Turn the phone off in the evening at least once a week, and see if you can get away with more.
- Give advance warning that you won't be around. If you don't, you may jeopardize your work relationships.
- While it is off, do something that is not work related. Don't look at a screen. Exercise or spend time with your family.

For kids: Kids' lives can be stuffed with so many different structured activities that they never get a chance to be bored. Boredom can be a good thing for children because it encourages them to use their working memory to fill the vacuum of excitement by inventing ways to amuse themselves. At least once a week, give kids a break from all that structure with free playtime. It is important to note that this shouldn't include watching television, which is a passive activity.

- Give them some pens and paper without any instructions and see what they come up with.
- Put them in the backyard with a water hose and a trowel.
- Let them rustle around in the costume box.
- Take them to the playground and avoid helicopter parenting. If they are old enough, let them use their own judgment about the risks they take. You can always step in if you think it is necessary. Indoor climbing walls are great places for them to learn to control their fear in a safe setting.

Simplify Your Goals Then Start at the End

Complexity is the archenemy of achievement. The more complex your goals, the less clear they are and the harder for your working memory to help you achieve them. Here we'll show you how to zero in on what you want and a smart way to achieve it.

- Whittle your goal down to just a couple of words, such as *Sales Manager* or *Android App*.

- Once you have refined your end goal, work backward to figure out what you need to do to get there. If publishing an Android App is your goal, put that at the top and below that, write out all of the previous steps necessary, all the way back to the starting point. For example:

Goal: Android App

↓

Review App

↓

Hire Programmer

↓

Develop App Idea

This process may seem simple, but that is the point. By simplifying the steps and writing them down, it transitions from "Oh, that'd be a great idea, but it'll never happen" to "I can do this." By actualizing your ideas, you are giving your working memory something concrete to work with.

This tactic can be effective at every level throughout the corporate ranks—helping mailroom interns streamline the mail delivery process while cutting postage costs and helping CEOs determine how to reach a company's financial goals.

Teachers can also use this strategy. For example:

Goal: C students get Bs

↓

Review test material with class

↓

Focus on test topics

Integrate working memory principles.

Simplify the Classroom

A classroom is a tough environment in which to learn. Kids chatter, pencils drop, and the lesson may be going too fast or too slow. And then there is the distracting stuff on the walls: the alphabet, formulas, maps, and decorations. As a result, a student's working memory has a lot of things to shut out before it can even begin working on the lesson. Here are some steps for integrating the principles of cognitive design in class:

- *Cut down on the stuff on the walls.* Ask yourself what is window dressing and what is necessary for the class to learn. If it isn't necessary, it makes it harder for you to keep their attention. Some teachers may want to trim it down to a bare wall, others may prefer having some things up to support their teaching style.

- *Stick to a routine.* By "mixing it up" and doing lessons at different times, you are placing a working memory demand on your students. To ensure that their working memory bandwidth is being spent on the lesson, keep them on track and aware of what to expect by sticking to a routine. For example, a teacher in the elementary grades who has the same students throughout the day, may like to regularly do math as the first lesson, geography the second, and reading the third. A single-subject teacher may like to follow a schedule accordingly: discuss yesterday's material, then give a quiz, then teach a new concept, and finally work in class to drill the proper method.

- *Get organized.* Don't make students guess where things are, and make sure they always put them back in the right place by using a color-coding system. For example, place a yellow dot on a book and indicate on the bookshelf where the yellow-dotted books should go with a yellow strip. Books with a red dot go on the section of the shelf with the red strip. Use this same color-coding system for books, toys, drawing materials, and more.

Strip It Down to the Essentials in Sports

Doing well in sports is all about being able to respond and act faster than the other guy. To do this, sometimes your working memory needs to be turned down, so that your motor cortex and cerebellum can react rapidly to the situation. If you insert your working memory into the mix, you run the risk of complicating matters, and slowing down.

- *Fill your cerebellum with the right moves.* If you want to learn to excel on a tennis court, learn the proper strokes, and drill, drill, drill. When these moves become second nature, it means that you aren't using your working memory to execute them.

- *Find a coach, find the right coach.* Find a coach that fits your goals. If you want to play tennis as well as your athletic uncle Bob, let him show you how to execute a backhand. If you want to play as well as Roger Federer, you'd better move up the coaching ladder. Bob is great for filling the weekend warrior's cerebellum with "good-enough" moves, but a professional coach is better for filling your cerebellum with elite technique.

- *Go for one-on-one lessons.* One-on-one lessons are best, because you have someone directly critiquing your form. In group lessons, the instructor can give you only a few moments' attention.

- *Focus on the feel.* Remove working memory from the learning process by feeling rather than thinking. If you are a coach, train your athletes with as few spoken instructions as you can get away with. Precise words get in the way of precise action. By talking and listening less, you can activate the C-MC loop.

- *Tire yourself out.* If you are too tired to think, your brain will drop the working memory and rely on the C-MC loop for learning new moves. The next time you train, you may find that the new moves are branded into your muscle memory.

Manipulation Exercises

Manipulation involves actively working with information using your working memory. The following exercises are aimed at enhancing your ability to use your working memory Conductor in a precise and efficient manner so that you can consciously grasp and direct (or ignore) information as the situation demands.

Techniques to Memorize More Than You Ever Thought You Could

Memorizing random lists of information. If you need to memorize a series of random information, such as order numbers, telephone numbers, the names of potential clients sitting around a board table, or dates, try the loci method. Here's how it works:

- Let's say you have to remember the numbers 29, 0, and 41, in that particular order. Use your working memory to combine the new information with something that you already know. Associate a number, like 29, with your 29-year-old friend *Tom*.

- Put Tom in a place with which you are familiar, like your favorite park.

- Then situate Tom in the place, like next to a grill.

- Add the next piece of information, for example, *Frodo* (who represents "0" because he carried a ring that looked like the number) by the beach volleyball court.

- Add the last piece of information, for example, *Laird Hamilton* (who represents 41 because you read about Laird Hamilton shredding a 41-foot wave).

- Make a story out of it: Tom burnt the hamburgers and threw them over the volleyball net to Frodo, who was about to eat them, when Laird scarfed them down. This translates to: 29, 0, and 41.

- Once you get the hang of it, the amount of information that you can remember will be much longer. Practice at home and then you can quickly use it on the fly.

Memorizing names. If you need to remember the names of people that you meet at a coffee break at a conference, where everyone is just milling around, the loci method isn't as useful. These situations tend to be a little more fluid, and it is easy to forget the name of a person who just introduced herself. Make people stick in your head by associating them with either a familiar word or image. If you tend to recall what you see better than what you hear, focus on the visual elements of that person and unite them with something that is visual and familiar to you, such as a color. For example, Bob drives a blue car, so make him "Blue Bob." If you tend to remember what you hear better than what you see, bring together information that you talk about, such as where a person lives, with their name. In this case, Bob, who is also from California, will be remembered as "California Bob."

Multiply on the Fly

Mental multiplication is a great stretch for your working memory because it requires you to hold a number of variables at the same time. A great way to do mental math is to multiply across the numbers, from left to right, adding up the results in between.

39 x 7 would be solved this way:

- 30 x 7 = 210
- 9 x 7 = 63
- 210 + 63 = 273

25 x 13 would be solved this way:

- 20 x 10 = 200
- 20 x 3 = 60
- 200 + 60 = 260
- 5 x 10 = 50
- 260 + 50 = 310
- 5 x 3 = 15
- 310 + 15 = 325

Become familiar with the technique with double-single multiplication like 69 x 8, 55 x 4, and 28 x 8, and then move on to the greater challenge of double-double digit multiplication, like 34 x 18, 47 x 19, and 28 x 33.

Why You Really Need to Start Reading More Than Just the Texts on Your Phone

Perhaps the most pleasurable way to manipulate information and give your working memory a workout at the same time is to read. Reading requires working memory because you have to use it not only to recall the information that has gone before and anticipate that which is to come but also to cobble together an interpretation of words and sentences, and new words. The secret to using reading as a working memory booster is to always challenge yourself. In the age that has given us texting and tweeting, we have become accustomed to reading shorter and shorter sentences with simplified content. The shorter and simpler, the easier it is for your working memory to process. If you want to challenge your working memory, you need to stretch it by reading more challenging stuff.

For Adults

Sit down with a good book, and preferably one that is more challenging for you to read than your usual fare. World literature is full of excellent tomes to challenge your working memory. It seems to be the case that the further you go back in time, to the twentieth, nineteenth, and eighteenth centuries, and before, the longer and more complex the sentences. Pick up a copy of Jane Austen, Robert Louis Stevenson, Charles Dickens, and dare to dip into the great poets like Shakespeare, Milton, or Dante. These writers will expand your mind, because the way they write is unfamiliar to us today and you will have to use your working memory to make sense of it.

For Younger Kids (2 to 5)

Read aloud to them and challenge them by reading new stories. Remember that the more well-worn the story, the more the children will rely on long-term memory rather than using their working memory to follow along. Keep them guessing for the sake of their working memory. If you read to children from an early age, you'll be surprised what they can make sense of. Use the following techniques to make sure kids are using their working memory:

- 2 to 3-year-olds: Ask them *facts* about the story. This will make them use their working memory to review what they know about the story. For example, "What color is the curious kitten?"

- 4 year-olds: Ask them to speculate on the *motivations* of the characters. For example, "Why do you think the curious kitten ran away from the brave mouse?" This will help exercise their working memory to stretch their sense of other-mindedness.

- 5-year-olds: Ask them to read stories on their own, but take note that this can be such a demanding working memory task on its own that depending on the child, you shouldn't necessarily expect more than a superficial understanding of the text.

For Older Kids (6 to 10)

These kids should be reading *easy* material on their own every day. What is easy for a ten-year-old is probably hard for a six-year-old, so exercise discretion. Parents should also read *harder* material with these children. In stretching their minds with you, the books they read on their own will seem much easier. Eventually, the challenging material will become familiar. Our six-year-old son reads the *Magic Treehouse* chapter books on his own, and Ross regularly reads *The Lord of the Rings* with him. Our son reads two pages, and Ross ten every night. While it is not always easy going, you may find that if you challenge your kids, they lap it up. One of the most encouraging things about the

Harry Potter phenomenon is that J. K. Rowling dared to make things hard on her readers. Children, yes children, bucked the adult trend for shorter and simpler and their working memory went wild for a complex and challenging read. This suggests that shorter and simpler is not inevitable.

Cooking Without Looking

Cooking is a great way to exercise your working memory in the manipulation of information, and you can eat the results! If you are an adult, read the recipe first and then try to cook the dish without looking back at it. This works great with meat dishes and can be even made more challenging with baking. For kids, search out simple recipes with as few steps as possible. Cooking without looking at the recipe forces you to keep both the ingredients and steps in mind, and at the same time carry them out. It's multitasking with flavor!

Get in Touch with Your Feelings

What you pay attention to affects how you feel. If you focus on negative things, you will be a negative individual. If you focus on positive things, you will be a positive individual. Sounds easy enough, right? Well, the tricky part is *how* to focus on the positive things, and that's where working memory comes into play. The first step is to familiarize your working memory with making conscious judgments about what is positive, negative, or neutral.

1. Have a friend read the list of words on the following page. **Don't look at the list yourself!**
2. Listen for repeating words. When you hear a repeated word that was read out two words before, snap your fingers and tell your friend whether it is positive, negative, or neutral (answers are bolded). Once you've done that, try it with words that were read out three words before.

2 Words	3 Words
computer	flower
confident	delight
fortunate	bright
confident	**flower**
fortunate	guilty
afraid	scissors
anguish	coerced
afraid	coerced
anguish	bright
camera	dismal
inspire	mad
hug	**bright**
inspire	**dismal**
joy	pain
lawnmower	confident
safe	tile
lawnmower	guilty
inspire	**confident**
inspire	**tile**

Now that your working memory is consciously assessing the emotional impact of words, you can make it familiar with filtering out the negative ones and focusing on the positive ones. In this exercise, connect the positive words by drawing a line between them, being careful not to touch the negative or neutral words. If you struggle with this exercise, have a few cups of coffee or tea, and see if it is easier for you to focus on the positive, as research shows that caffeine improves how fast and how accurately you can recognize positive words.

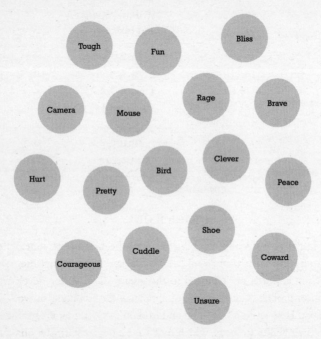

Support Working Memory at All Ages

Your working memory is an amazing tool, but just like any tool, it needs care. If you don't sharpen a knife, you can't complain that it doesn't cut. Just like a knife, your working memory requires maintenance to stay in top working order. In these exercises we offer tips on how to give your— or your child's or your students'—working memory the TLC it needs.

Size Up Your Audience

When giving instructions to students or children, don't give them more than their working memory can handle. By knowing how many instructions various age groups can hold in mind at one time, you can increase the likelihood that they will be able to carry out your instructions successfully. The following table shows how much you can expect according to age.

Age	Working Memory and Instructions
5 to 6	2 instructions
7 to 9	3 instructions
10 to 12	4 instructions
13 to 15	5 instructions
16 to 30s	6 instructions
40s	5 instructions
50s	4 instructions
60s to 70s	3 instructions

Switch It Off!

One of the most important things you can do to support your child's working memory is to turn off the TV. Research shows that the more television children are exposed to the greater the risk for developing attention problems, suggesting an abnormal development of working memory. How to do it? Be open and explain to them that it can undermine their ability to focus, which may have a negative impact on other aspects of their lives. Television should be a rare treat.

Sleep Yourself Smarter

When you skimp on sleep, your working memory gets as tired as you do. Plus, while it's fatigued it has to perform double duty, trying to make up for the slack when other areas of your brain are too pooped to perform as needed. Here's a repeat of the helpful list of the sleep you should be getting.

How Much Sleep Do You Need?

Age	Hours
Toddlers (1 to 3 years)	12 to 14 hours
Preschoolers (3 to 5 years)	11 to 13 hours
Kids (5 to 12 years)	10 to 11 hours
Teens	8.5 to 9.25
Adults	7 to 9 hours

Run for Your Working Memory

Science shows that running gives your PFC a workout. In part it's because running triggers greater blood flow to the PFC. We have found encouraging evidence that barefoot running may be one of the most beneficial forms of running in terms of working memory. Whether you prefer to lace up your shoes or go barefoot, making running a regular habit can enhance working memory. Just check with your physician before starting any exercise program.

Learn to Speak Français, Español, or Deutsch

Learning a new language is a working-memory-intensive skill. You have to use your working memory to shift a host of new words, sounds, and meanings into your long-term memory and then become familiar with manipulating them correctly. This works best for new languages. If you're already bilingual, become *tri*lingual. If you know English, give another language a try.

Retire Your Thoughts About Retirement

Working is great for keeping your working memory sharp. As the pace of life slows, and you are no longer required to adapt to the demands made of you in the workplace, your working memory isn't challenged like it once was, and what lays idle for too long will struggle to be roused when you need it. Retirement can damage your cognitive skills.

Feed Your Mind

What you eat is how you think. If you eat junk food, your working memory will perform like junk. One of the best things you can do to support your working memory is to avoid the regular consumption of junk foods that are laden with trans fats. A hot dog and a bag of chips at a ball game once in a while isn't as much of a problem as the everyday scarfing that will do a real number on your working memory. Here's the short list of good working memory foods and drinks to include in your diet:

omega-3 oils
lean red meat
oily fish
vegetables with color
berries
milk
red wine
berry wines
green tea, black tea

Eat Lightly

Evidence suggests that following a calorie-restricted diet is a good way to enhance your working memory. Intermittent fasting may also provide cognitive benefits. If you are interested in trying this out, consult your doctor first.

Get an Immediate Boost

The scents of rosemary and peppermint have cognitive-enhancing properties. Keep a vial of these essential oils on hand and at times when you need a quick boost, dab a couple of drops on a tissue, and put it near you when you are working. *Do not* apply the oil directly on your skin, as pure essential oils are very potent and can cause great discomfort.

Acknowledgments

WE ARE DEEPLY indebted to family, friends, and colleagues who supported us in myriad ways, directly and indirectly. Our parents, David and Karmen Packiam, and Ross and Beverly Alloway, inspired us to love and learn, and taught us that you can never ask too many questions. Through discovering together, laughing, and competing over the last M&M in the bowl, our siblings (Heather, Lark, Ian, Glenn) were the steel on which we were sharpened. We wouldn't be who we are without them. Glenn was always willing to lend his experienced ear and give welcome advice regarding the book.

Our friends and colleagues have been greatly supportive throughout this process. Verena and Thomas Ahnert gave Tracy a home to stay in when we were undergoing an international move and writing the book at the same time. Myron Penner and Kyle Russell spent hours discussing the philosophical implications of working memory and consciousness. Peter always knew better. Cédric Minel—the best cheesemonger/macaroon wizard in Edinburgh—got us thinking about the link between good food and a good working memory. Others whose keen intellects helped shape our questions and question our answers include Gwyneth Doherty-Sneddon, Nancy Anderson, Robert Logie, Sue Gathercole, Julian Elliott, Bill Bell, Peter Garside, Jonathan Wild, and Eyal Poleg. We are also grateful to Bill, Mark, and Wayne; Luke and Josh; Vaughn and Paul.

The team at Foundry Literary + Media has given amazing assistance in bringing this book out. The science of working memory would have languished among the stacks of research libraries if not for them. Mollie Glick's vision for our book was breathtaking and inspiring in its scope, and she encouraged us at every stage. Stéphanie Abou brought this book to an international readership and Kathleen Hamblin was always a friendly and helpful voice at the end of the phone. We are especially grateful to Frances Sharpe and Rachel Lehman-Haupt, who helped bring the material together and challenged us to step beyond our comfort zone.

Emily Loose and Karyn Marcus, our editors at Simon & Schuster, shepherded this book from beginning to end. Emily has been a cheerleader throughout. Her enthusiasm for this book was evident in every conversation, and her knack for smoothing out the rough edges was unparalleled. Karyn has been a wonderful support, and always quickly responded to our many questions. This book has been improved by her considerable publishing acumen.

Some of the scientists and authors whose bestselling work has shown us how to reach readers beyond the gates of the ivory tower include: Daniel Amen, Louann Brizendine, Dale Carnegie, Stephen R. Covey, Norman Doidge, Charles Duhigg, Timothy Ferriss, Daniel Gilbert, Malcolm Gladwell, Daniel Goleman, Chip and Dan Heath, Steven D. Levitt and Stephen J. Dubner, Christopher McDougall, John Medina, Steven Pinker, Gretchen Rubin, Oliver Sacks, William Sears, Daniel T. Willingham. Thanks for great books and great prose. We also want to give a special shout-out to the working memory masters: Rodney Mullen, Alex Honnold, Susan Polgar, Feross Aboukhadijeh, and Dominic O'Brien. Your willingness to share your stories with us put human faces on the science.

We owe much to those pioneers instrumental in discovering working memory, including nineteenth-century railway foreman Phineas Gage, whose survival of an iron rod blasting through his skull taught us that when the frontal cortex is damaged, so too is our working memory. Early brain scientist David Ferrier (from our alma mater at the University of Edinburgh) showed that electrocuting monkey brains could tell us more about our ability to think and act than you may expect. Alan Baddeley and Graham Hitch reintroduced working memory to the twentieth century. The many scientists whose work fills this book are only absent from the acknowledgments for reasons of brevity. Thank you for your fascinating insights and hard work.

We would also like to offer our most heartfelt thanks to the thousands whose participation in working memory experiments have expanded the frontiers of scientific knowledge. Without your sacrifice of time and effort, the hypotheses that inform working memory would have remained unexamined and unproven.

Finally, we'd like to acknowledge those brain regions that shaped this book. Amygdala, you were always there to motivate us with the fear of missing deadlines. Hippocampus, you provided an endless supply of stories, experiences, and meaningful moments from which we shamelessly borrowed. Broca's and Wernicke's areas, without your words, grammar, and turns of phrase, the pages would be blank; please don't embarrass us with typos or syntactical infelicities. Prefrontal Cortex and the working memory you provide, well, you two are the stars of the show, so we'll just say "cheers."

BIBLIOGRAPHY

Chapter 1: Welcome to the Working Memory Revolution

Alloway, T.P. 2007. *Automated Working Memory Assessment*. London: Pearson Assessment (15 translations).

Alloway, T.P. 2012. *Alloway Working Memory Assessment-II*. London: Pearson Assessment (5 translations).

BBC Business news. "FTSE Collapse Remains a Mystery." May 16, 2001. Last accessed November 7, 2012. http://news.bbc.co.uk/2/hi/business/1333405.stm.

Bindschaedler, C., Peter-Favre, C., Maeder, P., Hirsbrunner, T., Clarke, S. 2011. "Growing Up with Bilateral Hippocampal Atrophy: From Childhood to Teenage." *Cortex* 47:931–44.

Cooper, J., et al. 2012. "Dorsomedial Prefrontal Cortex Mediates Rapid Evaluations Predicting the Outcome of Romantic Interactions." *Journal of Neuroscience* 32:15647–15656.

D'Esposito, M. 2008. Working memory. *Handbook of clinical neurology*. Edited by P.J. Vinken and G.W. Bruyn. 88:237–47.

Jonides, J., et al. 1998. "The Role of Parietal Cortex in Verbal Working Memory." *Journal of Neuroscience* 18:5026–5034.

Kadosh, R., et al. 2007. "Virtual Dyscalculia Induced by Parietal-Lobe TMS Impairs Automatic Magnitude Processing." *Current Biology* 17:689–693.

Karremans, J., Verwijmeren, T., Pronk, T., Reitsma, M. 2009. "Interacting with Women Can Impair Men's Cognitive Functioning." *Journal of Experimental Social Psychology* 45:1041–1044.

Kevles, D. 1968. "Testing the Army's Intelligence: Psychologists and the Military in World War I." *The Journal of American History* 55: 565–581.

Luerding, R., Weigand, T., Bogdahn, U., Schmidt-Wilcke, T. 2008. "Working Memory Performance Is Correlated with Local Brain Morphology in the Medial Frontal and Anterior Cingulate Cortex in Fibromyalgia Patients: Structural Correlates of Pain–Cognition Interaction." *Brain* 131:3222–3231.

McCurry, J. "Too Fat, Too Fast. The £1.6bn finger." *Guardian,* December 8, 2005. Last accessed November 7, 2012. www.guardian.co.uk/business/2005/dec/09/japan.internationalnews.

McNab, F., Klingberg, T. 2008. "Prefrontal Cortex and Basal Ganglia Control Access to Working Memory." *Nature Neuroscience* 11: 103–107.

Roberts, N., et al. 2004. "The Impact of Orbital Prefrontal Cortex Damage on Emotional Activation to Unanticipated and Anticipated Acoustic Startle Stimuli." *Cognitive, Affective, and Behavioral Neuroscience* 4:307–316.

Chapter 2: Why Working Memory Is Crucial to Success

Craig's quote as reported in Dyson, F., Folger, T. 2010. *The Best American Science & Nature Writing*. New York: Mariner Books.

Acevedo, B., Aron, A., Fisher, H., Brown, L. 2012. "Neural Correlates of Focused Attention During a Brief Mindfulness Induction." *Social Cognitive Affective Neuroscience* 7:145–159.

Ainslie, G. 1975. "Specious Reward: A Behavioral Theory of Impulsiveness and Impulse Control." *Psychological Bulletin* 82: 463–496.

Amieva, H., Stoykova, R., Matharan, F., et al. 2010. "What Aspects of Social Network Are Protective for Dementia? Not the Quantity but the Quality of Social Interactions Is Protective Up to 15 Years Later." *Psychosomatic Medicine* 72:905–911.

Arnsten, A.F. 2009. "Stress Signalling Pathways that Impair Prefrontal Cortex Structure and Function." *Nature Reviews Neuroscience* 10:410–422.

Aron, A., Fisher, H., Mashek, D., et al. 2005. "Reward, Motivation, and Emotion Systems Associated with Early-Stage. Intense Romantic Love." *Journal of Neurophysiology* 94: 327–337.

Bimonte-Nelson, H.A., Hunter, C.L., Nelson, M.E., Granholm, A.C. 2003. "Frontal Cortex BDNF Levels Correlate with Working Memory in an Animal Model of Down Syndrome." *Behavioral Brain Research* 139:47–57.

Birnbaum, S.G., Yuan, P.X., Wang, M., Vijayraghavan, S., et al. 2004. "Protein Kinase C Overactivity Impairs Prefrontal Cortical Regulation of Working Memory." *Science* 306:882–884.

Casey, B.J., et al. 2011. "Behavioral and Neural Correlates of Delay of Gratification 40 Years Later." *Proceedings of the National Academy of Sciences of the USA* 108:14998–15003.

De Martino, B., Kumaran, D., Seymour, B., Dolan, R.J. 2006. "Frames Biases and Rational Decision-Making in the Human Brain." *Science* 313:684–687.

Dror, I.E., Busemeyer, J.R., Basola, B. 1999. "Decision Making Under Time Pressure: An Independent Test of Sequential Sampling Models." *Memory and Cognition* 27:713–725.

Fisher, H., Brown, L., Aron, A., Strong, G., Mashek, D. 2010. "Reward, Addiction, and Emotion Regulation Systems Associated with Rejection in Love." *Journal of Neurophysiology* 104: 51–60.

Fuster, J.M. 2008. *The Prefrontal Cortex, 4th Edition*. London: Academic Press.

Higgins, E.T. 2006. "Value from Hedonic Experience and Engagement." *Psychological Review* 113:439–460.

Hinson, J.M., Jameson, T.L., Whitney, P. 2003. "Impulsive Decision Making and Working Memory." *Journal of Experimental Psychology: Learning Memory and Cognition* 29:298–306.

Jacobsen, T., Schubotz, R.I., Höfel, L., Cramon, D.Y. 2006. "Brain Correlates of Aesthetic Judgment of Beauty." *NeuroImage* 29:276–285.

Kane, M.J., Brown, L.H., Little, J.C., Silvia, P.J., Myin-Germeys, I., Kwapil, T.R. 2007. "For Whom the Mind Wanders and When: An Experience-Sampling Study of Working Memory and Executive Control in Daily Life." *Psychological Science* 18:614–621.

Karremans, J., Verwijmeren, T. 2008. "Mimicking Attractive Opposite-Sex Others: The Role of Romantic Relationship Status." *Personality and Social Psychology Bulletin* 34:939–945.

Karremans, J., Verwijmeren, T., Pronk, T., Reitsma, M. 2009. "Interacting with Women Can Impair Men's Cognitive Functioning." *Journal of Experimental Social Psychology* 45:1041–1044.

Liefooghe, B., Barrouillet, P., Vandierendonck, A., Camos, V. 2008. "Working Memory Costs of Task Switching." *Journal of Experimental Psychology: Learning, Memory, & Cognition* 34: 478–494.

LoPresti, M.L., Schon, K., Tricarico, M.D., Swisher, J.D., Celone, K.A., Stern, C.E. 2008. "Working Memory for Social Cues Recruits Orbitofrontal Cortex and Amygdala: A Functional Magnetic Resonance Imaging Study of Delayed Matching to Sample for Emotional Expressions." *Journal of Neuroscience* 28:3718–3728.

Mischel, W., Ebbesen, E.B. 1970. "Attention in Delay of Gratification." *Journal of Personality and Social Psychology* 16:329–337.

Mischel, W., Ebbesen, E.B., Zeiss, A.R. 1972. "Cognitive and Attentional Mechanisms in Delay of Gratification." *Journal of Personality and Social Psychology* 21:204–218.

Phillips, L.H., Channon, S., Tunstall, M., Hedenstrom, A., Lyons, K. 2008. "The Role of Working Memory in Decoding Emotions." *Emotion* 8:184–191.

Porcelli, A., Delgado, M. 2009. "Acute Stress Modulates Risk Taking in Financial Decision Making." *Psychological Science* 20:278–283.

Pronk, T.M., Karremans, J.C., Overbeek, G., Vermulst, A.A., Wigboldus, D.H. 2010. "What It Takes to Forgive: When and Why Executive Functioning Facilitates Forgiveness." *Journal of Personality and Social Psychology* 981:119–131.

Rubia, K., Smith, A. 2004. "The Neural Correlates of Cognitive Time Management: A Review." *Acta Neurobiologiae* 64:329–340.

Shoda, Y., Mischel, W., Peake, P.K. 1990. "Predicting Adolescent Cognitive and Social Competence from Preschool Delay of Gratification: Identifying Diagnostic Conditions." *Developmental Psychology* 26:978–986.

Sprenger, A., Dougherty, M.R. 2006. "Differences Between Probability and Frequency Judgments: The Role of Individual Differences in Working Memory Capacity." *Organizational Behavior and Human Decision Processes* 99:202–221.

Tversky, A., Kahneman, D. 1981. "The Framing of Decisions and the Psychology of Choice." *Science* 211:453–458.

Watson, J.M., Strayer, D.L. 2010. Supertaskers: "Profiles in Extraordinary Multi-Tasking Ability." *Psychonomic Bulletin & Review* 17:479–485.

Whitney, P., Rinehart, C.A., Hinson, J.M. 2008. "Framing Effects Under Cognitive Load: The Role of Working Memory in Risky Decisions." *Psychonomic Bulletin & Review* 15:1179–1184.

Yehuda, R., Flory, J., Southwick, S., Charney, D. 2006. "Developing an Agenda for Translational Studies of Resilience and Vulnerability Following Trauma Exposure." *Annals of the New York Academy of Sciences* 1071:379–396.

Chapter 3: The Joker in the Mines

Alloway, T.P., Alloway, R.G., Horton, J.C. 2012. "Investigating the Link Between Working Memory and Optimism." Manuscript under Review.

Brefczynski-Lewis, J.A., Lutz, A., Schaefer, H.S., Levinson, D.B., Davidson, R. 2007. "Neural Correlates of Attentional Expertise in Long-Term Meditation Practitioners." *Proceedings of the National Academy of Sciences of the United States* 104:11483–11488.

Cools, R., Gibbs, S., Miyakawa, A., Jagust, W., D'Esposito, M. "Working Memory Capacity Predicts Dopamine Synthesis Capacity in the Human Striatum." *Journal of Neuroscience* 28:1208–1212.

Davidson, K.W., Mostofsky, E., Whang, W. 2010. "Don't Worry, Be Happy: Positive Affect and Reduced 10-Year Incident Coronary Heart Disease: The Canadian Nova Scotia Health Survey." *European Heart Journal* 319:1065–70.

Fitzgerald, T., Tennen, H., Affleck, G., Pransky, G.S. 1993. "The Relative Importance of Dispositional Optimism and Control Appraisals in Quality Of Life After Coronary Artery Bypass Surgery." *Journal of Behavioral Medicine* 16:25–43.

Frankl, V. 2006. *Man's Search for Meaning.* Boston: Beacon Press.

Grandt, R., Mueller, H.W., Hautzel, H. 2009. "Serotonin Release Induced by Working Memory: An [18F] Altanserin PET Study." *Journal of Nuclear Medicine* 50 (Supplement 2):1201.

Hester, R., Foxe, J., Molholm, S., Shpaner, M., Garavan, H. 2005. "Neural Mechanisms Involved in Error Processing: A Comparison of Errors Made with and without Awareness." *NeuroImage* 273:602–608.

Hester, R., Garavan, H. 2005. "Working Memory and Executive Function: The Influence of Content and Load on the Control of Attention." *Memory and Cognition* 33:221–233.

Jha, A.P., Stanley, E.A., Kiyonaga, A., Wong, L., Gelfand, L. 2010. "Examining the Protective Effects of Mindfulness Training on Working Memory Capacity and Affective Experience." *Emotion* 10:54–64.

Joormann, J., Dkane, M., Gotlib, I.H. 2006. "Adaptive and Maladaptive Components Of Rumination? Diagnostic Specificity and Relation to Depressive Biases." *Behaviour Therapy* 37:269–280.

Joormann, J., Gotlib, I.H. 2008. "Updating the Contents of Working Memory in Depression: Interference from Irrelevant Negative Material." *Journal of Abnormal Psychology* 117:182–192.

Krishnan, V., Han, M.H., Graham, D.L., et al. 2007. "Molecular Adaptations Underlying Susceptibility and Resistance to Social Defeat in Brain Reward Regions." *Cell* 131:391–404.

Kuchinke, L., Lux, V. 2012. "Caffeine Improves Left Hemisphere Processing of Positive Words." *PLoS ONE* 7: e48487.

Levens, S., Gotlib, I. 2010. "Updating Positive and Negative Stimuli in Working Memory in Depression." *Journal of Experimental Psychology: General* 139:654–664.

Levens, S., Muhtadie, L., Gotlib, I. 2009. "Impaired Resource Allocation and Rumination in Depression." *Journal of Abnormal Psychology* 118:757–766.

Levens, S.M., Phelps, E.A. 2010. "Insula and Orbital Frontal Cortex Activity Underlying Emotion Interference Resolution in Working Memory." *Journal of Cognitive Neuroscience* 22:2790–2803.

Levy, B.R., Slade, M.D., Kasl, S.V. 2002. "Longitudinal Benefit of Positive Self-Perceptions of Aging on Functioning Health." *Journal of Gerontology: Psychological Sciences* 57: 409–417.

Mario Sepulveda to Caroline Graham. "The Amazing First Interview with One of the Trapped Chilean Miners." *Daily Mail*, 17 October 2010. Last accessed November 7, 2012. www.dailymail.co.uk/news/article-1321230/Chilean-miners-World-exclusive-interview-Mario-Sepulveda.html.

Markus, H., Schwartz, B. 2010. "Does Choice Mean Freedom and Well-Being?" *Journal of Consumer Research* 37: 344–355.

Peterson, C. 2006. *A Primer in Positive Psychology*. New York: Oxford University Press.

Schieman, S., Young, M. 2010. "The Demands of Creative Work: Implications for Stress in the Work–Family Interface." *Social Science Research* 39:246–259.

Tindale, H.A., Chang, Y., Kuller, L.H., Manson, J.E., Robinson, J.G., Rosal, M.C., et al. 2009. "Optimism, Cynical Hostility, and Incident Coronary Heart Disease and Mortality in the Women's Health Initiative." *Circulation* 120: 656–662.

Treynor, W., Gonzalez, R., Nolen-Hoeksema, S. 2003. "Rumination Reconsidered: A Psychometric Analysis." *Cognitive Therapy and Research* 27: 247–259.

Van Reekum, C., Urry, H., Johnstone, T., et al. 2007. "Individual Differences in Amygdala and Ventromedial Prefrontal Cortex Activity Are Associated with Evaluation Speed and Psychological Well-Being." *Journal of Cognitive Neuroscience* 19:237–248.

Chapter 4: Failures, Bad Habits, and Missteps

American Society of Addiction Medicine. 2012. Last accessed November 7, 2012. www.asam.org.

Anna Patterson. Last accessed November 7, 2012. www.anorectic.fsnet.co.uk/.

Bailer, U., Narendran, R., Frankle, G., Himes, M., Duvvuri, V., Mathis, C., Kaye, W. 2012. "Amphetamine Induced Dopamine Release Increases Anxiety in Individuals Recovered from Anorexia Nervosa." *International Journal of Eating Disorders* 45:263–271.

Baumeister, R. 2002. "Yielding to Temptation: Self-Control Failure. Impulsive Purchasing, and Consumer Behavior." *Journal of Consumer Research* 28:670–676.

Centers for Disease Control and Prevention. "Obesity and Overweight." Last accessed November 7, 2012. www.cdc.gov/nchs/fastats/overwt.htm.

Cserje'si, R., Molnar, D., Luminet, O., Lenard, L. 2007. "Is There Any Relationship Between Obesity and Mental Flexibility in Children?" *Appetite* 49:675–678.

Elias, M.F., Elias, P.K., Sullivan, L.M., Wolf, P.A., D'Agostino, R.B. 2003. "Lower Cognitive Function in the Presence of Obesity and Hypertension: The Framingham Heart Study." *International Journal of Obesity* 27:260–268.

Finn, P. 2002. "Motivation, Working Memory, and Decision Making: A Cognitive-

Motivational Theory of Personality Vulnerability to Alcoholism." *Behavioral and Cognitive Neuroscience Reviews* 1:183–205.

Gonzales, M., Tarumi, T., Miles, S., Tanaka, H., Shah, F., Haley, F. 2010. "Insulin Sensitivity as a Mediator of the Relationship Between BMI and Working Memory-Related Brain Activation." *Obesity* 18:2131–2137.

Hoch, S., Loewenstein, G. 1991. "Time-Inconsistent Preferences and Consumer Self-Control." *Journal of Consumer Research* 4: 492–507.

Hofmann, W., Friese, M., Strack, F. 2009. "Impulse and Self-Control from a Dual-Systems Perspectives." *Psychological Science* 4:162–176.

Internet Porn Addiction. Last accessed November 7, 2012. www.safefamilies.org/sfStats.php.

Johnson, P., Kenny, P. 2010. "Dopamine D2 receptors in Addiction-Like Reward Dysfunction and Compulsive Eating in Obese Rats." *Nature Neuroscience* 13:635–641.

Kemps, E., Tiggemann, M., Wade, T., Tovim, B., Isaac, D., Breyer, R. 2006. "Selective Working Memory Deficits in Anorexia Nervosa." *European Eating Disorders Review* 14:97–103.

Kessler, D. 2010. *The End of Overeating: Taking Control of the Insatiable American Appetite.* New York: Rodale Books.

Ko, C.H., Liu, G.C., Hsiao, S., et al. 2009. "Brain Activities Associated with Gaming Urge of Online Gaming Addiction." *Journal of Psychiatric Research* 43:739–747.

Lenoir, M., Serre, L., Cantin, F., Ahmed, S. 2007. "Intense Sweetness Surpasses Cocaine Reward." *PLoS ONE* 2:e698.

Lubman, D.I., Yücel, M., Pantelis, C. 2004. "Addiction, a Condition of Compulsive behaviour? Neuroimaging and Neuropsychological Evidence of Inhibitory Dysregulation." *Addiction* 99: 1491–1502.

Michael. Last accessed November 7, 2012. www.dimensionsmagazine.com/dimtext/kjn/people/heaviest.htm.

Murray, A., Knight, N., Cochlin, L., et al. 2009. "Deterioration of Physical Performance and Cognitive Function in Rats with Short-Term High-Fat Feeding." *FASEB Journal* 23:1–8.

National Council on Problem Gambling. 2012. Last accessed November 7, 2012. www.ncpgambling.org/i4a/pages/index.cfm?pageid=3314.

Ogden, C., Carroll, M., Kit, B., Flegal, K. 2012. "Prevalence of Obesity in the United States, 2009–2010." *NCHS Data Brief*, No. 82.

Silvera, D., Lavack, A., Kropp, F. 2008. "Impulse Buying: The Role of Affect, Social Influence, and Subjective Well-Being." *Journal of Consumer Marketing* 25:23–33.

Substance Abuse and Mental Health Services Administration. *Results from the 2011 National Survey on Drug Use and Health: Summary of National Findings,* NSDUH Series H-44, HHS Publication No. (SMA) 12-4713. Rockville, MD: Substance Abuse and Mental Health Services Administration, 2012.

Valerie Compan to Gura T. "Addicted to Starvation: The Neurological Roots of Anorexia." *Scientific American,* June/July 2008.

Volkow, N.D., Fowler, J., Wang, G. 2003. "The Addicted Human Brain: Insights from Imaging Studies." *Journal of Clinical Investigation* 111:1444–1451.

Volkow, N.D., Fowler, J., Wang, G. 2004. "The Addicted Human Brain Viewed in the Light of Imaging Studies: Brain Circuits and Treatment Strategies." *Neuropharmacology* 47:3–13.

Wang, G. J., Yang, J., Volkow, N. 2006. "Gastric Stimulation in Obese Subjects Activates the Hippocampus and Other Regions Involved in Brain Reward Circuitry." *Proceedings of the National Academy of Sciences* 103:15641–15645.

Whitmer, R.A., Gunderson, E.P., Quesenberry, C.P. Jr., Zhou, J., Yaffe, K. 2007. "Body Mass Index in Midlife and Risk of Alzheimer Disease and Vascular Dementia." *Current Alzheimer's Research* 4:103–109.

Witt, A. "Rich Man, Poor Man." *The Washington Post,* January 30, 2005. Last accessed on November 7, 2012. www.washingtonpost.com/wp-dyn/articles/A36338-2005 Jan25.html.

World of Warcraft gamers addiction stories. Last accessed November 7, 2012. www .gamefront.com/world-of-warcraft-addiction-stories/.

Zastrow, A., Kaiser, K., Stippich, C., et al. 2009. "Neural Correlates of Impaired Cognitive-Behavioral Flexibility in Anorexia Nervosa." *The American Journal of Psychiatry* 166:608–616.

Zoroya, G. "One Wild Ride for Jackpot Winner." *USA Today,* February 12, 2004. Last accessed on November 7, 2012. http://usatoday30.usatoday.com/news/ nation/2004-02-12-lottery-winner_x.htm.

Chapter 5: The Most Important Learning Tool

Alloway, T.P., Alloway, R.G., Wooten S. 2012. "Home Sweet Home: The Impact of Zipcode on Cognitive Skills." Manuscript under Review.

Alloway, T.P., Alloway, R.G. 2010. "Investigating the Predictive Roles of Working Memory and IQ in Academic Attainment." *Journal of Experimental Child Psychology* 106:20–29.

Alloway, T.P., Archibald, L.M. 2008. "Working Memory and Learning in Children with Developmental Coordination Disorder and Specific Language Impairment." *Journal of Learning Disabilities* 41:251–262.

Alloway, T.P., Banner, G., Smith, P. 2010. "Working Memory and Cognitive Styles in Adolescents' Attainment." *British Journal of Educational Psychology* 80:567–581.

Alloway, T.P., Bibile, V., Lau, G. 2012. "Computerized Working Memory Training: Can it Lead to Gains in Cognitive Skills in Students?" *Computers & Human Behavior.*

Alloway, T.P., Cockcroft, K. 2012. "Working Memory in ADHD: A Comparison of British and South African Children." *Journal of Attention Disorders* doi: 10.1177/1087054711417397.

Alloway, T.P., Elliott, J., Holmes, J. 2010. "The Prevalence of ADHD-Like Symptoms in a Community Sample." *Journal of Attention Disorders* 14:52–56.

Alloway, T.P., Elliott, J., Place, M. 2010. "Investigating the Relationship Between Attention and Working Memory in Clinical and Community Samples." *Child Neuropsychology* 16:242–254.

Alloway, T.P., Gathercole, S.E., Adams, A.M., Willis, C., Eaglen, R., Lamont, E. 2005. "Working Memory and Other Cognitive Skills as Predictors of Progress Towards Early Learning Goals at School Entry." *British Journal of Developmental Psychology* 23:417–426.

Alloway, T.P., Gathercole, S.E., Elliott, J. 2010. "Examining the Link Between Working

Memory Behavior and Academic Attainment in Children with ADHD." *Developmental Medicine & Child Neurology* 52:632–636.

Alloway, T.P., Gathercole, S.E., Holmes, J., Place, M., Elliott, J. 2009. "The Diagnostic Utility of Behavioral Checklists in Identifying Children with ADHD and Children with Working Memory Deficits." *Child Psychiatry & Human Development* 40:353–366.

Alloway, T.P., Gathercole, S.E., Kirkwood, H.J., Elliott, J.E. 2009. "The Cognitive and Behavioral Characteristics of Children with Low Working Memory." *Child Development* 80:606–621.

Alloway, T.P., Gathercole, S.E., Kirkwood, H.J., Elliott, J.E. 2009. "The Working Memory Rating Scale: A Classroom-Based Behavioral Assessment of Working Memory." *Learning and Individual Differences* 19:242–245.

Alloway, T.P., Gathercole, S.E., Pickering, S.J. 2006. "Verbal and Visuo-Spatial Short-Term and Working Memory in Children: Are They Separable?" *Child Development* 77:1698–1716.

Alloway, T.P., Gathercole, S.E., Willis, C., Adams, A.M. 2005. "Working Memory and Special Educational Needs." *Educational and Child Psychology* 22:56–67.

Alloway, T.P., Gathercole, S.E. 2006. "How Does Working Memory Work in the Classroom?" *Educational Research and Reviews* 1:134–139.

Alloway, T.P., Passolunghi, M.C. 2011. "The Relations Between Working Memory and Arithmetical Abilities: A Comparison Between Italian and British Children." *Learning and Individual Differences* 21:133–137.

Alloway, T.P., Rajendran, G., Archibald, L.M. 2009. "Working Memory Profiles of Children with Developmental Disorders." *Journal of Learning Difficulties* 42:372–382.

Alloway, T.P., Wootan, S., Deane, P. 2012. "Investigating Working Memory and Sustained Attention in Dyslexic Adults." *Learning and Individual Differences.*

Alloway, T.P. 2009. "Working Memory but Not IQ Predicts Subsequent Learning in Children with Learning Difficulties." *European Journal of Psychological Assessment* 25:92–98.

Alloway, T.P. 2010. *Improving Working Memory: Supporting Students' Learning.* London: Sage Press.

Alloway, T.P. 2010. "Working Memory and Executive Function Profiles of Students with Borderline Intellectual Functioning." *Journal of Intellectual Disability Research* 54:448–456.

Alloway, T.P. 2011. "A Comparison of Working Memory Profiles in Children with ADHD and DCD." *Child Neuropsychology* 21:1–12.

Alloway, T.P. 2011. "The Benefits of Computerized Working Memory Assessment." *Educational and Child Psychology* 28:8–17.

Alloway, T.P. 2012. "Can interactive Working Memory Training Improving Learning?" *Journal of Interactive Learning Research* 23:1–11.

Alloway, T.P. 2012. "Fluid Intelligence. In N Seel, Ed." *Encyclopedia of the Sciences of Learning.* New York: Springer.

Alloway, T.P., Elsworth, M. 2012. "A Comparison of IQ and Working Memory Across High, Average, and Low Ability Students." *Learning and Individual Differences.* 22:891–895.

Alloway, T.P., Gathercole, S.E. 2006. "How Does Working Memory Work in the Classroom?" *Educational Research and Reviews.* 1:134–139.

Alloway, T.P., Gregory, D. 2012. "The Predictive Ability of IQ and Working Memory Scores in Literacy in an Adult Population." *International Journal of Educational Research.*

Alloway, T.P., Gathercole, S.E., Willis, C., & Adams, A.M. 2004. "A Structural Analysis of Working Memory and Related Cognitive Skills in Early Childhood." *Journal of Experimental Child Psychology* 87: 85–106.

Archibald, L.M., Alloway, T.P. 2008. "Comparing Language Profiles: Children with Specific Language Impairment and Developmental Coordination Disorder." *International Journal of Communication and Language Disorders* 43:165–180.

Arnsten, A.F. 2008. "Genetics of Childhood Disorders: XVIII. ADHD, Part. 2: Norepinephrine Has a Critical Modulatory Influence on Prefrontal Cortical Function." *Journal of the American Academy of Child and Adolescent Psychiatry* 39:1201–1203.

Baltruschat, L., et al. 2011. "Addressing Working Memory in Children with Autism Through Behavioral Intervention." *Research in Autistic Spectrum Disorders* 5:267–276, 2011.

Baron-Cohen, S. 2004. "The Cognitive Neuroscience of Autism." *Journal of Neurology Neurosurgery Psychiatry* 75:945–948.

Baron-Cohen, S. 2006. "Two New Theories of Autism: Hyper-Systemizing and Assortative Mating." *Archives of Diseases in Childhood* 91:2–5.

Brody, G., Flor, D. 1998. "Maternal Resources, Parenting Practices, and Child Competence in Rural, Single-Parent African American Families." *Child Development* 69:803–816.

Bugden, S., Price, G.R., McLean, D.A., Ansari, D. 2012. "The Role of the Left Intraparietal Sulcus in the Relationship Between Symbolic Number Processing and Children's Arithmetic Competence." *Developmental Cognitive Neuroscience* 2:448–57.

Bull, R., Scerif, G.. 2001. "Executive Functioning as a Predictor of Children's Mathematics Ability: Inhibition, Switching, and Working Memory." *Developmental Neuropsychology* 19:273–93.

Casanova, M.F., Buxhoeveden, D.P., Switala, A.E., Roy, E. 2002. "Minicolumnar Pathology in Autism." *Neurology* 58:428–432.

Casey, B.J., Castellanos, F.X., Giedd, et al. 1997. "Implication of Right Frontostriatal Circuitry in Response Inhibition and Attention-Deficit/Hyperactivity Disorder." *American Academy Child and Adolescent Psychiatry* 36:374–383.

Christakis, D., Zimmerman, F., DiGiuseppe, D., McCarthy, C. 2004. "Early Television Exposure and Subsequent Attentional Problems in Children." *Pediatrics* 113:708–713.

Courchesne, E., Mouton, P., Calhoun, M., et al. 2011. "Neuron Number and Size in Prefrontal Cortex of Children with Autism." *Journal of the American Medical Association* 306:2001–2010.

Cowan, N., Alloway, T.P. 2008. "The Development of Working Memory in Childhood," in *Development of Memory in Infancy and Childhood,* 2nd edition, M. Courage & N. Cowan, Eds. pp. 303–342. Hove, England: Psychology Press.

de Vries, M., Geurts, H.M. 2012. "Cognitive Flexibility in ASD; Task Switching with Emotional Faces." *Journal of Autism and Developmental Disorders* 42:2558–68.

Dronkers, et al. 2007. "Paul Broca's Historic Cases: High Resolution MR Imaging of the Brains of Leborgne and Lelong." *Brain* 130:1432–1441.

Ellis Weismer, S., Evans, J., Hesketh, L. 1999. "An Examination of Working Memory Capacity in Children with Specific Language Impairment." *Journal of Speech, Language, and Hearing Research* 42:1249–1260.

Ellis Weismer, S., Tomblin, J.B., Zhang, X., Buckwalter, P., Gaura Chynoweth, J., Jones, M. 2000. "Nonword Repetition Performance in School-Age Children with and without Language Impairment." *Journal of Speech, Language, and Hearing Research* 43:865–878.

Fuster, J.M. 2008. *The Prefrontal Cortex*, 4th Edition. London: Academic Press.

Gathercole, S., Durling, M., Evans, S., Jeffcock, S., Stone, E. 2008. "Working Memory Abilities and Children's Performance in Laboratory Analogues of Classroom Activities." *Applied Cognitive Psychology* 22:1019–1037.

Gathercole, S.E., Alloway, T.P., Willis, C., Adams, A.M. 2006. "Working Memory in Children With Reading Disabilities." *Journal of Experimental Child Psychology* 93:265–281.

Geary, D.C., Hoard, M.K., Nugent, L., Bailey, D. 2012. "Mathematical Cognition Deficits in Children with Learning Disabilities and Persistent Low Achievement: A Five Year Prospective Study." *Journal of Educational Psychology* 104:206–223.

Gross, L. 2006. "A Neural Seat for Math?" *PLoS Biology.* 4:e149.

Groth, N. 1975. "Mothers of Gifted." *The Gifted Child Quarterly* 19:217–222.

Hasher, L., Zacks, R. 1988. "Working Memory, Comprehension, and Aging: A Review and a New View," in *The Psychology of Learning and Motivation*, G. H. Bower, Ed., vol. 22, pp. 193–225. New York: Academic Press.

Holmes, J., Gathercole, S., Place, M., Alloway, T.P., & Elliott, J. 2010. "An Assessment of the Diagnostic Utility of EF Assessments in the Identification of ADHD in Children." *Child & Adolescent Mental Health* 15: 37–43.

Horn, J.L., Cattell, R.B. 1967. "Age Differences in Fluid and Crystallized Intelligence." *Acta Psychologica* 26:107–129. http://nces.ed.gov/surveys/pisa/. www.americaspromise.org/. www.usatoday.com/news/education/2010-12-07-us-students-international-ranking_N.htm.

Jaeggi, S. M., Buschkuehl, M., Jonides, J., & Shah, P. 2011. "Short- and Long-term Benefits of Cognitive Training." *PNAS*, 108:25.

Lesser, R.P., Lueders, H., Dinner, D.S., et al. 1984. "The Location of Speech and Writing Functions in the Frontal Language Area. Results of Extraoperative Cortical Stimulation." *Brain* 107: 275–291.

Luciana, M., Conklin, H.M., Hooper, C.J., Yarger, R.S. 2005. "The Development of Nonverbal Working Memory and Executive Control Processes in Adolescents." *Child Development* 76:697–712.

Mutter, B., Alcorn, M.B., Welsh, M. 2006. "Theory of Mind and Executive Function: Working-Memory Capacity and Inhibitory Control as Predictors of False-Belief Task Performance." *Perceptual and Motor Skills* 102:819–835.

National Resource Center on ADHD. 2012. "Statistical Prevalence." Last accessed November 7, 2012. www.help4adhd.org/about/statistics.

Ni, W., Constable, R.T., Mencl, W., Pugh, K., Fulbright, R., Shaywitz, S., Shaywitz, B., Gore, J., Shankweiler, D. 2000. "An Event-Related Neuroimaging Study Distinguishing Form and Content in Sentence Processing." *Journal of Cognitive Neuroscience* 12:120–133.

Novick, J.M., Trueswell, J.C., Thompson-Schill, S.L. 2005. "Cognitive Control and Parsing: Reexamining the Role of Broca's Area in Sentence Comprehension." *Cognitive, Affective, and Behavioral Neuroscience* 5:263–281.

Oden, M. 1968. "The Fulfillment of Promise: 40-year Follow-Up of the Terman Gifted Group." *Genetic Psychology Monographs* 77:3–93.

Pickering, S. "Working Memory in Dyslexia," in *Working Memory and Neurodevelopmental Conditions*, T. Alloway & S. Gathercole, Eds., pp. 10–72. London: Psychology Press.

Raghubara, K., Barnes, M., Hecht, S. 2010. "Working Memory and Mathematics: A Review of Developmental, Individual Difference, and Cognitive Approaches." *Learning and Individual Differences* 20:110–122.

Reynolds, C., Willson, V., Ramsey, M. 1999. "Intellectual Differences Among Mexican Americans, Papagos and Whites, Independent of G." *Personality and Individual Differences* 27:1181–1187.

Riding, R. 1991. *Cognitive styles analysis*. Birmingham: Learning and Training Technology.

Riding, R., Grimley, M., Dahraei, H., Banner, G., 2003. "Cognitive Style, Working Memory, and Learning Behaviour and Attainment in School Subjects." *British Journal of Educational Psychology* 73:149–169.

Rogalsky, C., Matchin, W., Hickok, G. 2008. "Broca's Area, Sentence Comprehension, and Working Memory: An fMRI Study." *Frontiers in Human Neuroscience* 2:14.

Sahin, N.T., Pinker, S., Halgren, E. 2006. "Abstract Grammatical Processing of Nouns and Verbs in Broca's Area: Evidence from fMRI." *Cortex* 42: 540–562.

Shipstead, Z., Redick, T., Engle, R. 2012. "Is Working Memory Training Effective?" *Psychological Bulletin* 138:628–54.

Siegel, L., Ryan, E. 1989. "The Development of Working Memory in Normally Achieving and Subtypes of Learning Disabled Children." *Child Development* 60:973–980.

Stanley, J., Kipp, H., Greisenegger, E., et al. 2008. "Evidence of Developmental Alterations in Cortical and Subcortical Regions of Children with Attention-Deficit/Hyperactivity Disorder." *Archives of General Psychiatry* 65:1419–1428.

Swanson, H.L., Jerman, O. 2007. "The Influence of Working Memory on Reading Growth in Subgroups of Children with Reading Disabilities." *Journal of Experimental Child Psychology* 96:249–283.

Swanson, L., Alloway, T.P. 2011. "Working Memory Learning and Academic Achievement," in *APA Educational Psychology Handbook,* K. Harris, T. Urdan, & S. Graham, Eds. vol 1. New York: American Psychological Society.

Terman, L., Madison, M., Oden, M. 1947. *Genetic Studies of Genius: The Gifted Child Grows Up; Twenty-Five Years' Follow-up of a Superior Group*, 4th edition. Stanford, CA: Stanford University Press.

Terman, L. 1926. *Mental and Physical Traits of a Thousand Gifted Children.* Vol. 1. *Genetic studies of genius*, 2nd edition. Stanford, CA: Stanford University Press.

Vidal, C.N. et al., 2006. "Mapping Corpus Callosum Deficits in Autism: An Index of Aberrant Cortical Connectivity." *Biological Psychiatry* 60:218–25.

Chapter 6: The New Mind-Body Connection

Alex Honnold. Interview with Ross Alloway, August 2011.

Al'Absi, M., Hugdahl, K., Lovallo, W.R. 2002. "Adrenocortical Stress Responses and Altered Working Memory Performance." *Psychophysiology* 39:95–99.

Babya, M., Blumenthal, J.A., Herman, S., Khatri, P., Doraiswamy, M., et al. 2000. "Exercise Treatment for Major Depression: Maintenance of Therapeutic Benefit at 10 Months." *Psychosomatic Medicine* 62:633–638.

Berger, Lee R., et al. 2010. "Australopithecus sediba: A New Species of Homo-like Australopith from South Africa." *Science* 328: 195.

Boecker, H., et al. 2008. "The Runner's High: Opioidergic Mechanisms in the Human Brain." *Cerebral Cortex* 18:2523–31.

Brené, S., Bjørnebekk, A., Aberg, E., Mathé, A.A., Olson, L., Werme, M. 2007. "Running Is Rewarding and Antidepressive." *Physiology & Behavior* 92:136–140.

Casey, S. 2010. *The Wave: In Pursuit of the Rogues, Freaks and Giants of the Ocean.* New York: Doubleday.

Clark, P.J., Bhattacharya, T.K., Miller, D.S., Kohman, R.A., DeYoung, E.K., and Rhodes, J.S. 2012. "New Neurons Generated from Running Are Broadly Recruited into Neuronal Activation Associated with Three Different Hippocampus-Involved Tasks." *Hippocampus.* 22:1860–67.

Doyne, E.J., Ossip-Klein, D.J., Bowman, E.D., Osborn, K.M., McDougall-Wilson, I.B., Neimeyer, R.A. 1987. "Running Versus Weight Lifting in the Treatment of Depression." *Journal of Consulting and Clinical Psychology* 55:748–754.

Echlin, P.S. 2010. "Return to Play After an Initial or Recurrent Concussion in a Prospective Study of Physician-Observed Junior Ice Hockey Concussions: Implications for Return to Play After a Concussion." *Neurosurgical Focus* 29:E5.

Echlin, P.S., Upshur, R.E., Peck, D.M., Skopelja, E.N. 2005. "Craniomaxillofacial Injury in Sport: A Review of Prevention Research." *British Journal of Sports Medicine* 39:254–263.

Giza, C., Hovda, D. 2001. "The Neurometabolic Cascade of Concussion." *Journal of Athletic Training* 363:228–235.

Goldman-Rakic, P.S. 1995. "Cellular Basis of Working Memory." *Neuron* 14:447–485.

Goldman-Rakic, P.S.1988. "Topography of Cognition: Parallel Distributed Networks in Primate Association Cortex." *Annual Review of Neuroscience* 11:137–156.

Gow, A., et al. 2012. "Neuroprotective Lifestyles and the Aging Brain: Activity, Atrophy, and White Matter Integrity." *Neurology* 79:1802.

Jordan, B.D., Matser, J.T., Zimmerman, R., Zazula, T. 1996. "Sparring and Cognitive Function in Professional Boxers." *The Physician and Sports Medicine* 24:87–98.

Hamilton, L. 2008. *Force of Nature: Mind, Body, Soul (And, of Course, Surfing).* New York: Rodale Books.

Lieberman, D.E., Bramble, D.M., Raichlen, D.A., Shea, J.J. 2009. "Brains, Brawn and the Evolution of Human Endurance Running Capabilities," in *The First Humans: Origin and Early Evolution of the Genus Homo,* F.E. Grine, J.G. Fleagle, R.E. Leakey, Eds. pp. 77–98. New York: Springer.

Lieberman, D.E., Venkadesan, M., Werbel, W.A., Daoud, A.I., D'Andrea, S., Davis, I.S., Mang'eni, R.O., Pitsiladis, Y. 2010. "Foot Strike Patterns and Collision Forces in Habitually Barefoot Versus Shod Runners." *Nature* 463:531–535.

Matser, J.T., Kessels, A.G.H., Jordan, B.D., Lezak, M.D., Troost, J. 1998. Chronic traumatic brain injury in professional soccer players. *Neurology* 51:791–796.

Matser, J.T., Kessels, A.G.H., Lezak, M.D., Jordan, B.D., Troost, J. 1999. "Neuropsychological Impairment in Amateur Soccer Players." *Journal of American Medical Association* 282:971–973.

Maxwell, J., Masters, R., Eves, F. 2003. "The Role of Working Memory in Motor Learning and Performance." *Consciousness and Cognition* 12:376–402.

McDougall, C. 2009. *Born to Run.* New York: Knopf.

McKee, A.C., Cantu, R.C., Nowinski, C.J., Hedley-Whyte, E.T., Gavett, B.E., Budson, A.E., Santini, V.E., Lee, H-Y., Kubilus, C.A., Stern, R.A. 2009. "Chronic Traumatic Encephalopathy in Athletes: Progressive Tauopathy after Repetitive Head Injury." *Journal of Neuropathology & Experimental Neurology* 68:709–735.

McMorris, T., Swain, J., Smith, M., Corbett, J., Delves, S., Sale, C., Harris, R.C., Potter, J. 2006. "Heat Stress Plasma Concentrations of Adrenaline Noradrenaline 5-Hydroxytryptamine and Cortisol Mood State and Cognitive Performance." *International Journal of Psychophysiology* 61:204–215.

Pontifex, M.B., Hillman, C.H., Fernhall, B., Thompson, K.M., Valentini, T.A. 2009. "The Effect of Acute Aerobic and Resistance Exercise on Working Memory." *Medicine and Science in Sport and Exercise* 41:927–934.

Robinson, S.J., Sünram-Lea, S.I., Leach, J., Owen-Lynch, P.J. 2007. "The Effects of Exposure to an Acute Naturalistic Stressor on Working Memory State Anxiety and Salivary Cortisol Concentrations." *Stress* 11:115–124.

Rodney Mullen. Interview with Ross Alloway, August 2011.

Roland, P.E. *1984.* "Organization of Motor Control by the Normal Human Brain." *Human Neurobiology* 2:205–216.

Suzuki, M., Miyai, I., Ono, T., Oda, I., Konishi, I., Kochiyama, T., et al. 2004. "Prefrontal and Premotor Cortices Are Involved in Adapting Walking and Running Speed on the Treadmill: An Optical Topography Study." *NeuroImage* 23:1020–1026.

Talavage, T., Nauman, E., Breedlove, E., et al. 2010. "Functionally-Detected Cognitive Impairment in High School Football Players Without Clinically-Diagnosed Concussion." *Journal of Neurotrauma,* DOI: 10.1089/neu.2010.1512.

Vandervert, L. 2003. "The Neurophysiological Basis of Innovation," in *The International Handbook on Innovation,* L.V. Shavinina, Ed., pp. 17–30. Oxford, England: Elsevier Science.

Vandervert, L.R., Schimpf, P.H., Liu, H. 2007. "How Working Memory and the Cerebellum Collaborate to Produce Creativity and Innovation." *Creativity Research Journal* 9:1–18.

Vestberg, T., Gustafson, R., Maurex, L., Ingvar, M., Petrovic, P. 2012. "Executive Functions Predict the Success of Top-Soccer Players." *PLoS ONE* 7:e34731.

Chapter 7: Working Memory Across the Life Span

Abrahám, H., Vincze, A., Jewgenow, I., Veszprémi, B., Kravják, A., Gömöri, E., Seress, L. 2010. "Myelination In the Human Hippocampal Formation from Midgestation to Adulthood." *International Journal of Developmental Neuroscience* 28:401–410.

Alloway, T.P., Alloway, R.G. (in press). "Working Memory in the Lifespan: A Cross-Sectional Approach." *Journal of Cognitive Psychology.*

Alloway, T.P., Horton, J., Alloway, R.G., Dawson C. In press. "The Impact of Technology and Social Networking on Working Memory." *Computers & Education.*

Alloway, T.P., McCallum, F., Hoika, E., Alloway, R.G. 2012. "Working Memory and Children's Lie-Telling Skills." Manuscript under review.

Alzheimer's Association. 2012. "Alzheimer's Facts and Figures." Last accessed November 7, 2012. www.alz.org/alzheimers_disease_facts_and_figures.asp

Alzheimer's Disease International. 2009. World Alzheimer Report. Last accessed May 16, 2013. http://www.alz.co.uk/research/files/WorldAlzheimerReport-ExecutiveSummary.pdf

Alzheimer's Society. 2012. Dementia 2012. http://www.alzheimers.org.uk/site/scripts/documents_info.php?documentID=412

Asendorpf, J., Warkentin, V., Baudonniere, P.M. 1996. "Self-Awareness and Other-Awareness II: Mirror Self-Recognition, Social Contingency Awareness, and Synchronic Imitation." *Developmental Psychology* 32: 313–321.

Baddeley, A.D., Bressi, S., Della Sala, S., Logie, R., Spinnler, H. 1991. "The Decline of Working Memory in Alzheimer's Disease: A Longitudinal Study." *Brain* 114:2521–2542.

Baddeley, A.D., Bressi, S., Della Sala, S., Spinnler, H. 1986. "Dementia and Working Memory." *Quarterly Journal of Experimental Psychology* 38A:603–618.

Bateman, R.J., et al. 2012. "Clinical and Biomarker Changes in Dominantly Inherited Alzheimer's Disease." *The New England Journal of Medicine* 367:795–804.

Bell, M. 2002. "Power Changes in Infant Eeg Frequency Bands During a Spatial Working Memory Task." *Psychophysiology* 39:450–458.

Bialystok, E., Craik, F., Luk, G. 2012. "Bilingualism: Consequences for Mind and Brain." *Trends in Cognitive Science* 16:240–250.

Blakemore, S.J., Choudhury, S. 2006. "Brain Development During Puberty: State of the Science." *Developmental Science* 9:11–14.

Bookheimer, S.Y., et al. 2000. "Patterns of Brain Activation in People at Risk for Alzheimer's Disease." *New England Journal of Medicine* 343: 450–456.

Bunge, S., Wright, S. 2007. "Neurodevelopmental Changes in Working Memory and Cognitive Control." *Current Biology* 17:243–250.

Carlson, S., Moses, L. 2001. "Individual Differences in Inhibitory Control and Theory of Mind." *Child Development* 72:1032–1053.

Carlson, S., Moses, L., Claxton, L.J. 2004. "Individual Differences in Executive Functioning and Theory of Mind: An Investigation of Inhibitory Control and Planning Ability." *Journal of Experimental Child Psychology* 87: 299–319.

Casey, B.J., Jones, R.M., Hare, T.A. 2008. "The Adolescent Brain." *Ann NY Acad Sci* 1124: 111–126.

Christ, S., Van Essen, D., Watson, J., Brubaker, L., McDermott, K. 2009. "The Contributions of Prefrontal Cortex and Executive Control to Deception: Evidence from Activation Likelihood Estimate Meta-Analyses." *Cerebral Cortex* 19:1557–1566.

Conel, J. 1963. *The Postnatal Development of the Human Cerebral Cortex*, Vols. 1–6. Cambridge, MA: Harvard University Press.

Courchesne, E., Mouton, P., Calhoun, M., et al. 2011. "Neuron Number and Size in Prefrontal Cortex of Children with Autism." *Journal of the American Medical Association* 306:2001–2010.

Crone, E.A., Wendelken, C., Donohue, S.E., Bunge, S.A. 2006. "Neurocognitive Development of the Ability to Manipulate Information in Working Memory." *Proceedings of the National Academy of Sciences of the United States* 103:9315–9320.

Davis, S., Dennis, N., Buchler, N., Madden, D., White, L., Cabeza, R. 2009. "Assessing the Effects of Aging on Long White Matter Tracts Using Diffusion Tensor Imaging (DTI) Tractography." *Neuroimage* 46:530–541.

Davis, S., Kragel, J., Madden, D., Cabeza, R. In press. "Cross-Hemispheric Communication and Aging: Linking Behavior, Brain Activity, Functional Connectivity, and White Matter Integrity." *Cerebral Cortex.*

Diamond, A. 2002. "Normal Development of Prefrontal Cortex from Birth to Young Adulthood: Cognitive Functions, Anatomy, and Biochemistry," in *Principles of Frontal Lobe Function,* D.T. Stuss and R.T. Knight, Eds., pp. 466–503. London: Oxford University Press.

Dick, B., Rashiq, S. 2007. "Disruption of Attention and Working Memory Traces in Individuals with Chronic Pain." *Anesthesia & Analgesia* 104:1223–1229.

Drabble, Emily. 2013. Our ageing population: news and resources round up. *Guardian,* March 17, 2013. Last accessed May 16, 2013. http://www.guardian.co.uk/teacher-network/teacher-blog/2013/mar/17/ageing-population-school-teaching-news-resources

Ertel, K.A., Glymour, M.M., Berkman, L. 2008. "Effects of Social Integration on Preserving Memory Function in a Nationally Representative US Elderly Population." *American Journal of Public Health* 98:1215–1220.

Fuster, J.M. 2008. *The Prefrontal Cortex,* 4th Edition. London: Academic Press.

Gallup, G. 1970. "Chimpanzees: Self-Recognition." *Science* 167: 86–87.

Giedd, J.N. 2004. "Structural Magnetic Resonance Imaging of the Adolescent Brain." *Ann NY Acad Sci* 1021:77.

Giedd, J., et al. 1999. "Brain Development During Childhood and Adolescence: A Longitudinal MRI Study." *Nature Neuroscience* 2:861–863.

Glynn, L., Sandman, C. 2011. "Prenatal Origins of Neurological Development. *Current Directions in Psychological Science* 20:384–389.

Hampton, Keith., et al. 2009. "Social Isolation and New Technology." *Pew Internet and American Life Project* 4 Nov. 2009. Web. 18 Aug. 2010. www.pewinternet.org/Reports/2009/18--Social-Isolation-and-New-Technology.aspx.

Iacono, D., Markesbery, W.R., Gross, M., Pletnikova, O., Rudow, G. Zandi, P., Troncoso, J. 2009. "The Nun Study: Clinically Silent AD Neuronal Hypertrophy and Linguistic Skills in Early Life." *Neurology* 739:665–673.

Joseph Coughlin to Clifford S. "Online, 'a Reason to Keep on Going'." *New York Times,* June 1, 2009. Last accessed November 7, 2012. www.nytimes.com/2009/06/02/health/02face.html.

Kemper, S., Greiner, L.H., Marquis, J.G., Prenovost, K., Mitzner, T.L. 2001. "Language Decline Across the Life Span: Findings from the Nun Study." *Psychology and Aging* 16: 227–239.

Kensinger, E.A., Shearer, D.K., Locascio, J.J., Growdon, J.H., Corkin, S. 2003. "Working Memory in Mild Alzheimer's Disease and Early Parkinson's Disease." *Neuropsychology* 17:230–239.

Legrain, V., Crombez, G., Mouraux, A. 2011. "Controlling Attention to Nociceptive Stimuli with Working Memory." *PLoS One* 66:e20926.

Legrain, V., Crombez, G., Verhoeven, K., Mouraux, A. 2011. "The Role of Working Memory in the Attentional Control of Pain." *Pain* 152:453–459.

Lenroot, R.K., Giedd, J.N. 2006. "Brain Development in Children and Adolescents: Insights from Anatomical Magnetic Resonance Imaging." *Neuroscience and Biobehavioral Reviews* 30:718–729.

Lisa Perlow: http://hbr.org/2009/10/making-time-off-predictable-and-required/ar/1.

Liu, W., Yuen, E.Y., Yan, Z. 2009. "Acute Stress Enhances Glutamatergic Transmission in Prefrontal Cortex and Facilitates Working Memory." *Proceedings of the National Academy of Sciences of the USA* 106:14075–14079.

McPherson, M., Smith-Lovin, L., Brashears, M. 2006. "Social Isolation in America: Changes in Core Discussion Networks." *American Sociological Review* 71:353–375.

Mrzljak, L., Uylings, H., Van Eden, C.G., Judás, M. 1990. "Neuronal Development in Human Prefrontal Cortex in Prenatal and Postnatal Stages," in *The Prefrontal Cortex: Its Structure, Function and Pathology*, H. Uylings, C. Van Eden, J. De Bruin, M. A. Corner, and M. G. P. Feenstra (Eds). Amsterdam: Elsevier, p. 185.

Munnell, A. 2011. "What Is the Average Retirement Age?" Report produced for the Center for Retirement Research, Boston College. Last accessed November 8, 2012. http://crr.bc.edu/wp-content/uploads/2011/08/IB_11-11.pdf.

Perner, J., Frith, U., Leslie, A.M., Leekam, S.R. 1989. "Exploration of the Autistic Child's Theory of Mind: Knowledge, Belief, and Communication." *Child Development* 60:688–700.

Radel, C. "At 100 Years Old, an Ohio Doctor Is Still In." *MSNBC News*, December 18, 2011. Last accessed November 7, 2012. www.msnbc.msn.com/id/45715573/ns/health-aging/t/years-old-ohio-doctor-still/.

Rajah, M.N., D'Esposito, M. 2005. "Region-Specific Changes in Prefrontal Function with Age: A Review of PET and fMRI Studies on Working and Episodic Memory." *Brain* 128: 1964–1983.

Richards, M., Sacker, A. 2003. "Lifetime Antecedents of Cognitive Reserve." *Journal of Clinical and Experimental Neuropsychology* 25:614–624.

Riley, K.P., Snowdon, D.A., Markesbery, W.R. 2002. "Alzheimer's Neurofibrillary Pathology and the Spectrum of Cognitive Function: Findings from the Nun Study." *Annals Neurology* 51:567–77.

Rohwedder, S., Willis, R. 2011. "Mental Retirement." *Journal of Economic Perspectives* 24:119–138.

Ross-Sheehy, S., Oakes, L., Luck, S. 2003. "The Development of Visual Short-Term Memory in Infancy." *Child Development* 74:1807–1822.

Rubin, L. 1997. "Neuronal Cell Death: When, Why and How." *British Medical Bulletin* 53:617–631.

Ruggles, S., et al. 2010. Integrated Public Use Microdata Series: Version 5.0 [Machine-readable database]. Minneapolis, MN: University of Minnesota.

Rypma, B., D'Esposito, M. 2000. "Isolating the Neural Mechanisms of Age-related Changes in Human Working Memory." *Nature Neuroscience* 3:509–515.

Saito, S. 2001. "The Phonological Loop and Memory for Rhythms: An Individual Differences Approach." *Memory* 94:313–322.

Sanchez, C. 2011. "Working Through the Pain: Working Memory Capacity and Differences in Processing and Storage Under Pain." *Memory* 19:226–232.

Snowdon, D., et al. 2000. "Serum Folate and the Severity of Atrophy of the Neocortex in Alzheimer's Disease: Findings From The Nun Study." *American Journal of Clinical Nutrition* 71:993–98.

Snowdon, D.A., Kemper, S.J., Mortimer, J.A., Greiner, L.H., Wekstein, D.R., Markesbery, W.R. 1996. "Linguistic Ability in Early Life and Cognitive Function and Alzheimer's Disease in Late Life: Findings from the Nun Study." *Journal of the American Medical Association* 275:528–532.

Snowdon, D.A. 2001. *Aging with Grace: What the Nun Study Teaches Us About Leading Longer, Healthier, and More Meaningful Lives.* New York: Bantam Books.

Sowell, E.R., Thompson, P.M., Tessner, K.D., Toga, A.W. 2001. "Mapping Continued Brain Growth and Gray Matter Density Reduction in Dorsal Frontal Cortex: Inverse Relationships during Postadolescent Brain Maturation." *Journal of Neuroscience* 2122: 8819–8829.

Stalwart, V., Lee, K. 2008. "Social and Cognitive Correlates of Children's Lying Behavior." *Child Development* 79:866–881.

Wimmer, H., Perner, J. 1983. "Beliefs about Beliefs: Representation and Constraining Function of Wrong Beliefs in Young Children's Understanding of Deception." *Cognition* 13:103–128.

Zelazo, P. 2004. "The Development of Conscious Control in Childhood." *Trends in Cognitive Sciences* 8:12–17.

Ziegler, D., et al. 2010. "Cognition in Healthy Aging is Related to Regional White Matter Integrity, but Not Cortical Thickness." *Neurobiology of Aging* 31:1921–1926.

Chapter 8: Working Memory Training 101

Ackerman, P.L., Kanfer, R., Calderwood, C. 2010. "Use It or Lose It? Wii Brain Exercise Practice and Reading for Domain Knowledge." *Psychology and Aging* 25:753–766.

Alloway, T.P. 2012. "Can Interactive Working Memory Training Improve Learning?" *Journal of Interactive Learning Research* 23:1–11.

Alloway, T.P., Bibile, V., Lau, G. In press. "Computerized Working Memory Training: Can It Lead to Gains in Cognitive Skills in Students?" *Computers & Human Behavior.*

Boot, W., Kramer, A., Simons, D., Fabiana, M., Gratton, G. 2008. "The Effects of Video Game Playing on Attention Memory and Executive Control." *Acta Psychologica* 129:387–398.

Buschkuehl, M., Jaeggi, S., Jonides, J. 2012. "Neuronal Effects Following Working Memory Training." *Developmental Cognitive Neuroscience* 25:S167–S179.

Clark, J.E., Lanphear, A.K., Riddick, C.C. 1987. "The Effects of Videogame Playing on the Response Selection Processing of Elderly Adults." *Journals of Gerontology* 42:82–85.

De Lisi, R., Wolford, J.L. 2002. "Improving Children's Mental Rotation Accuracy with Computer Game Playing." *The Journal of Genetic Psychology* 163:272–282.

Grabbe, J. 2012. "Sudoku and Working Memory Performance for Older Adults." *Activities Adaptation & Aging* 35:241–254.

Jaeggi, S.M., Buschkuehl, M., Jonides, J., Perrig, W.J. 2008. "Improving Fluid Intelligence with Training on Working Memory." *Proceedings of the National Academy of Sciences, USA* 105:6829–6833.

Jaeggi, S.M., Buschkuehl, M., Jonides, J., Shah, P. 2011. "Short- and Long-Term Benefits of Cognitive Training." *Proceedings of the National Academy of Sciences of the USA* 108: 10081–10086.

Lorant-Royer, S., Munch, C., Mesclé, H., Lieury, A. 2010. "Kawashima vs 'Super Mario'! Should a Game Be Serious in Order to Stimulate Cognitive Aptitudes?" *European Review of Applied Psychology* 60:221–232.

Lorant-Royer, S., Spiess, V., Goncalves, J., Lieury, A. 2008. "Programmes d'entraînement cérébral et performances cognitives: efficacité ou marketing? De la gym-cerveau au programme du Dr Kawashima." *Bulletin de Psychologie* 61:531–549.

Nouichi, R., Taki, Y., Takeuchi, H., et al. 2012. "Brain Training Game Improves Executive Functions and Processing Speed in the Elderly: A Randomized Controlled Trial." *PLoS ONE* 71:e29676.

Redick, T. S., Shipstead, Z., Harrison, T. L., Hicks, K. L., Fried, D.E., Hambrick, D. Z., Kane, M. J., & Engle, R. W. 2013. No Evidence of Intelligence Improvement After Working Memory Training: A Randomized, Placebo-Controlled Study. *Journal of Experimental Psychology: General* 142: 359–379.

Sims, V.K., Mayer, R.E. 2002. "Domain Specificity of Spatial Expertise: The Case of Video Game Players." *Applied Cognitive Psychology* 161:97–115.

Whitlock, L., McLaughlin, A., Allaire, J. 2012. "Individual Differences in Response to Cognitive Training: Using a Multi-Modal Attentionally Demanding Game-Based Intervention for Older Adults." *Computers in Human Behavior* 28:1091–1096.

Chapter 9: Secrets of Working Memory Specialists

Amidzic, O., Riehle, H.J., Fehr, T., Wienbruch, C., Elbert, T. 2001. "Pattern of Focal [gamma]-Bursts in Chess Players." *Nature* 412:603–604.

Beam, C. "Bubble Boys." *New York Magazine*, September 11, 2011, last accessed November 6, 2012. http://nymag.com/news/features/silicon-valley-2011-9/.

Bentley, P. "It Takes Mark Zuckerberg Two Hours to Do What Takes us Five Minutes: Causing a Stir in Silicon Valley, the Young Entrepreneurs Who Stay Up All Night Doing Lines (of code)." *Daily Mail*, September 12, 2011, last accessed November 6, 2012. www.dailymail.co.uk/news/article-2036586/Meet-precocious-Mark-Zuckerbergs-future-causing-stir-Silicon-Valley.html.

Chase, W.G., Simon, H.A. 1973. "Perception in Chess." *Cognitive Psychology* 4:55–81.

Chase, W.G., Simon, H.A. 1973. "The Mind's Eye in Chess," in *Visual information processing*, W.G. Chase, Ed., pp. 215–281. New York: Academic Press.

de Groot, A., Gobet, F. 1996. *Perception and Memory in Chess. Heuristics of the Professional Eye.* Assen:Van Gorcum.

Dominic O'Brien. Interview with Tracy Alloway, November 2011.

Ericsson, K.A., Staszewski, J.J. 1989. "Skilled Memory and Expertise: Mechanisms of Exceptional Performance," in *Complex Information Processing: The Impact of Herbert A. Simon*, D. Klahr and K. Kotovsky, Eds., pp. 235–267. Hillsdale NJ: Lawrence Erlbaum.

Feross Aboukhadijeh. Interview with Ross Alloway, December 2011.

Gobet, F. 1997. "A Pattern-Recognition Theory of Search in Expert Problem Solving." *Thinking and Reasoning* 3:291–313.

Gobet, F. 1998. "Expert memory: A Comparison of Four Theories." *Cognition* 66:115–152.

Gobet, F., Simon, H. 1996. "The Roles of Recognition Processes and Look-Ahead Search in Time-Constrained Expert Problem Solving: Evidence from Grand-Master-Level Chess." *Psychological Science* 7:52–55.

Julius, E. 1992. *Rapid Math Tricks and Tips.* NJ: Wiley Press.

Lane, G. 2008. *Mind Games: Amazing Mental Arithmetic Made Easy.* London: John Blake.

Maguire, E.A., Valentine, E.R., Wilding, J.M., Kapur, N. 2003. "Routes to Remembering: The Brains Behind Superior Memory." *Nature Neuroscience* 6:90–95.

Pesenti, M., Zago, L., Crivello, F., et al. 2001. "Mental Calculation in a Prodigy Is Sustained by Right Prefrontal and Medial Temporal Areas." *Nature Neuroscience* 4:103–107.

Robbins, T.W., Anderson, E.J., Barker, D.R., Bradley, A.C., Fearnyhough, C., Henson, R., Hudson, S.R. 1996. "Working Memory in Chess." *Memory and Cognition* 24:83–93.

Susan Polgar. Interview with Tracy Alloway, November 2011.

Chapter 10: Feed Your Brain, Fuel Your Working Memory

BBC 2005. "The Omega Wave." Last accessed November 7, 2012. www.bbc.co.uk/science/humanbody/mind/articles/intelligenceandmemory/omega_three.shtml.

Bruce-Keller, A.J., Umberger, G., McFall, R., Mattson, M. 1999. "Food Restriction Reduces Brain Damage and Improves Behavioral Outcome Following Excitotoxic and Metabolic Insults." *Annals Neurology* 45:8–15.

Crawford, M., Bloom, M., Broadhurst, C., Schmidt, W., Cunnane, S., Galli, C., Ghebremeskel, K., Linseisen, F., Lloyd-Smith, J., Parkington, J. 2000. "Evidence for the Unique Function of Docosahexanoic Acid DHA During the Evolution of the Modern Hominid Brain." *Lipids* 34:S39–S47.

Crichton, G.E., Elias, M., Dore, G., Robbins, M. 2012. "Relation Between Dairy Food Intake and Cognitive Function: The Maine-Syracuse Longitudinal Study." *International Dairy Journal* 22:15–23.

Crichton, G.E., Murphy, K.J., Bryan, J. 2010. "Dairy Intake and Cognitive Health in Middle-Aged South Australians." *Asia Pacific Journal of Clinical Nutrition* 192:161–71.

Crichton, G.E., Murphy, K.J., Howe, P.R., Buckley, J.D., Bryan, J. 2012. "Dairy Consumption and Working Memory Performance in Overweight and Obese Adults." *Appetite.*

Cunnane, S.C., Crawford, M. 2003. "Survival of the Fattest: Fat Babies Were the Key to Evolution of the Large Human Brain." *Comparative Biochemistry and Physiology* 136:17–26.

Daniel, D.R., Thompson, L., Hoover, L.C. 2000. "Nutrition Composition of Emu Compares Favorably with That of Other Lean Meats." *Journal American Dietetic Association* 100:836–8.

Duan, W., Guo, Z., Jiang, H., Ware, M., Li, X.J., Mattson, M.P. 2003 "Dietary Restriction Normalizes Glucose Metabolism and BDNF Levels Slows Disease Progression and Increases Survival in Huntington Mutant Mice." *Proceedings of the National Academy of Sciences of the USA* 100:2911–2916.

Francis, S.T., Head, K., Morris, P.G., Macdonald, I.A. 2006. "The Effect of Flavanol-Rich Cocoa on the fMRI Response to a Cognitive Task in Healthy Young People." *Journal of Cardiovascular Pharmacology* 47:S215–S220.

Galloway, S., Broad, E. 2005. "Oral L-Carnitine Supplementation and Exercise Metabolism." *Chemical Monthly* 136:1391–1410.

Granholm, A.C., Bimonte-Nelson, H.A., Moore, A.B., et al. 2008. "Effects of a Saturated Fat and High Cholesterol Diet on Memory and Hippocampal Morphology in the Middle-Aged Rat." *Journal of Alzheimer's Disease* 142:133–145.

Kelly, C., Polich, J. 2009. "Binge Drinking in Young Adults: Data Definitions and Determinants." *Psychological Bulletin* 135:142–156.

Lustig, R. 2009. "Sugar: The Bitter Truth." Public lecture at the University of California-San Francisco "Mini Medical School for the Public" on May 26, 2009.

Macready, A., Kennedy, O., Ellis, J., Williams, C., Spencer, J., Butler, L. 2009. "Flavonoids and Cognitive Function: A Review of Human Randomized Controlled Trial Studies and Recommendations for Future Studies." *Genes & Nutrition* 4:227–242.

Mattison, J., et al. 2012. "Impact of Caloric Restriction on Health and Survival in Rhesus Monkeys from the NIA Study." *Nature* 489:318–321.

Mattson, M., Duan, W., Lee, J., Guo, Z. 2001. "Suppression of Brain Aging and Neurodegenerative Disorders by Dietary Restriction and Environmental Enrichment: Molecular Mechanisms." *Mechanisms of Ageing and Development* 122:757–778.

Meydani, M., Das, S., Band, M., Epstein, S., Roberts, S. 2011. "The Effect of Caloric Restriction and Glycemic Load on Measures of Oxidative Stress and Antioxidants in Humans: Results From the CALERIE Trial of Human Caloric Restriction." *Journal of Nutrition Health and Aging* 156:456–460.

Moss, M., Cook, J., Wesnes, K., Duckett, P. 2003. "Aromas of Rosemary and Lavender Essential Oils Differentially Affect Cognition and Mood in Healthy Adults." *International Journal of Neuroscience* 113:15–38.

Moss, M., Hewitt, S., Moss, L., Wesnes, K. 2008. "Modulation of Cognitive Performance and Mood by Aromas of Peppermint and Ylang-Ylang." *International Journal of Neuroscience* 118:59–77.

Moss, M., Oliver, L. 2012. "Plasma 18-Cineole Correlates with Cognitive Performance Following Exposure to Rosemary Essential Oil Aroma." *Therapeutic Advances in Psychopharmacology* doi:10.1177/2045125312436573.

Narendran, R., et al. 2012. "Improved Working Memory but No Effect on Striatal Vesicular Monoamine Transporter Type 2 after Omega-3 Polyunsaturated Fatty Acid Supplementation." *PLOS ONE* 7: e46832.

Nehlig, A. 2010. "Is Caffeine a Cognitive Enhancer?" *Journal of Alzheimer's Disease* 20:S85–S94.

Saults, J.S., Cowan, N., Sher, K.J., Moreno, M. 2007. "Differential Effects of Alcohol on Working Memory: Distinguishing Multiple Processes." *Experimental and Clinical Psychopharmacology* 156:576–587.

Smith, M., Rigby, L., Van Eekelen, A., Foster, J. 2011. "Glucose Enhancement of Human Memory: A Comprehensive Research Review of the Glucose Memory Facilitation Effect." *Neuroscience and Biobehavioral Reviews* 35:770–783.

Tan, Z.S., Harris, W.S., Beiser, A.S., Au, R., Himali, J.J., Debette, S., et al. 2012. "Red Blood Cell Omega-3 Fatty Acid Levels and Markers of Accelerated Brain Aging." *Neurology* 78:658–64.

Tangney, C.C., Aggarwal, N., Li, H., et al. 2011. "Vitamin B12 Cognition and Brain MRI Measures: A Cross-Sectional Examination." *Neurology* 77:1276–1282.

USDA Database for the Flavonoid Content of Selected Foods, Release 3. 2011. Last accessed November 7, 2012. http://www.ars.usda.gov/Services/docs.htm?docid=6231

Wittea, V., Fobkerb, M., Gellnerc, R., Knechta, S., Floel, A. 2009. "Caloric Restriction Improves Memory in Elderly Humans." *Proceedings of the National Academy of Sciences of the USA* 106:1255–1260.

Chapter 11: Seven Habits to Supercharge Working Memory . . . and a Few to Avoid

Alloway, T.P., Alloway, R.G. 2012. "Attentional Control and Engagement with Digital Technology." *Computers and Human Behavior.*

Andrade, J. 2010. "What Does Doodling Do?" *Applied Cognitive Psychology* 24:100–106.

Berman, M., Jonides, J., Kaplan, S. 2008. "The Cognitive Benefits of Interacting with Nature." *Psychological Science* 19:1207–1212.

Carskadon, M.A., Harvey, K., Dement, W.C. 1981. "Acute Restriction of Nocturnal Sleep in Children." *Perceptual Motor Skills* 53:103–112.

Carskadon, M.A., Harvey, K., Dement, W.C. 1981. "Sleep Loss in Young Adolescents." *Sleep* 4:299–312.

Chee, M., Choo, W. 2004. "Functional Imaging of Working Memory after 24 Hr of Total Sleep Deprivation." *Journal of Neuroscience* 2419:4560–4567.

Chuah, L.Y.M., Dolcos, F., Chen, A.K., Zheng, H., Parimal, S., Chee, M.W.L. 2010. "Sleep Deprivation and Interference by Emotional Distracters." *Sleep* 33:1305–1313.

Dager Schweinsburg, A.D., Nagel, B., Schweinsburg, B., Parke, A., Theilmann, R., Tapert, S. 2008. "Abstinent Adolescent Marijuana Users Show Altered fMRI Response During Spatial Working Memory." *Psychiatry Research: Neuroimaging* 163:40–51.

Drummond, S.P., Gillin, J.C., Brown, G.G. 2001. "Increased Cerebral Response During a Divided Attention Task Following Sleep Deprivation." *Journal of Sleep Research* 10:85–92.

Ersche, K.D., Clark, L., London, M., Robbins, T.V., Sahakian, B.J. 2006. "Profile of Executive and Memory Function Associated with Amphetamine and Opiate Dependence." *Neuropsychopharmacology* 315:1036–1047.

Ersche, K.D., Sahakian, B.J. 2007. "The Neuropsychology of Amphetamine and Opiate Dependence: Implications for Treatment." *Neuropsychology Review* 17:317–336.

Fink, A., Grabner, R.H., Benedek, M., Reishofer, G., Hauswirth, V., Fally, M., Neuper, C., Ebner, F., Neubauer, A. 2009. "The Creative Brain: Investigation of Brain Activity During Creative Problem Solving by Means of EEG and FMRI." *Human Brain Mapping.* 303:734–748.

Frank, M.G., Issa, N.P., Stryker, M.P. 2001. "Sleep Enhances Plasticity in the Developing Visual Cortex." *Neuron* 30:275–87.

Hart, C.L., van Gorp, W.G., Haney, M., Foltin, R.W., Fischman, M.W. 2001. "Effects of Acute Smoked Marijuana on Complex Cognitive Performance." *Neuropsychopharmacology* 25: 757–765.

Heishman, S.J., Kleykamp, B.A., Singleton, E.G. 2010. "Meta-Analysis of the Acute Effects of Nicotine and Smoking on Human Performance." *Psychopharmacology* 210:453–469.

Hofmann, W., Vohs, K., Baumeister, R. 2012. "What People Desire, Feel Conflicted About, and Try to Resist in Everyday Life." *Psychological Science* 23:582–588.

Jonelis, M., Drummond, S., Salamat, J., et al. 2012. "Age-Related Influences of Prior Sleep on Brain Activation during Verbal Encoding." *Frontiers in Neurology* 3:1–8.

Kopasz, M., Loessl, B., Hornyak, M., Riemann, D., Nissen, C., Piosczyk, H., Voderholzer, U. 2010. "Sleep and Memory in Healthy Children and Adolescents—A Critical Review." *Sleep Medicine Reviews* 14:167–177.

Lyoo, I.K., Pollack, M.H., Silveri, M.M., Ahn, K.H., Diaz, C.I., Hwang, J., et al. 2006. "Prefrontal and Temporal Gray Matter Density Decreases in Opiate Dependence." *Psychopharmacology* 184:139–144.

MovNat. Last accessed November 7, 2012. http://movnat.com/.

National Sleep Foundation. Last accessed November 7, 2012. www.sleepfoundation.org/.

National Association of Professional Organizers. Last accessed November 7, 2012. www.napo.net/

Owens, J., Belon, K., Moss, P. 2010. "Impact of Delaying School Start Time on Adolescent Sleep Mood and Behavior." *Archives of Pediatrics & Adolescent Medicine* 164:608–614.

Payne, J.D., Tucker, M.A., Ellenbogen, J.M., Wamsley, E.J., Walker, M.P., Schacter, D.L., Stickgold, R. 2012. "Memory for Semantically Related and Unrelated Declarative Information: The Benefit of Sleep the Cost of Wake." *PLoS ONE* 73: e33079.

Pilcher, J., Huffcutt, A. 1996. "Effects of Sleep Deprivation on Performance: A Meta Analysis." *Sleep* 19:318–326.

Steenari, M.R., Vuontela, V., Paavonen, E.J., Carlson, S., Fjallberg, M., Aronen, E. 2003. "Working Memory and Sleep in 6- to 13-Year-Old Schoolchildren." *Journal of the American Academy of Child and Adolescent Psychiatry* 42:85–92.

Wahlstrom, K. 2010. "School Start Time and Sleepy Teens." *Archives of Pediatrics & Adolescent Medicine* 164:676–677.

Whitney, P., Rosen, P. 2012. "Sleep Deprivation and Performance: The Role of Working Memory," in *Working Memory: The Connected Intelligence*, T.P. Alloway and R.G. Alloway, Eds. New York: Psychology Press.

Chapter 12: Designing the World for Working Memory

Barros, R., Silver, E., Stein, R. 2009. "School Recess and Group Classroom Behavior." *Pediatrics* 123:431436.

Gardiner, V. "24 Rooms Tucked in One." *New York Times*, January 14, 2009. Last accessed November 7, 2012. www.nytimes.com/2009/01/15/garden/15hongkong.html?pagewanted=all&_r=0

Ginsburg, K. 2007. "The Importance of Play in Promoting Healthy Child Development and Maintaining Strong Parent-Child Bonds." *Pediatrics* 119: 182–191.

Jahnke, H., Hygge, S., Halin, N., Green, A.M., Dimberg, K. 2011. "Open-Plan Office

Noise: Cognitive Performance and Restoration." *Journal of Environmental Psychology* 31:373–382.

Litman, L., Davachi, L. 2008. "Distributed Learning Enhances Relational Memory Consolidation." *Learning and Memory* 15:711–716.

Seppänen, O., Fisk, W., Lei, Q. 2006. "Ventilation and Performance in Office Work." *Indoor Air* 6:28–36.

Chapter 13: The Dawn of Working Memory

Azéma, M., Rivère, F. 2012. "Animation in Palaeolithic Art: A Pre-Echo of Cinema." *Antiquity* 86:316–32.

Barabás, P., Director. 2005. *Pururambo* (documentary).

Bates, T.C., Luciano, M., Lind, P., Wright, M.J., Montgomery, G.W., Martin, N.G. 2008. "Recently-derived Variants of Brain-size Genes ASPM MCPH1 CDK5RAP and BRCA1 Not Associated with General Cognition Reading or Language." *Intelligence* 36:689–693.

Binford, L.R., Binford, S. 1966. "A Preliminary Analysis of Functional Variability in the Mousterian of Levallois Facies." *American Anthropologist* 68:238–295.

Bruner, E. 2010. "Morphological Differences in the Parietal Lobes Within the Human Genus: A Neurofunctional Perspective." *Current Anthropology* 51:S77–S88.

Chauvet, J.M., Deschamps, E., Hillaire, C. 1996. *Dawn of Art: The Chauvet Cave the Oldest Known Paintings in the World*. New York: Harry N. Abrams, Inc.

Clottes, J. 2003. *Chauvet Cave: The Art of Earliest Times*. Utah: University of Utah Press.

Conard, N., Malina, M., Münzel, S. 2009. "New Flutes Document the Earliest Musical Tradition in Southwestern Germany." *Nature* 460:737–740.

Coolidge, F., Wynn, T. 2001. "Executive Functions of the Frontal Lobes and the Evolutionary Ascendancy of *Homo sapiens*." *Cambridge Archaeological Journal* 11:255–260.

Coolidge, F., Wynn, T. 2005. "Working Memory: Its Executive Functions and the Emergence of Modern Thinking." *Cambridge Archaeological Journal* 15:5–26.

Coolidge, F., Wynn, T. 2009. *The Rise of Homo sapiens: The Evolution of Modern Thinking*. Chichester, UK: Wiley-Blackwell.

Coolidge, F., Wynn, T. 2011. *How to Think Like a Neandertal*. Oxford University Press, USA.

Dalén, L., Orlando, L., Shapiro, B., et al. 2012. "Partial Genetic Turnover in Neandertals: Continuity in the East and Population Replacement in the West." *Molecular Biology and Evolution* doi: 10.1093/molbev/mss074.

Darling, S., Havelka, J. 2010. "Visuo-Spatial Bootstrapping: Evidence for Binding of Verbal and Spatial Information in Working Memory." *Quarterly Journal of Experimental Psychology* 63:239–245.

Enard, W., Przeworski, M., Fisher, S., Lai, C., Wiebe, V., Kitano, T., Monaco, A., Pääbo, S. 2002. "Molecular Evolution of *FOXP2* a Gene Involved in Speech and Language." *Nature* 418:869–872.

Evans, P.D., Mekel-Bobrov, N., Vallender, E.J., Hudson, R.R., Lahn, B.T. 2006. "Evidence That the Adaptive Allele of the Brain Size Gene *Microcephalin* Introgressed into *Homo Sapiens* from an Archaic *Homo* Lineage." *Proceedings of the National Academy of Sciences of the United States* 103:18178.

Fincham, J., Carter, C., van Veen, V., Stenger, V., Anderson, J. 2002. "Neural Mechanisms of Planning: A Computational Analysis Using Event-Related fMRI." *Proceedings of the National Academy of Sciences* 99:3346–3351.

Fisher, S.E., Vargha-Khadem, F., Watkins, K.E., Monaco, A.P., Pembrey, M.E. 1998. "Localisation of a Gene Implicated in a Severe Speech and Language Disorder." *Nature Genetics* 18: 168–70.

Green, R., Krause, J., Briggs, A., et al. 2010. "A Draft Sequence of the Neandertal Genome." *Science* 328:710–22.

Herzog, W., director. 2011. *Cave of Forgotten Dreams* (documentary).

Howard Hughes Medical Institute. "Human Brain Evolution Was a 'Special Event,'" December 29, 2004, last accessed November 6, 2012. www.hhmi.org/news/lahn3.html

Inoue, S., Matsuzawa, T. 2007. "Working Memory of Numerals in Chimpanzees." *Current Biology* 17:R1004–R1005.

Jurmain, R., Kilgore, L., Trevathan, W. 2012. *Essentials of Physical Anthropology*. Wadsworth Publishing.

Karlsen, P.J., Allen, R.J., Baddeley, A.D., Hitch, G.J. 2010. "Binding Across Space and Time in Visual Working Memory." *Memory and Cognition* 38:292–303.

Klein, R. 2003. "Whither the Neanderthals?" *Science* 299:1525–1527.

Kubrick, S., director. 1968. *2001: A Space Odyssey* (movie).

Lai, C., Fisher, S., Hurst, J., Vargha-Khadem, F., Monaco, A. 2001. "A Fork-head-domain Gene is Mutated in a Severe Speech and Language Disorder." *Nature* 413:519–523.

Lalueza-Fox, C., Krause, J., Caramelli, D., et al. 2006. "Mitochondrial DNA of an Iberian Neandertal Suggests a Population Affinity with other European Neandertals." *Current Biology* 16:R629–630.

Mekel-Bobrov, N., Gilbert, S.L., Evans, P.D., Vallender, E.J., Anderson, J.R., Hudson, R.R., Tishkoff, S.A., Lahn, B.T. 2005. "Ongoing Adaptive Evolution of *ASPM* a Brain Size Determinant in *Homo sapiens.*" *Science* 309:1720.

Pääbo, S. 1985. "Molecular Cloning of Ancient Egyptian Mummy DNA." *Nature* 314:644–645.

Reyburn, S. "Hirst Shark Sells for 9.6 Million Pounds at Sotheby's." *Bloomberg,* September 15, 2008, last accessed November 6, 2012. www.bloomberg.com/apps/news?sid=aw9UAnyzyFB4&pid=newsarchive

Söderqvist, S., McNab, F., Peyrard-Janvid, M., Matsson, H., Humphreys, K., Kere, J., Klingberg, T. 2010. "The SNAP25 Gene Is Linked to Working Memory Capacity and Maturation of the Posterior Cingulate Cortex During Childhood." *Biological Psychiatry* 68:1120–1125.

Vernes, S., Nicod, J., Elahi, F., Coventry, J., Kenny, N., Coupe, A., Bird, L., Davies, K., Fisher, S. 2006. "Functional Genetic Analysis of Mutations Implicated in a Human Speech and Language Disorder." *Human Molecular Genetics* 15:3154–3167.

Wilford, J. "Flutes Offer Clues to Stone-Age Music." *New York Times,* June 24, 2009, last accessed November 6, 2012. www.nytimes.com/2009/06/25/science/25flute.html.

Wynn, T. 2008. "A Stone-Age Meeting of Minds." *American Scientist* 96:44.

Wynn, T., Coolidge F. 2004. "The Expert Neandertal Mind." *Journal of Human Evolution* 46:467–487.

INDEX